Collection Development

in College Libraries

Collection
Development
in College Libraries

Edited by
Joanne Schneider Hill,
William E. Hannaford, Jr., and
Ronald H. Epp

AMERICAN LIBRARY ASSOCIATION

Chicago and London   1991

Designed by Charles Bozett

Composed by Achorn Graphic Services, Inc.
in Goudy Old Style on a Miles 33 typesetting system.

Printed on 50-pound Glatfelter, a pH-neutral stock, and bound in
10-point Carolina cover stock by Braun-Brumfield, Inc.

The paper used in this publication meets the minimum requirements of
American National Standard for Information Sciences—Permanence of
Paper for Printed Library Materials, ANSI Z39.48-1984. ∞

Library of Congress Cataloging-in-Publication Data

Collection development in college libraries / edited by Joanne Lopez
   Hill, William E. Hannaford, Jr., and Ronald H. Epp.
     p.   cm.
   ISBN 0-8389-0559-5
   1. Libraries, University and college—Collection development.
 I. Hill, Joanne Lopez. II. Hannaford, William E. III. Epp, Ronald
H.
Z675.U5C6423 1991
025.2'1877—dc20   90-27006
                                               CIP

Printed in the United States of America.

95 94 93 92 91   5 4 3 2 1

Contents

Introduction

During the last quarter century, much has been written about collection development—what it should be called, just what it is, who should do it, and the like. Most of the relevant articles and books on collection development have been geared to the large university and research libraries. Only a very small proportion has been directed to college libraries. Our attempt is to remedy, at least in part, this state of affairs and to start the dialogue necessary for continued concern.

There are two fundamental reasons why a book is needed focusing on collection development in college libraries: (1) the overwhelming bias toward "big" in library literature, and (2) the assumption that "big" easily translates into or trickles down to "small." The result of these biases over the years has been a dearth of material on collection development in college libraries.

Although it is notoriously difficult to adequately define a college library, for the most part these libraries share the following common factors: finite collection size (generally well under one million); small student body (usually about 2,000); principal focus on undergraduate students and instructional programs; secondary focus on research needs of faculty; small materials budget (again, well under $1 million); library staff of two to fifteen professionals; and the absence of subject bibliographers on the library staff. It is significant that a college library may have 65,000 volumes, 400 students, a $45,000 materials budget, and a professional staff of two, or it may have one million volumes, 2,800 students, a materials budget of $1 million or more, and a professional staff of seventeen. The range is enormous. The one commonality that separates colleges from universities is purpose—colleges exist (or should) primarily to educate undergraduates.

For many reasons, mostly related to size, the treatment of collection development in professional literature traditionally focuses on the university library experience. Generally, sizes of collections and of materials budgets and the numbers of librarians involved in collection development are much larger for university libraries than for college libraries. Furthermore, the prevalence of faculty status for librarians in university libraries, as opposed to the lack of such status in most college libraries, has provided much of the impetus for research on this topic.

A search of the literature shows that there is, indeed, a bias; of the many books, articles, or chapters in books on collection development written during the last twenty-five years, very few directly address college libraries. It is surprising that so little research and writing in this area has been done, considering the fact that collection development may be more difficult to do well in colleges than in universities.

A review of existing literature fails to uncover a single monographic work specifically devoted to college library collection development. There are several that come close, including *Library Resources for College Scholars: Transactions of a Conference Held at Washington and Lee University, Lexington, Virginia, February 14–15, 1980*, though this work does not pretend to discuss a full range of issues relating to collection development. Several other works concentrate on college librarianship and include a chapter or two on collection development or at least on one or more of the several activities that make it up. These include Lyle's *The President, the Professor, and the College Library* and *Administration of the College Library*; Miller and Rockwood's *College Librarianship*; and a recent work edited by G. B. McCabe, *The Smaller Academic Library: A Management Handbook*. The journal literature is a bit kinder to collection development in colleges, but not much more so. A good review of the extant literature is given by Richard Johnson in his paper "The College Library Collection." A careful look at the bibliography included in this article will make clear just how profound is the bias against "small."

The second reason for our book is to present an alternative to the assumption that what works in large libraries will also work in small ones. This view, which has held sway for many years, has been dubbed by Evan Farber the "university-library syndrome." Anyone who has worked in both university and college libraries knows that assumption is questionable. To be sure, there are significant similarities between university and college libraries, and much is to be gained by the comparison. Yet, without setting college libraries apart and examining them separately, one runs the risk of assuming that what applies to research libraries also applies to college libraries, except reduced in scale. This syndrome operates by using university libraries as the model and then comparing college libraries to them, generalizing from what has been learned from the study of universities to the operation of colleges.

Rather than dwell exclusively on how colleges diverge from or conform to attributes associated with universities, we will concentrate on those qualities that are unique to college libraries. Although resulting differences in self-definition may not divide strictly along institutional lines, it is clear that many more college than university libraries will identify themselves with the papers in this book. When research results, theory, practice, and even basic assumptions of library operations are reexamined through the lens of college library perspectives and values, new conclusions can be drawn and new directions forged that have implications for college, and perhaps even university, libraries.

Our focus is on the heart of any library—its collections—and the context in which and activities by which these collections are developed and maintained. We have chosen to use the term *collection development* rather than *collection management*, which is currently in vogue. *Collection development* seems more properly to mean just the set of activities that results in the intentional and systematic building of a library collection, whereas *collection management* seems to relate more to the management of these activities. Obviously, both go hand-in-hand, but collection management is itself a collection development activity. Thus, it can be said that collection development involves the activities of evaluation, budgeting, selection, weeding, storage, preservation, and management.

The present work is limited to some of the problematic areas in collection development, and so a word must be said about the method behind this book and about the contributors and their papers. We intentionally sought some of the best college librarians, many of whom have vast experience in both libraries and writing, and asked them to write about what they think is important to collection development in college libraries. The result is not so much a methodological survey as an attempt to include librarians from as many different kinds of college libraries and with as many different interests and views as possible. In short, this book is not a text. We do not pretend that every issue in the gamut of collection development concerns has been covered. A major area left to the more rapid reporting of professional journals is the effect of technological innovation on library collections, a subject which seems to change too rapidly for inclusion in a monograph. Although the glue may not always stick, these previously unpublished papers overall are an important contribution to a largely ignored area of librarianship.

College Libraries:
Are They Different?

The essays in Part 1 provide snapshots of issues that have either tradition-ally faced college libraries or just recently become concerns. At the same time, they present a group portrait of the numerous ways in which collec-tion development in the college library differs from that of the university library.

Several vantage points have been used to provide evidence of those aspects of collection development that are unique to college libraries.

In "Collection Development in College and University Libraries: A Comparison," Mary F. Casserly identifies some of the qualitative differ-ences between college and research library collection development by focusing on specific philosophies and practices. She notes that these differ-ences are not as clearcut and well defined as much of the literature on collection development would suggest. Casserly explores philosophical differences regarding the concept of primary clientele; student, faculty, and administrator expectations; and immediate use versus future research needs. She then compares and contrasts collection development practices and procedures related to library organization and staffing, materials selec-tion, and collection assessment. Casserly concludes that, since few collec-tion development librarians operate in archetypal college or research li-braries, it is important for librarians to understand and appreciate the collection development process as it is conducted in both of those settings.

Like the rich, who are different because they have money, college libraries differ from other academic libraries because they are small. Joan H. Worley, in "The Importance of Being Small: Collection Development in the College Library," explores the collection implications of "being small in academe," where *small* denotes undergraduate, liberal arts col-leges with enrollments under 2,000. Such libraries, though more numer-ous than comprehensive university libraries, have a low visibility; how-ever, Worley maintains, they are able to accomplish things large institutions could not easily manage. For example, successful college libraries have a well-defined mission and greater knowledge of their constituencies, and respond more readily to user needs. Distanced from other degree-granting institutions by their focus on undergraduates and the liberal arts, college library collections reflect essential differences in programs, faculty behaviors, and student attitudes. For Worley, college library collection development is driven not necessarily by the courses taught but by how they are taught, and, because undergraduate library use is largely faculty motivated, faculty habits have unusual implications for college libraries.

Clearly, the bias of this book is that there is, indeed, something specific about college libraries that requires examination and elaboration separate from the study of research libraries. At first glance, C. Roger Davis appears to be playing devil's advocate by refuting this central theme. A closer look at his thesis, however, reveals a qualification, not a refutation, of this bias. In "No Difference but Dollars: Collection Development in College versus University Libraries," Davis maintains that curriculum is the basis for collection development decisions at both college and university libraries. Therefore, questions of format, indexing, recommender, level, use, language, country of origin, and even price are viewed as secondary. Davis speculates that, in using the term "college and university," some writers may mean "small and large" academic libraries. Even so, selection and deselection are viewed as proceeding from the same theoretical base and with the same title-by-title attention in both large and small academic libraries. While he admits that differences in collection development do exist (for example, with regard to attitude toward goals, of collection method by field, and in working conditions that affect the context in which decisions are made), Davis concludes that the overall approaches and principles are the same. At bottom, he finds the chief difference is dollars, meaning the size of the materials budget, with all other differences flowing from it.

This initial section provides dialogue about the nature of college library collection development. Points are made both for and against the premise of the book, which is that sufficient differences exist between college and university libraries to warrant separate consideration for collection development. How well the case has been made should not be judged, however, until the entire book has been read and digested.

Collection Development in College and University Libraries: A Comparison

by Mary F. Casserly

Throughout the 1960s and 1970s, much of the professional literature and most of the conferences on collection issues focused exclusively on collection development in the research library. By the late 1970s, however, the literature began to reflect an awareness that collection development in the college library is and should be substantively and qualitatively different from the process as it is conducted in the university or research library.[1] The purpose of this chapter is to contribute to the growing body of professional literature comparing and contrasting collection development theory and practice in these two settings.

Logically, the first step should be to define what is meant by *college library* and *research library*. Although it often appears from the way the terms are used in the literature on collection development that the distinction between these categories is clear and well understood, this is not the case. In terms of any of the quantitative measures (i.e., staff, collection, and budget) by which libraries are commonly compared, great diversity exists among the libraries serving institutions that call themselves colleges. These libraries also differ dramatically in such subjective characteristics as mission, goals, and organizational culture. Similarly, the approximately one hundred university libraries, which through their membership in the Research Libraries Group (RLG) are recognized as research libraries, and the hundreds of libraries in small and medium-sized universities vary considerably in relation to these objective and subjective characteristics. By developing different sets of standards for college and university libraries, the profession has acknowledged that there are fundamental and important differences between them.[2] Unfortunately, these documents do not provide definitions that can be used to place academic libraries into one group or another and are not helpful in determining where the dividing line between these two types of libraries should be drawn. The use of these terms in this chapter notwithstanding, *college libraries* and *research libraries* are far from being cohesive, homogeneous categories.

The following comparisons illustrate some of the philosophical and practical differences between collection development in the college and research library settings. However, in light of the lack of homogeneity within these categories, such comparisons also demonstrate that these differences are not as clearcut and straightforward as they are often portrayed.

PHILOSOPHY

It is generally accepted that the differences in collection development as it is practiced in college and research library settings result directly from the differences in the missions of the institutions that these libraries serve. Specifically, while the typical four-year college emphasizes teaching, the university has a broader mission and emphasizes research. As a result of this distinction, collection development librarians in these environments have different perspectives on their primary clientele and consequently on the purposes of the collection they must build.

To best serve its primary clientele, the college library collection is closely tied to the curriculum. This collection is built to be used and, in this context, value is measured by usage. In contrast, the collection built for the research library setting is intended to support not only curricular needs but, more important, the research needs of the faculty and graduate students. The research library's mandate is therefore broader than that of the college. Although college libraries are able to focus on the short run, research libraries must provide for both long- and short-term needs. Consequently, for the collection development officer in the research library setting, value cannot be measured by the number of times, or even whether, materials receive immediate use.[3]

These philosophical differences are an often-stated theme in the professional literature and are especially common in articles written about collection development in the college setting. However, outside the archetypal college and research libraries, these differences may be less distinct. In these settings, competing library and institutional goals give rise to many conflicts between collection priorities and the needs or demands of students, faculty, and administration, as well as between collection priorities and immediate and future needs.

Students

The concept of primary clientele, especially within the college library setting, would be fairly straightforward if it were not for the complications caused by student and program diversity. Undergraduates, both among institutions as well as within a single institution, vary considerably in terms of their educational preparedness and general sophistication. Colleges have added new undergraduate courses and programs without necessarily dropping other offerings. In addition to this activity on the undergraduate level, many colleges have expanded their offerings to include master's and professional degrees. As a result, fewer institutions currently offer only bachelor's degrees.[4] The implication of this expansion is that most college collections are being called on to support more, and more varied, curriculum-related needs than ever before.

While college libraries often face problems providing for graduate-level needs, undergraduate needs are problematic for research libraries. The literature on collection development in the research library setting often gives the impression that as a research collection is built and maintained the needs of the undergraduate are automatically addressed and met. One reason for this perception may be that the relatively unglamorous problems of providing resources for undergraduates are rarely discussed in this literature. In reality, however, the needs of university undergraduates for relatively low-level materials, duplicate copies, audiovisual materials, and new formats, such as CD–ROM products, compete with the needs of graduate students and faculty members for materials to support their research efforts.

Faculty and Administrators

Faculty and administrators generate expectations for research libraries through changes in institutional objectives and in program and research emphases. These changes may occur in a variety of ways. Faculty may be hired with unique research interests and/or graduate programs may be added. Similarly, the institution may become involved in grants or other types of funded projects in research areas that are new to the institution and consequently to the library. These occurrences often require the acquisition of numerous arcane, expensive, and difficult-to-obtain resources. However, it is not always clear whether such changes represent long- or short-range institutional commitments, and it may be very difficult for the collection development librarian to determine the amount of fiscal and staff resources to commit to these subject areas.

The library-related expectations of college faculty and administrators are different from but no less intense than those of their counterparts in research institutions. Although in the college setting faculty research needs take second place to the instructional needs of the students, the political reality is that faculty needs exert strong pressures and influences on collection development. Farber has coined the expression "university library syndrome" to describe the views held by faculty and administrators with respect to the role of the librarian and the library in the undergraduate teaching process.[5] This concept could easily be expanded to include expectations about the size and content of the collection.

Ph.D. candidates are trained at universities with research collections. Consequently, faculty often bring to the college environment expectations concerning the library that are derived from their previous employment as well as from their graduate, and sometimes undergraduate, experiences. Further, as a result of their training, they come to these positions with unique research interests and often expect that they will have access in the college to the same types of resources that they used in their previous educational environment.

Another faculty expectation that can be problematic for the college library may be closer to the instructional mission of the archetypal undergraduate institution. It can be argued that, in order to achieve excellence in instruction, faculty members must remain *au courant* in their fields. In many colleges the administration provides some of the resources, such as money for travel, release time, and sabbaticals, needed to support a well-informed faculty. The library may also be expected to provide journals and monographs that, although too specialized for undergraduate students, address faculty members' current awareness needs.

The expectations of college administrators can further exacerbate the faculty pressures just described. Although the mission of a college is generally acknowledged to be undergraduate education, in most college settings faculty are retained, promoted, and tenured on the basis of their teaching, research, and professional service.[6] The relative weight given to these criteria is dependent on a number of variables, an important one being the stance of the administration. In colleges where evidence of research (i.e., publication) is a highly valued promotion and retention criterion, the pressure on the library to acquire the resources needed for such research may be substantial, requiring that collection development librarians make difficult trade-offs between faculty and student needs.

Immediate versus Future Use

The truism that collections, like Rome, are not built in a day applies in varying degrees to both college and research libraries. College library collections are built to support current or impending use by a largely undergraduate clientele. Research libraries, on the other hand, are charged with the task of meeting not only current but future research needs. The collection development librarian in this setting must acquire materials that will give depth to the research collection of the future. There is, then, an element of clairvoyance involved in this process. In addition it pits the need to collect comprehensively against the need to reinforce areas in the collection that are currently being used.[7]

College libraries also face challenges concerning collection depth. One of these is related to the development of special collections. Many college libraries are committed to building comprehensive collections on subjects of local interest. Such collections must be built over time and therefore these libraries must acquire some rather esoteric materials at the expense of resources that would address immediate needs, albeit to a lesser degree than their more research-oriented counterparts.

The second challenge concerns the problematic concept of a collection based on usage. Usage is often regarded as going hand-in-hand with the notion of a curriculum-based collection. Some authors have even advocated that materials budgets be wed to this concept.[8] However, collection development librarians, including those in institutions most nearly resembling the archetypal college library, have to resist the pressure to pursue a strategy of strengthening only those areas of the collection that are currently being used. Easy access to circulation and often to in-house use statistics make this an attractive strategy. Unfortunately, it can result in a Catch-22 situation in which areas of the collection are not used because they are weak—or perceived as being weak—and yet cannot be strengthened because they are not used.

PRACTICES AND PROCEDURES

In addition to, and arguably as the result of, the previously outlined philosophical distinctions, there are many differences in the manner in which collection development is carried out in the college and research setting. These differences can be found in the amount and type of authority and control exercised by the collection development officer, in the amount and type of responsibility assigned to the collection development staff, and in the methods of selecting and acquiring materials and assessing collection adequacy.

Organization

In the archetypal college library, collection development may not be a full-time position. Instead, collection development responsibilities may be assumed by the director or assigned to another professional, such as a reference or acquisitions librarian.[9] The reasons for this may vary, but contributing factors include a small professional staff, possibly consisting of only one or two librarians; a low materials budget; and a selection process controlled by faculty. However, in all but the smallest college library the trend is toward devoting more resources to collection development processes. The literature suggests that in these settings there is a shift away from faculty control of the selection process and toward the creation of full-time collection development positions.

For many years academic libraries at the other end of the continuum have devoted considerable staff resources to the collection development process. A recent survey of fifty-three libraries, members of the Association of Research Libraries (ARL), confirms that they continue to do so. The survey also provides a picture of the archetypal research library's collection development organization. Collection development in this setting is a separate unit or department within the library and has a core of four to six full-time bibliographers complemented by twenty to twenty-five part-time selectors.[10]

Contrary to how it may appear to envious collection development librarians in college settings, relatively few of their counterparts in university libraries enjoy this type of full-time staffing arrangement. In fact, a wide range of organizational models for collection development in large and medium-sized academic libraries has been identified. Cogswell, analyzing the responses to a survey of thirty-one research university libraries, found that collection development was conducted in a variety of settings ranging in structure from highly centralized, such as that previously described, to a decentralized model where selection responsibility is assigned to librarians and faculty and where the library director supervises all collection development activities.[11] Although Cogswell does not indicate the frequency of the occurrence of these models, there is evidence that in the majority of the medium-sized libraries (i.e., those with a professional staff of between eighteen and thirty librarians), collection development is not conducted in a separate unit and that participants in the process are culled from other departments in the library.[12]

Staffing

Research libraries are more likely than college libraries to have separate collection development units with full-time bibliographers. Further, in this environment members of the collection development staff, even those having only part-time collection responsibilities, usually have to meet stringent requirements relating to their collection development roles as part of the hiring process. In contrast to this, librarians in the college library setting are often hired on the basis of their abilities to perform other library responsibilities and are then placed into the collection development structure according to their educational background and/or interests.[13] As a result, they frequently do not have formal subject backgrounds in the area(s) that they are expected to coordinate. This phenomenon has prompted one author to draw a distinction between "subject specialists" and those who have "subject responsibilities."[14] It can also result in a collection development "team" in which selection responsibilities are constantly being shifted to accommodate new librarians with new educational backgrounds and/or interests. Consequently, librarians may not be responsible for the same subject areas long enough to develop needed expertise, and faculty may be confused about who their library contact person or liaison is.

As a result of these different staffing patterns, the roles of the librarians in charge of collection development in college and research libraries differ substantially. The role of the college librarian is likely to be one of coordinator. Often this librarian is in the difficult position of having responsibility for collection development without the corresponding control or authority over any of the librarians to whom subject responsibilities have been assigned. Further, because of the pressures of other responsibilities, these librarians may have a very limited role in the collection development process.[15] The collection development librarian must be prepared to deal with this type of ambiguity.

In contrast, the collection development officer in the research library setting, commonly a unit or department head, is intimately involved in the recruitment and performance evaluation of all or most of the librarians involved in collection development. This staff is also more likely to be involved in the full range of collection development or collection management activities. However, less desirable by-products of this organizational model may include problems related to full-time subject specialists who become isolated from the university community, as well as difficulties in communicating effectively with part-time bibliographers who are spread over large staffs and may be separated by formidable geographical distances.

Some have suggested that library professionals who work in the college setting should possess qualifications different from those of librarians who work in the larger, more research-oriented setting, and that consequently they should be trained differently.[16] The differences in the staffing and organization for collection development in these two settings further suggest that there are substantive differences in the qualifications needed to effectively manage these collection development processes. For example, the coordinating talents needed to successfully manage the collection development process in the typical college library setting are not the same as the skills needed to organize and supervise a unit or department. The growing amount of attention being focused on staff training for collection development in the research library setting[17] and the absence of attention to this aspect of collection development in the college-related literature suggest that different aptitudes and abilities are needed by collection development officers in these two settings. Further credence is given to this supposition when one observes that librarians are not usually recruited from collection development positions in college library settings to manage collection development units in large university libraries.

Selection

The evolution of selection practices in university libraries from the nineteenth century to the present has been chronicled by a number of authors,
including Orne, Kaser, and Edelman and Tatum, and consequently it is
well documented that the primary responsibility for selection now resides
with the library staff in the research library setting.[18] The librarians in
this archetypal setting not only are accountable for the collection but also
have control over the budget and the selection process. In the smallest
of the college libraries, selection may also be fully controlled by the library
staff. However, in the research library setting this circumstance is due in
part to the growth of fiscal resources, whereas in the small college library
setting it is generally the result of an extremely small budget.

Since the vast majority of academic libraries fall between these two
extremes, it is difficult to generalize about methods of selecting materials.
The question of who selects varies widely among institutions and remains
one of the most sensitive areas in the collection development process.[19]
However, as a rule (with the extremely small academic library being an
aberration), the larger the academic library's collection, the smaller the
role played by faculty in the selection process.[20]

The comparison of the selection processes in college and research libraries cannot, however, be summed up in a general statement concerning
the relationship between collection size and faculty involvement in selection. In most institutions, regardless of size, materials are selected cooper-
atively. Further, on some campuses, faculty involvement, or noninvolve-
ment for that matter, may be part of the tradition or culture of the
institution. Finally, faculty involvement in selection "may vary with the
intended use of the materials."[21] Even in large research libraries, faculty
will be very involved in selecting for reserve collections, and may be
heavily involved in selecting film and videos, especially if the primary
purpose of this collection is to provide materials for classroom use.

The distinction between selection processes in college and research
libraries goes beyond the relative amount of selection performed by faculty. There are differences in the aspects of selection in which faculty are
involved as well as in the level of faculty participation found in these
settings.

Faculty involvement in book selection in the small college setting is
typically direct and personal. Money is generally allocated for the purpose
of processing faculty orders. Although the librarian supervises the pre-
order searching and selection of the vendor, there may be little or no
review of the request in terms of suitability for the collection. On the
other hand, faculty involvement in selection in the research library setting
can be quite indirect. In this environment faculty requests may be just
that. They may be considered suggestions and reviewed by a department
library committee and/or a bibliographer. These faculty, however, may

participate in selection through consultation with bibliographers and involvement in policy decisions.[22]

Another way in which faculty participation may differ in the college and research library setting is in faculty responsibility for selecting curriculum-related materials. Although faculty may participate in or even dominate this process in the college library setting, many of these materials are likely to be acquired either by the bibliographers or through some form of mechanical selection in the research library setting. Under these circumstances, faculty selection is focused more exclusively on special subject and/or research interests, and librarians have more time to become involved in other aspects of collection development.

One method of mechanical selection, the approval plan, has long been almost exclusively the province of the research library. However, this type of plan has become increasingly popular with college libraries. In addition to the previously noted advantage of saving staff time, an approval plan is one way to escape the predicament of faculty domination of selection and as such it may be attractive to growing college libraries.[23]

An important difference between approval plans in college and research libraries centers on the types of plans used. Although many large university and research libraries rely on subject-based plans, these may not be suitable for smaller libraries. Schmidt found this to be true at the University of Illinois–Urbana,[24] and the University of Maine had a similar experience. College and small-to-medium-sized university libraries may find that for current, domestic imprints, publisher-based plans (including university press plans) are more affordable, more easily managed, and more politically acceptable to faculty and administration.

Collection Assessment

Grover has observed that collection assessment has moved in two directions that clearly reflect the differences in college and research library collection philosophies.[25] The first approach, the pragmatic, encompasses those techniques that enable the library to gather information about the collection and its relationship to the institution's curriculum, program, and constituency. For college libraries, this approach may be the most useful, since the techniques that fall within this category, such as circulation and use studies, measure the extent to which the collection meets the current curriculum-related needs of its patrons.

The second approach to collection assessment is collection centered rather than patron or curriculum centered. It is less concerned with applicability to one institution than it is with contributing to the overall understanding of the discipline. The RLG Conspectus Project uses this second approach; consequently, most of the efforts of large university libraries have been focused on this approach for the past decade.

The Conspectus Project is the collection-centered approach that research libraries employ to describe their past and current collecting practices. These descriptions are then compared to determine where the institution stands with respect to other research libraries. Collection development officers form some judgments concerning the quality of their collections based on the data generated from these projects. However, these data do not tell the individual library how well or how poorly it is meeting the needs of its clientele.

As with all other aspects of collection development, assessment efforts in college and research libraries do not fall neatly into one or the other of these approaches. Research libraries use many different assessment techniques and some pragmatic approaches are even incorporated into conspectus-based projects. At the same time, many state and regional projects involving small academic as well as public libraries have been modeled after the RLG Conspectus Project (e.g., the Alaska Statewide Inventory Project, METRO, and LIRN). Some libraries (e.g., Albion College) have also undertaken assessment projects using an instrument modeled after the Conspectus.[26]

Participants in Conspectus-based projects cite a number of staff process-benefits, including an increased level of knowledge about the collection, improved priority setting and staff allocation, and strengthened working relationships with faculty.[27] When such benefits are supplemented by advantages gained through resource sharing and cooperative acquisitions programs, this technique may be valuable for many college and small university libraries. However, it is not the most efficient or effective method of assessing the strengths and weaknesses of predominantly usage-based collections. Since most college library collections are built to support undergraduate use, we must turn to other methods—such as circulation and use studies that measure the extent to which the collection meets curricular needs of patrons—that may be more useful.

CONCLUSIONS

This essay identifies areas of collection development philosophy and practice in which qualitative, not simply quantitative, differences exist. This is far from an exhaustive inventory. There are many other differences, particularly in collection development practice, that deserve to be explored, including deselection and methods of selecting and acquiring special materials, such as out-of-print titles and foreign imprints.

Very few academic librarians involved in collection development do so in the quintessential college or research library. Rather, most librarians function in a setting that occupies a place on a continuum anchored by these archetypes. Further, this place may shift across the continuum, closer to one anchor or the other, as different aspects of philosophy and practice are considered. It is therefore important that librarians understand and appreciate collection development not only from the research library perspective but also from the perspective of the college library setting. It is hoped that this comparison has provided some of the information that collection development librarians will need to select from each of these archetypal settings what might be most valuable and applicable to their unique situations.

NOTES

1. William Miller and D. Stephen Rockwood, "Collection Development from a College Perspective," in *College Librarianship*, ed. William Miller and D. Stephen Rockwood (Metuchen, N.J.: Scarecrow Press, 1981), 138.

2. Association of College and Research Libraries, *Standards for College Libraries* (Chicago: ALA, 1986); Association of College and Research Libraries, *Standards for University Libraries* (Chicago: ALA, 1979).

3. Barbara B. Moran, "Library Collections and Cooperation," in *Academic Libraries: The Changing Knowledge Centers of Colleges and Universities*, ed. Barbara B. Moran (Washington, D.C.: Association for the Study of Higher Education, 1984), 65.

4. *Fact Book on Higher Education 1989–90* (New York: American Council on Education, 1989), 134.

5. Evan Ira Farber, "College Librarians and the University Library Syndrome," in *The Academic Library: Essays in Honor of Guy R. Lyle*, ed. Evan Ira Farber and Ruth Walling (Metuchen, N.J.: Scarecrow Press, 1974), 12–28.

6. Peter Seldin, *Changing Practices in Faculty Evaluation* (Washington, D.C.: Jossey-Bass, 1985), 35–45.

7. William H. Axford, "Collection Management: A New Dimension," *Journal of Academic Librarianship* 6 (January 1981): 324–29.

8. Miller and Rockwood, "Collection Development from a College Perspective," 143.

9. Bonita Bryant, "Allocation of Human Resources for Collection Development," *Library Resources and Technical Services* 30 (April–June 1986): 152.

10. *Collection Development Organization and Staffing in ARL Libraries*, SPEC kit, no. 131 (Washington, D.C.: Office of Management Studies, 1987).

11. James A. Cogswell, "The Organization of Collection Management Functions in Academic Research Libraries," *Journal of Academic Librarianship* 13 (November 1987): 268–76.

12. Carol W. Cubberly, "Organization for Collection Development in Medium-sized Academic Libraries," *Library Acquisitions: Practice & Theory* 11 (1987): 305.

13. Ibid., 312. Also Dennis W. Dickinson, "Subject Specialists in Academic Libraries: The Once and Future Dinosaurs," in *New Horizons for Academic Libraries*, ed. American Library Association (New York: Saur, 1979), 440.

14. J. E. Scrivner, "Subject Specialization in Academic Libraries—Some British Practices," *Australian Academic and Research Libraries* 5 (September 1974): 113–22.

15. Cubberly, "Organization for Collection Development," 313.

16. Evan Ira Farber, "College Libraries," in *Education for Professional Librarians*, ed. Herbert S. White (White Plains, N.Y.: Knowledge Industry Publications, 1986), 49–65; Herbert S. White, "Summary and Conclusions," in ibid., 256.

17. *Collection Development Organization and Staffing*, 1987.

18. Jerrold Orne, "The Evolution of Academic Library Staff in the United States," in *University Library History: An International Review*, ed. James Thompson (New York: Saur, 1980), 77–91; David Kaser, "Collection Building in American Universities," in ibid., 33–55; Hendrick Edelman and G. Marvin Tatum, "The Development of Collections in American University Libraries," *College and Research Libraries* 37 (May 1976): 222–45.

19. Patrick J. Wreath, "Collection Development—Generalizations and a Decentralized Model," *Library Acquisitions: Practice & Theory* 1 (1977): 165.

20. Elizabeth Futas, ed. *Library Acquisition Policies and Procedures*, 2d ed. (Phoenix, Ariz.: Oryx Press, 1984), xvi.

21. Robert N. Broadus, "Selection and Acquisition (Excerpts)," in *Background Readings in Building Library Collections*, 2d ed., ed. Phyllis Van Orden and Edith B. Phillips (Metuchen, N.J.: Scarecrow Press, 1979), 238.

22. Pam Cenzer, "Library/Faculty Relations in the Acquisitions and Collection Development Process," *Library Acquisitions: Theory & Practice* 7 (1983): 216.

23. R. Charles Wittenberg, "The Approval Plan: An Idea Whose Time Has Gone? and Come Again?" *Library Acquisitions: Practice and Theory* 12 (1988): 240.

24. Karen A. Schmidt, "Capturing the Mainstream: Publisher-based and Subject-based Approval Plans in Academic Libraries," *College and Research Libraries* 47 (July 1986): 365–69.

25. Mark L. Grover, "Collection Assessment in the 1980s," *Collection Building* 8, no. 4 (1987): 23–26.

26. Larry R. Oberg, "Evaluating the Conspectus Approach for Smaller Library Collections," *College and Research Libraries* 49 (May 1988): 187–96.

27. Ibid., 195; Anthony W. Ferguson, Joan Grant, and Joel Rutstein, "Internal Use of the RLG Conspectus," *Journal of Library Administration* 8 (Summer 1987): 35–40.

The Importance of Being Small: Collection Development in the College Library

by Joan H. Worley

Near my house are four grocery stores: a comprehensive Kroger's, which sells cut flowers and cheap perfume along with groceries, prescription drugs, and banking services; the White Store, one of a hometown chain of mid-sized supermarkets; Gourmet Market, a coffee and tea emporium with a line of imported delicacies; and Reeds' Fine Foods, an unusual neighborhood grocer. In size and complexity one may imagine them analogous to the libraries of the University of Illinois, Vanderbilt, the Folger, and an imaginary college, respectively. Stores not unlike them may be found in cities across the country, except for Reeds'. Reeds' is a trip backward in time.

There is a butcher named Buford who cuts meat to suit your preference and wraps it in reddish-brown paper. Produce is sold bulk, with the price marked in crayon on paper bags. "Those oranges come from California," Mr. Reed will say. "I haven't tried them, but these over here are real sweet. From Florida." There is special ordering of any item not in stock—white-wine vinegar, juniper mustard, you name it. And because Reeds' is in a "nice neighborhood," the store caters to nice neighborhood appetites, with fresh fish, English tea, and Belgian chocolates. There is home delivery. No lines at the cash register. Check-cashing without I.D.'s. Parking by the door. Smiling clerks.

But it is small. Reeds' can't compete with modern supermarket technology—with barcoded inventory and networked cash registers. And it can't compete in the number or variety of stock: where Kroger's has four or five brands of tomato juice, Reeds' has one or two. But although there are times when I shop at each of the other stores, depending on their special strengths and the items I need, for day-in, day-out shopping, I go to Reeds'—for service, convenience, and, mainly, because Reeds' has what I need. Most of those miles of shelving and thousands of items at the larger stores might as well not be there. I never buy them. The surfeit of goods is a deterrent, in fact; too many choices create noise on the shelf. Reeds' has fewer items, but it has the right ones.

The lessons of commerce will not be lost on college librarians: as Reeds' is to Kroger's, so the college library is to the research library. It will have fewer items, and (one hopes) the right ones, those needed by its users. There are compensatory advantages to being small, and many of them relate to collection management. This essay will explore the collection implications of "being small in academe,"[1] where *small* denotes undergraduate liberal arts colleges with enrollments no larger than 2,000. My perspective is that of a library serving a small student population on a shoestring budget.

Although college libraries have low visibility and the distinctive issues affecting them are seldom discussed in library literature, colleges outnumber larger, more comprehensive universities. In Ohio, for example, 44 of 70 institutions granting baccalaureate degrees have enrollments under 2,000, with an average of 915 students; in Oregon, 15 of 24 institutions have enrollments under 2,000, with an average of 746 students; and in Tennessee, 30 of 42, with an average enrollment of 904.[2] Being small is not uncommon.

Like the rich, who are different because they have money, colleges are different because they are small. In addition to small student populations, they have small faculties and relatively small numbers of course offerings; their libraries typically have collections under 200,000 volumes, current periodicals lists numbering under 1,000, few staff members (and fewer professional librarians), and, not invariably but frequently, limited budgets. Small can be beautiful (Georgian architecture on a tree-shaded campus), friendly and congenial (a faculty and staff of compatible hearts and minds), academically sound (a select student body), responsive to individual student needs (in loco parentis), and creative (scope for innovation without the hindrance of a large bureaucracy). In the past decade, small has often meant struggling, too: Because most colleges are private, and by definition more expensive than state-supported institutions, they have been adversely affected by declining federal aid to students and by a troubled economy. Certainly there are colleges with large endowments or other income that have not felt budget constraints in recent years, but they are atypical.

Either because of their size or their relative poverty, there is a temptingly facile inclination to consider college libraries poor relations of the Association of Research Libraries (ARL) giants and to dismiss their activities and interests as professionally irrelevant.[3] However, college libraries are of particular interest because many of them have developed independently, in relative isolation, with a variety of solutions to fundamentally similar problems. More important, logistically they are able to do things large institutions could not manage. And, on point for collection management issues, successful college libraries have a well-defined mission, know their constituencies, and are responsive to user needs.

Knowledge is the hallmark of intelligent collection management, and it begins at home. The college library must know its purpose well—on campus, for the wider community (if any), and in the network of information providers in the area and region. Although each college library's mission statement, or statement of purpose, may differ markedly from others, depending on the degree offered, the curriculum, nearby libraries, and other factors, it is important for every college library to establish its individual identity, both for itself and its users: these things we do/do not do, these materials and services we will/will not seek to provide.

THE MISSION

The mission of the college library is determined in large part by the institutional mission, which typically sets forth in lofty rhetoric the undergraduate and liberal arts nature of its program. Those two terms, *undergraduate* and *liberal arts,* conceptually distance the college from other degree-granting institutions; the essential differences in program, faculty behaviors, and student attitudes between primarily four-year liberal arts colleges and comprehensive universities will be reflected in the library collections.

The most important characteristic defining the mission of both the college and the library is the baccalaureate degree: The college is centered on *teaching,* while the university is centered on *research.* Of course, research can be and is carried out at the college level, and teaching goes on at universities, but the primary focus of the institution is inexorably shaped by the degrees it offers. Where there are graduate programs, one may expect to find an emphasis on research, with concomitant interest in outside sources of funding (often from the federal government), a reward structure for faculty who publish, and highly motivated students whose waking moments are spent in the library and the lab. Libraries supporting graduate programs must identify, locate, and acquire materials on a comprehensive level. In contrast, the task of college libraries is one of careful selection: to identify and select materials needed to support undergraduate studies—and, where budgets are severely restricted, to select *only* those materials.

The mission of the college library is shaped significantly by its curriculum, too. Traditionally, liberal arts colleges offer programs strong in the humanities, social sciences, fine arts, and natural sciences. In the past twenty-five years, colleges have added nontraditional courses, majors, and degrees in order to compete successfully for more students (e.g., business majors and nursing [B.S.N.] degrees); but, in general, few colleges offer many professional courses of study. Typically, liberal arts colleges adhere to a back-to-the-basics curriculum, or, more correctly, a basic curriculum that was never abandoned. Courses in hotel management, architecture, agricultural economics, and fashion design, for example, will be uncommon. And with small enrollments, course offerings are likely to be limited in number as well as scope. Obviously, many materials ordered routinely to support a comprehensive curriculum are not essential for the college library. Indeed, there may be little "routine" ordering; where book budgets are small, selection is necessarily needs-based and often course-specific.

The mission of the college library is also shaped by geography—specifically, the proximity of other libraries and/or membership in area consortia. If nearby research and special libraries share resources through a network or allow on-site use by off-campus users, there are obvious implications for selection, weeding, and retention. For example, with a research library in the same city, the archival role of the college library will be sharply reduced or absent. The library may choose to work toward a high-use collection of collegiate materials, deselecting those that do not circulate.

Other factors that influence the definition of mission have to do with local circumstances, traditions, and the nature of the library's constituency. An (unusual) emphasis on faculty publication, for example, would be reflected in a mission statement as well as in the collection.

And last, one must take note of what isn't there: Underlying every statement of purpose, or mission statement, are unexamined assumptions so fundamental or so ingrained in librarians through their professional education that they serve as guiding principles whether they are included in published documents or not, and whether they are appropriate for a given library. Regrettably, unwittingly, large academic libraries set collection development agendas and practices for *all* academic libraries (and for public libraries, too, according to one library leader[4]). The predominance of library authors from large institutions has resulted in the widespread publication and acceptance of generalizations about collection development that simply do not hold true for small colleges.

A recent, sophisticated discussion of the challenge of collection development is a case in point. "The academic library has neither a single mission nor a homogeneous constituency," one reads.[5] *The* academic library assumes an unwarranted and unrealistic catholicity, as does the following statement on the "five essential functions which the academic library attempts and is expected to fulfill":

1. The notification function. The academic library continues to serve as the principal (although never exclusive) means by which scholars communicate the results of their research to each other across space and time.
2. The documentation function. The academic library maintains the essential raw data upon which many disciplines base their research.
3. The historical function. *To all libraries, but to the academic library*

especially [italics added], falls the responsibility for maintaining the records of civilization, without which the future will be denied access to the past.

4. The instructional function. The students, whose education is after all the primary purpose of all academic institutions, depend upon the library as a means to supplement and enrich their learning.

5. The bibliographic metafunction. In order to achieve the preceding four functions, the library must promote and facilitate access to information sources.[6]

These five functions are essential for *academic libraries serving comprehensive universities*. They are not essential for every academic library. Indeed, it is likely that some college libraries will serve their constituencies more effectively by *not* serving two or three of the named functions. In any case, it is imperative that professional librarians should question any and all received wisdom on collection development in the careful review of library practice.

If the college is centered on teaching undergraduates (and presumably this is axiomatic), the primary focus of the college library is support for the curriculum. For collection management purposes, however, the curriculum is not the courses taught but *how* they are taught. Since student study is almost exclusively faculty-driven at the undergraduate level, the "curriculum" the library supports is determined not only by the college catalog but equally by faculty behaviors.

THE FACULTY

Teaching faculty most often are closely involved with the college library. Indeed, there is speculation that interest in the library increases as the size of the college enrollment decreases,[7] for a variety of reasons:

1. Campus culture at the small college will enhance faculty involvement: Faculty will be personally acquainted with the entire library staff, well informed about the library, and perhaps proud of specific holdings.

2. At liberal arts colleges, the dominant faculty (e.g., those whose voices will be heard) are likely to be faculty in traditionally book-oriented disciplines.

3. The emphasis on teaching increases the likelihood of significant one-on-one work with students. Instructors across the curriculum may require rough drafts of papers, reviewing bibliographies with some care. At one college, and possibly many others, instructors of freshman English meet with each student in the library to check citations against the materials cited. In situations involving closely watched research, faculty, like librarians, experience student

search success or failure secondhand, and, like librarians, they learn collection strengths and weaknesses in such esoterica as AIDS, abortion, smoking and health, crack/cocaine, back-to-the-basics (education), gun control, child abuse, acid rain, and the tropical forest—topics rather far afield of Wordsworth and Faulkner studies.

4. Independent study projects, senior theses, and honors studies involving some or all students will require intensive library use and tutorial time, and as these program options are often present at liberal arts colleges, faculty—even in non-book-oriented fields—will be unusually well aware of library resources.

5. The difficulties students experience in finding information will be reported to their instructors, as happens everywhere. At a college, however, instructors are apt to personally check library holdings to verify the reported need, perhaps because of their apparent involvement in the selection of materials.

6. It may be, too, that faculty interest in the library is fueled by necessity. Where resources are limited, faculty may lack confidence that the collection can support a spontaneous assignment. They may routinely research topics in the catalog and stacks before making assignments.

7. Faculty may provide reference assistance for their students, either by personally guiding them through reference tools and indexes, or by "remote control," suggesting specific titles during office conferences with students. Some faculty maintain card files of acquisitions in their areas of interest in order to offer this "shoebox reference." The practice is more commonly found where a reference or information desk is not staffed or is staffed for limited hours only, but such is the involvement of college faculty with students, at least at some colleges, that it may occur where there is a flourishing reference service.

8. Faculty are involved in selecting materials at many college libraries, much more involved than at university libraries. They choose materials because they feel uniquely qualified to do so, because they fear that needed or desirable materials may not be ordered otherwise, because ordering materials is a traditional faculty prerogative at the college, because ordering books represents power, or for any one or combination of a hundred reasons that have been advanced. For whatever reason, selection by faculty heightens involvement in the library; faculty have an investment in the process and an interest in the cause.

Other factors that affect faculty behaviors, attitudes, and use of the library include the tenure and seniority of faculty; faculty participation in college governance, if any; and the existence and/or effectiveness of library liaison activities.

College librarians have mixed reactions regarding faculty involvement, according to local conditions (e.g., the acquisitions budget and particular faculty members of their acquaintance). Again, size is a determining factor: Opinions undoubtedly will vary according to the size of the library, the budget, and the staff. If it is reasonably well funded, the library may use a vendor approval plan; without such a plan, it is difficult for librarians alone to manage selection for course support, basic materials in fields not taught, recreational reading, and the multitude of subjects that fall between departmental areas of interest. At many colleges there simply are not enough librarians to do the job properly. (Although it is rarely acknowledged in the literature, one needs an omnifarious knowledge of publishers, vendors, disciplines, and courses taught to select a few materials that will be well used instead of gathering by the armload, as at large libraries, anything that might be useful some day.)

Despite the well-advertised efforts of librarians to play an increasingly active role in collection development in college libraries,[8] few would spurn faculty participation. Indeed, most college librarians welcome faculty interest in the library, although many might wish that faculty thinking on the selection (and retention) of materials were more congruent with their own—more realistic about student use of materials, more knowledgeable of library access points, more alert to freshman and sophomore needs, less elitist about popular and trade books, less inclined to view the college library as a miniature Library of Congress, and so forth.

The challenge confronting college librarians is not how to wrest control of book selection from the grasping hands of misguided faculty, but how to effectively organize faculty expertise for the library's benefit. Granted, every college faculty includes people who are not involved or even interested in the library. Librarians must decide, case by case, if their time is well spent encouraging such people to participate when working with new faculty and faculty who are interested requires as much time as one can give.

College librarians invest enormous energy in their collections. Few would differ with the director who wrote, "After providing strong leadership and able management—collection building is the library director's primary responsibility, one upon which all else hangs."[9] Efforts made to inform faculty of collection development issues should be—and one suspects are—unstinting at college libraries. Librarians talk with faculty about student work, materials recently published or received, circulation records, or general and specific collection needs. They may send book jackets, advertisements, reviews, photocopied title or contents pages of new books, bibliographies, and checklists annotated with library holdings as part of an informal, in-house current awareness service for faculty. They highlight new titles or subscription services (CD-ROMs, for example) in library memos or newsletters. They generate new title lists of books and periodicals to send to departments or individuals. They meet with faculty both formally at departmental meetings and informally. They keep up with individual faculty research interests and projects. These activities keep faculty *and* librarians abreast of collection development interests and concerns; if they are effective, such activities will improve teaching, increase library use, and enhance collection development.

THE STUDENTS

Speculation on the characteristics of students at small colleges will be left to braver writers. Student needs may differ among colleges, or not; and students at colleges may exhibit library behaviors different from those at universities, or perhaps not. Whatever the nature of students, they are (or should be) the chief beneficiaries of collection development activities. Faculty and library selectors act as proxies representing anticipated student demand, according to their best guess, and the primary users, students, have little direct involvement with the actual development of the collection.

By necessity, selection of materials is done well in advance of need. Even with generous funding for acquisitions, however, selectors cannot anticipate every need. Interlibrary loan and reference staff can negotiate or offer alternative sources of information on a topic, but inevitably, occasions arise—more often than librarians care to admit—when even large libraries are unable to meet legitimate needs within time constraints. The college library, because of its size, is in a position to act very quickly in filling requests. The (potentially) rapid response time is due in large part to the college library's service capabilities. However, the direct communication between the student and a small library staff known by name increases the likelihood of problems being recognized; in a small situation, library failures are likely to be reported to staff and in turn to the library administration. When a student expresses a valid need for information, the director may well be staffing the reference desk; if not, he or she will be notified directly, and, if the item is available, the acquisitions department will have a phone or electronic order out that day . . . or get the item from a local bookstore. Such an extraordinary effort made for an individual user is not an everyday occurrence, of course, but it happens, and it is more likely to happen in the college library.

Students who comment on the small-world atmosphere of the college, where "everyone knows you" and "you're not just a number," affirm an advantage of scale so obvious that it is rarely articulated: Small libraries tend to offer humane service. Rules get bent because library staff members know their users and take responsibility for exceptions. The mission of the college may not be as comprehensive or as encompassing as that of the university, but in fact, there is significant overlap between the two. What is markedly distinct about the collegiate environment is the focus on the individual undergraduate where all teaching and academic support services are directed. In the library, these needlepoint homilies are translated into an everyday commitment to service.

CONCLUSION

As the key to the success of Reeds' Fine Foods is its size and its commitment to service, so too, the college library has the potential for superior service to the academic community. With a clear purpose, knowledge of its campus constituents, and a willingness to go the extra mile for students and faculty, the college library will be the library of choice—because of service and convenience, but mainly because it offers what its users need. It will have fewer books, but it will have the right ones.

NOTES

1. William A. Moffatt, "Reflections of a College Librarian: Looking for Life and Redemption This Side of ARL," *College and Research Libraries* 45 (September 1984): 338–47.

2. Constance Healey Torregrosa, ed., *1989 Higher Education Directory* (Falls Church, Va.: Higher Education Publications), 246–61, 266–71, 302–11.

3. Moffatt, "Reflections of a College Librarian," *passim.*

4. Charles Robinson, "Can We Save the Public's Library?" *Library Journal* 114 (September 1, 1989): 147–48.

5. Ross Atkinson, "Old Forms, New Forms: The Challenge of Collection Development," *College and Research Libraries* 50 (September 1989): 507.

6. Ibid., 508.

7. Joan Worley, "Collection Development in the Small College Library: Can Less Be More?" *Choice* 25 (June 1988): 1513.

8. William Miller and D. Stephen Rockwood, "Collection Development from a College Perspective," *College and Research Libraries* 40 (July 1979): 324.

9. Moffatt, "Reflections of a College Librarian," 346.

No Difference but Dollars: Collection Development in College versus University Libraries

by C. Roger Davis

This is the devil's advocate chapter. Readers who find this approach disconcerting, especially so early on, are urged to spring ahead and fall back later as time permits and second thoughts, seasoned thoughts, prevail.

The premise of this book follows appropriately from Miller and Rockwood's *College Librarianship,* especially its three sections on "Collection Development from a College Perspective."[1] Miller and Rockwood maintain that collection development is, or ought to be, fundamentally different in college and university libraries. In the present anthology, Hill, Hannaford, and Epp agree and have here opened the windows on a variety of positions in support of this thesis. This chapter will review statements from the Miller and Rockwood book, list and comment on the positions in the present book to which exception is taken, cite those claims that are inconsistent with this book's thesis, and conclude with a personal perspective.

MILLER AND ROCKWOOD: ACCURATE OR MISLEADING?

In attempting to set forth the fundamental differences between college and university libraries, Miller and Rockwood maintain that in colleges "the primary client is the student and not the faculty member" and that the college library should be (in Evan Farber's words) "a collection of cultural and recreational materials that can expand students' horizons."[2] Miller and Rockwood argue that "university collection-development officers . . . have the comfort of aiming for total coverage in many, or perhaps even in every field; they might even have the funds to acquire near total coverage."[3] In addition, "university librarians need not worry very much about the rationale for their periodicals collection."[4] Miller and Rockwood also state that subject specialists and collection development librarians in universities can "proceed in an abstract intellectual vacuum."[5] The authors and others imply that collection development librarians in a college setting know or should know their collections better than their counterparts at a university. Overall, Miller and Rockwood seek an objective set of criteria to counter the twin policy perils of "whims, hunches, and prejudices" on the one hand and "ordering anything any faculty member actually does request" on the other.[6]

The questions of whether books are bought mainly for students in a college and for faculty in a university, and whether either of these alleged "primary clients" actually uses or can be led to use the books thus bought, can be set aside if we consider not what the students should need or what the faculty might want but what links them both—the curriculum. The curriculum is the appropriate basis for collection development decisions serving students and faculty at college *and* university libraries. All other questions are secondary: format (paperback, microfilm, computer disc, videocassette), indexing (where and how often cited?), recommender (someone important?), level (juvenile? "research"? whose?), use (last checked out when? by whom?), language, country of origin, and even price. These are secondary to the curriculum.

Evan Farber's suggestion that the college library today can afford to collect "cultural and recreational materials" that do not relate to the curriculum is surely as surreal as the belief that universities aim (or with rare exceptions have ever aimed) for "total coverage." Many college librarians bemoan budgets that barely cover essentials, and in recent years even the University of Texas and Stanford University, never mind Yale, Princeton, and other major research universities, have had significant budget crunches affecting library acquisitions. The University of Massachusetts announced an $8.6-million loss in its operating budget for 1989–90, involving cancellation of 957 class sections, a cut of twenty-four faculty and two hundred administrative and staff positions, and a cut of $1.3 million in the library budget.[7] "Not worry very much about . . . periodicals"? In the past fifteen years, this same university has had at least six extensive reviews of periodical subscriptions and serial standing orders, requiring a 16.5 percent cut in 1974–76 alone and severe, across-the-board, quota-based cuts in other years.[8] This case may be extreme, but "steady-state serials" (the need to cancel a title of equal cost for every one added) has been the rule at many state and private university libraries throughout the past fifteen years.[9]

It is unimaginable that, in times of increased accountability throughout academe, a collection development officer would proceed "in a vacuum" without continual consultation with those shaping and using the curriculum. Has no one seen Stanford's internal faculty contact forms or read Texas's manual for bibliographers?[10] The assertion that college collection development people know their collection better than their university counterparts is unwarranted and possibly a red herring. As sole bibliographer for an 800,000-volume library, is it likely that I know as much about this collection as when I was one of six area bibliographers at a university library of not quite two million volumes? It can be argued that college librarians know little about the contents of even relatively *small* collections, and are responsible for less, because book selection is dominated by the faculty.[11] On the other hand, are we really to imagine that selectors anywhere are not responsible for what is added—on standing orders, approval orders, by gift, or whatever—just because they handle a *large* number of titles? Review of approval orders in a university library is a title-by-title process as much as is any other selecting.

Finally, the twin policy perils Miller and Rockwood wish colleges to avoid exist for universities, too, but, as with other polarities presented, a resolution—a middle way or a different way—exists. It could be as simple as following the practices they dismiss as "self-evident":

> Use *Choice*, use standard lists, involve faculty in collection decisions, give special attention to the existing strengths of [the] library, consider the holdings of other area institutions and the willingness of such institutions to extend their resources to others, make interlibrary loan arrangements, and try to anticipate the changing nature of the college curriculum.[12]

TEN VIEWPOINTS RECONSIDERED

In their introduction to this book, Hill, Hannaford, and Epp suggest that "collection development in colleges may be more difficult to do well." This is flattering but suspect, if one listens to the magnitude, diversity, and unpredictability of the forces ARL libraries need to react to, as told twice yearly at the Association for Library Collections and Technical Services (ALCTS), Resources Section, Chief Collection Development Officers of Large Research Libraries (a.k.a. "the Big Heads") discussion group meetings. More substantive, from the work of my colleagues in these pages, are the following ten views, with my comments:

1. *Adaptation of university to college collection development is "more than mere downscaling."* *Downscaling* sounds like *downgrading* and may imply it. The collection development process, however, must be matched to each institution with regard to its integrity; colleges need not wait for "trickle-down" from university libraries to address their own needs and goals. Still, it is wasteful to invent solutions if one can see a range of policies, practices, and possibilities in job descriptions, selection tools, vendors, weeding and storage, teaching, data access, and cooperative efforts at a larger library and intelligently choose, combine, and compact them into

one's own space, staff, and time requirements. We need not think of this as "scaling" at all, but simply adopting or adapting essential features of needed services. Are you starting a Russian Studies program? A preservation program? Have you been offered an extraordinary collection of Spanish Golden-Age drama and wonder how to proceed? Should you not consult someone who has experienced such events?

2. *Collection development in college libraries can be simplified.* Or: *Collection development is complex enough to merit a look at its components and a contingency model.* Collection development can be about as simple or as complex as the people most concerned wish it to be, whether at a college *or* a university. At some point, all could probably benefit from the kind of atomization of duties and rationalization of resources that comes from a self-study. A contingency model could identify key variables in an organizational situation and allow one to tailor or customize one's response or one's collection to local needs and interests. This could be preferable to hard-and-fast formulas for budget allocations; hard-and-fast rules for accepting gifts, replacing lost books, or calling Security; or set-in-concrete periodical ratios by student or subject ("two financial journals for every fifty economics students or for every sexual-issue journal"). But if so, such a contingency model would be equally helpful in university libraries that, with other elements of society, are moving from a strictly hierarchical arrangement to one organized more by function.[13] Like college libraries, they increasingly need to prove responsiveness to a changing financial, political, and curricular environment.

3. *Collection development based on demand or use may be wrong, but collection development itself can be morally right.* Collection development based on demand or use may be "wrong," but in a time of tight budgets one must wonder at the alternative: the wisdom and utility of arguing for material that nobody actively wants. Does moral duty here call for presenting to one's potential as well as probable users a broad or representative range of the issues of the day? The reality is determined by the goals of the library and by politics—that is, politics in the good sense of dealing with people who have needs and trying to meet them. Paul Mosher has spoken of collection development as essentially a political process.[14] If collection development is also a moral activity, this must be true in university as well as college libraries.

4. *Censorship can have worse effects in a college library because of its limited budget.* Part of the high moral ground in collection development is concern over censorship—inappropriate influences of student groups, faculty, staff, and one's own biases as selector (which, however, one may have been hired for). The potential harmful

effects of censorship, however, are greater in a large library because that censorship may go undetected more easily and affect
more people.

5. *Limited funds and changeable course offerings require focus on undergraduate rather than research materials.* Limited funds and changeable course offerings are by no means proprietary to colleges: universities have them too, writ large. What that fact requires of
collection developers is that there be a focus on the curriculum.

6. *Scarce resources should focus on developing "student-centered" core
collections rather than "faculty-research-related" ones.* To persist in
distinguishing between student-centered core collections and
faculty-research-related ones is to give short shrift to one's wor-
thier faculty *and* student clients in the research-teaching-learning
triangle. One may agree that, given budget constraints, esoteric
purchases in support of the research of individual faculty members
is a luxury best left to university libraries, but there are other
constraints to consider: (*a*) the limits of recruiting, or the need
to attract and retain good faculty; and (*b*) the cost of the second-
rate, or the need to encourage state-of-the-art presentations in
lecture and lab. There is, in short, a need to recognize the tie
that exists between active research and good teaching, and to
make the latter more likely by making the former more easy. At
Smith College, junior faculty are permitted to teach a seminar
in their specialty very early; thus their research interest and the
curricular need can be seen as combined and corresponding, con-
flating not conflicting.

I reject the negativism implied when one speaks of teaching faculties
as "coming under pressure" to do research and to publish. To offer useful
information, interpretations, methodologies, available strategies or technology, interdisciplinary bridges, and enthusiasm, one cannot teach well
without doing research. As William Dickinson, geosciences chair at the
University of Arizona, writes:

> In my heart, I think that the discovery inherent in research and the trans-
> mission inherent in teaching are truly two sides of the same coin. Teacher
> and student are both engaged in the same kind of inquiry, and the habits
> of hypothesis and analysis embodied in what we call research are essential
> to the process. . . . In my mind research is a key source of vitality and a
> prime touchstone with reality.[15]

Kingman Brewster of Yale wrote, "If teaching is to be more than the
retailing of the known, and if research is to seek real breakthroughs in
the explanation of man and the cosmos, then teachers must be scholars,
and scholarship must be more than the refinement of the inherited store
of knowledge."[16] In any case, the better undergraduate students can and

do use faculty-research-level materials in every field. This said, however, it is still useful to perform daily in one's own institution—college *or* university—a kind of triage on expressed research needs to identify those that can be met locally, those that can be met through a sharing or loan arrangement, and those best left for travel fellowships.

7. *Bibliographic instruction is central to student success with library resources.* Bibliographic instruction is the best tool, or tactic, to promote the informed use of academic library resources, and Evan Farber deserves much credit for his long championing of it. However, to suppose that, for example, suburban upper-middle-class kids in attractive, accessible liberal arts colleges need such instruction any more than farm kids or inner-city kids attempting to use large, impersonal, and sometimes forbidding university libraries is simply wrong.

8. *A large portion of books in college libraries are seldom used.* One contributor states that historically book selection in college libraries has been chiefly a faculty duty and cites studies showing that a great many of these books are seldom used. If he intends to imply that librarians do better, unfortunately other studies found the reverse, or at least that "there was no significant difference in the circulation patterns of books selected by faculty and those selected by librarians."[17] We need not fight to divide the spoils; use of materials no matter by whom selected should be much greater at every academic library, and any methods that achieve a better fit between selector and user should be welcomed.

9. *College faculty are more likely to be sympathetic and supportive.* Are faculty more supportive in a college library? It is my experience that, if times are tight and the situation is perceived as "them or us," faculty will look out for themselves and let the library (staff, at least) be cut. At other times, appropriately motivated faculty will rally 'round the library when it is under the gun, speaking against cuts in hours, materials budgets, or interlibrary loan services—considerations that affect them directly. Apart from the annual ebb and flow of particular political issues, how supportive faculty are may also relate to how autonomous the library is and how much authority it has to perform its mission. Thus Patricia Battin observes, "The most striking feature of traditional academic organizations . . . is the virtual isolation of the library. . . . Despite the rhetoric about it being the heart of the university, the library and librarians have been for years isolated from the policy councils of most institutions."[18] And J. Gormly Miller at Cornell notes, "In the first place the university library administration did not usually have the degree of authority to make the allocations effectively nor were sufficient additional funds forthcoming."[19]

10. *Collection development in college libraries requires a higher level of organization and structure to incorporate a closer working relationship with faculty.* If it is true, as one contributor writes, that college libraries have a closer working relationship with faculty than do university libraries, that is simply a shame. Are a much higher percentage of faculty really library-conscious in a college of 2,000 than in a university of 20,000? As for the call for "a higher level of organization and structure" in the college librarian's working relationship with faculty, would not an informed faculty library liaison from each department do the trick—for college *or* university library? That, and innumerable personal encounters (unstructured) between selection staff and individual faculty.

SIMILAR GOALS—SIMILAR APPROACHES

Several chapters in this book pursue unassailable goals for college libraries—a "fair and intellectually sound" apportioning of funds, good communication with faculty about academic program changes, systematic growth when opportunity beckons, effective use of approval plans, and a manageable preservation effort. These are equally good goals for university libraries.

Regarding allocation formulas, Jasper Schad reminds us that "individuals apply their own particular standards of fairness, which is to say that fairness cannot be measured against a single, absolute principle. It is pretty much what people think it is."[20] Data are important but in the end they may be shaped to whatever ends the presenter wishes. Inescapably, no matter how quantified, the result, to be acceptable (whether fair or intellectually sound or not), must be the result of a political process—and one no different in essence in a college, university, or research library.

Similarly, communicating about changes in the college curriculum involves the same process and variables as in the university setting. The only difference is dollars, the scale of the disruption if a major program or an important faculty member is added or dropped. Regarding systematic growth, Richard Werking's Trinity University essay is instructive and cheering, but how different would the basic steps in the expansion process have been in a much larger library?

Those who argue for approval plans in essence argue on my side, that there need not be a difference between college libraries and other libraries in their ability to make effective use of approval plans. Informed profiling, constant monitoring, and careful review of approval plans must be the rule if they are to succeed in any setting. Given a fair chance, they can be a godsend. Similarly, those who argue for preservation efforts are saying that college libraries can be like research libraries in having materials that are appropriate candidates for this attention.

CONCLUSION

A. Bartlett Giamatti, in his farewell baccalaureate address at Yale, re-marked, "We know we are alone. It is how we connect or combine that should interest us."[21] One can stress divisions, distinctions, and differences. Between college and research libraries, however, there is a blurring or blending of such differences, as in Italo Calvino's *Invisible Cities*, where the cities Marco Polo visits seem to take on aspects of each other over time.[22] In a society moving toward inclusiveness and diversity, it may be wiser to look for shared characteristics, mutual interests, and commonalities. Small and large academic libraries may have more in common with "their own kind" than with each other, but to seek always one's solutions in the peer group invites stagnation, not standard-raising.

There are differences in attitude toward collection development goals at both university and college libraries. The extremes of these can be found represented in fiction: Stanisław Lem's story *The Cyberiad* features an insatiable robot named Pug, enthused about all previous facts and feeling that all knowledge is priceless; then there is the librarian in B. F. Skinner's *Walden Two* who prides himself on having the best if not the most, and consigns the rest to an old barn.[23]

There are differences in the collection development process by field. As J. Gormly Miller notes, "The procedures and sub-systems within these processes and the characteristics of the materials being handled are very different among the various disciplines, subject matters, and geographical areas being served."[24] In other words, fine arts is different from labor relations. The differences may be in characteristics of the documentation, the way information is handled, the pattern of research and teaching, or, most important, the needs of the users within particular client groups.

There are major differences between college and research libraries in working conditions that affect the context in which collection development decisions are made, but the overall approaches and principles are the same. The chief difference is dollars. All other differences flow from it.

Otherwise, what can be made of the fact that, year after year, many more guests—collection development librarians from medium-sized and small libraries—attend the "Big Heads" meeting than do members? Or that after some years the RTSD (now ALCTS) Resources Section (RS) Chief Collection Development Officers of Medium-sized Research Libraries discussion group changed its name to that of the Collection Development Librarians of Academic Libraries? Or that staff from a wide mix of institutions profitably attend meetings of the ALCTS RS Gifts and Exchange and Acquisition Librarians/Vendors of Library Materials discussion groups? Or that Sheila Creth can address personnel issues all "along the academic library continuum from the small college library to the largest university library"?[25] Or that Larry Oberg can report successful use of the RLG Conspectus by smaller libraries?[26] Or that many of the contributors to this volume have worked well at both college and university libraries? Surely nothing if not that the experience is transferable.

Librarians unhappy with their uneven collection or their present mix of research and undergraduate library practices may find appealing the client-centered model presented by Bart Harloe. It "creates a decision-making structure whereby important collection development initiatives are taken by the library, with the advice and consent of the . . . faculty."[27] Best of all, it is conciliatory and collegial.

Advocacy is not an abstract good. Indeed, both innocence and experience argue for an end to the perception of the collection development officer as advocate—for librarians as selectors, for higher budgets, for unrepresented areas or authors—and a restored understanding of that leader as an ombudsman for quality. "Innocence," because such leaders do not want or need power and authority; "experience," because having fought with faculty, they know enough not to, or how to, or to choose their fights and causes carefully, with the aim of better service.

Kafka says, "We must have books which come upon us like ill fortune and distress us deeply. . . . A book must be an ice axe to break the sea frozen inside us."[28] This book is not quite that, but perhaps my distress over its premise will inspire a closer reading by others.

NOTES

1. William Miller and D. Stephen Rockwood, eds., *College Librarianship* (Metuchen, N.J., and London: Scarecrow, 1981), 135–53.

2. Ibid., 137, 139. Miller and Rockwood cite Evan Farber, "Limiting College Library Growth: Bane or Boon?" in *Farewell to Alexandria*, ed. Daniel Gore (Westport, Conn.: Greenwood, 1976), 39.

3. Miller and Rockwood, *College Librarianship*, 135.

4. Ibid., 141.

5. Ibid., 142.

6. Ibid., 151–52.

7. Robert Grabar, "UMass Slashing Several Hundred Jobs," *Daily Hampshire Gazette* 203 (July 21, 1989): 1, 8.

8. See Siegfried Feller, "Library Serial Cancellectomies at the University of Massachusetts, Amherst," *Serials Librarian* 1 (Winter 1976–77): 140–52.

9. From a survey report by Carl Deal (University of Illinois at Urbana-Champaign) for the chief collection development officers of large research libraries, June 20, 1989: "Twenty-two [research] libraries cancelled from 4 to 2,155 serials titles in 1988/89. . . . The ratio of serials allocations to monographs continues to grow, and serial cancellations have been very serious for many research collections, especially since 1986/87." From a 132-page Cornell report funded by the Mellon Foundation: "The typical responses that had been made previously at Cornell and elsewhere under the circumstances of increasing needs

and decreasing resources were to reduce duplication, cut back journal and serial subscriptions, improve staff efficiency, reduce staff positions, allow for some deterioration of collections and services, defer or suspend retrospective acquisitions, and eliminate allocation of general funds for support of special collections." J. Gormly Miller, *Collection Development and Management at Cornell* (Ithaca, N.Y.: Cornell University Libraries, 1981), 11.

10. A revised and expanded version of the work begun by Carolyn Bucknall (University of Texas–Austin) and her subcommittee of the Resource and Technical Services Division Collection Management and Development Committee is available as *A Guide for Writing a Bibliographer's Manual* (Chicago: ALA, 1987).

11. Charles A. Gardner, "Book Selection Policies in the College Library: A Reappraisal," *College and Research Libraries* 46 (March 1985): 140–46; quoted in Larry R. Oberg, Mary Kay Schleiter, and Michael Van Houten, "Faculty Perceptions of Librarians at Albion College: Status, Role, Contribution, and Contacts," *College and Research Libraries* 50 (March 1989): 220.

12. Miller and Rockwood, *College Librarianship,* 139.

13. Filtering eventually to a library near you: "Fast-rising business whizzes expect radically decentralized organizations, machines that suggest alternatives, and managers who lead through negotiation rather than rule by authority." Brian Dumaine, "What the Leaders of Tomorrow See," *Fortune* 120 (July 3, 1989): 2, 48–62.

14. Paul Mosher (Director, University of Pennsylvania Libraries) contributed significantly to a larger discussion of strategies for securing book funds at the Chief Collection Development Offices of Large Research Libraries meeting at San Antonio, January 9, 1988. He spoke of establishing support, forming a social contract that has financial bases, finding symbols and images that move the administration, working with the development office to ensure compatible aims, spotting persuasive faculty with savvy, making sure the head librarian is supportive, and creating a climate of understanding to oppose "management by exasperation."

15. "The Spirit of Inquiry," an insert to *Lo Que Pasa* (the University of Arizona faculty/staff newsletter), March 23, 1987, p. 4; cited in Rebecca Kellogg, "Faculty Members and Academic Librarians: Distinctive Differences," *College and Research Libraries News* 48 (November 1987): 603.

16. *The Report of the President; Yale University: 1971–72* (New Haven, Conn.: Yale University, 1972), 14.

17. Mary Sellen, "Book Selection in the College Library: The Faculty Perspective," *Collection Building* 7 (Spring 1985): 4; quoted in David L. Vidor and Elizabeth Futas, "Effective Collection Developers: Librarians or Faculty?" *Library Resources and Technical Services* 32 (April 1988): 135; and see page 136: "The hypothesis that librarians are more effective collection developers than faculty members has not been upheld." See also Oberg, Schleiter, and Van Houten, "Faculty Perceptions," 220: "[These studies] do not prove that librarians are better selectors. In fact, most of the charges leveled at the faculty also apply to librarians."

18. Patricia Battin, "The Library: Center of the Restructured University," in *Colleges Enter the Information Society*, ed. Russel Edgerton (Washington, D.C.: American Association for Higher Education, 1983), 26; quoted in Dennis P. Carrigan, "The Political Economy of the Academic Library," *College and Research Libraries* 49 (July 1988): 330.

19. Miller, *Collection Development*, 57.

20. Jasper G. Schad, "Fairness in Book Fund Allocation," *College and Research Libraries* 48 (November 1987): 480.

21. A. Bartlett Giamatti, "On Congregations, Their Pleasures and Perils," *Yale Alumni Magazine* 49 (June 1986): 18.

22. Italo Calvino, *Invisible Cities*, trans. William Weaver (New York and London: Harcourt Brace Jovanovich, 1974).

23. Stanisław Lem, *The Cyberiad: Fables for the Cybernetic Age*, trans. Michael Kandel (New York: Seabury, 1974); B. F. Skinner, *Walden Two* (New York: Macmillan, 1948; new prefaces 1969, 1976).

24. Miller, *Collection Development*, 11–12.

25. Sheila D. Creth, "Personnel Issues for Academic Librarians: A Review and Perspectives for the Future," *College and Research Libraries* 50 (March 1989): 144.

26. Larry R. Oberg, "Evaluating the Conspectus Approach for Smaller Library Collections," *College and Research Libraries* 49 (May 1988): 187–96.

27. Bart Harloe, "Achieving Client-Centered Collection Development in Small and Medium-Sized Academic Libraries," *College and Research Libraries* 50 (May 1989): 344–53.

28. Letter to Oskar Pollak, January 27, 1904, in Franz Kafka, *I Am a Memory Come Alive: Autobiographical Writings*, ed. Nahum N. Glatzer (New York: Schocken, 1974), 7.

Part 2

Emerging Issues

The late 1970s was an era of great innovation in collection development, at least for medium-sized and large academic and research libraries. Policies and guidelines were written, and the journal literature was full of substantive articles.

Although college libraries benefited from much that was written about larger libraries, showing that the trickle-down theory is not entirely without merit, there are some emerging issues that seem to affect smaller academic libraries with more imminent force, or at least differently. Several of these emerging issues in collection development in college libraries are discussed in this section: parsimony vis-à-vis collection development, management structure, and ethics.

Thomas Leonhardt, in his paper "Ockham's Razor and Collection Development," argues that collection development has become too complex in the last few years and that librarians are like the crew of the *Vincennes,* using an expensive, complex Aegis system to try to identify enemy aircraft when a good pair of binoculars might have done the job better, faster, and less expensively. He further argues that Ockham's razor can be applied to collection development, thus simplifying it, and that this, in turn, will lead to more effective collection development at a lower cost. Leonhardt specifies some of the ways in which collection development has been made needlessly complicated (e.g., the conspectus), and details various methods of simplification.

Large academic libraries have tried a number of organizational approaches to collection development, and these have been reported in the literature. However, there is little in the published literature on approaches to the organization of collection development in small academic libraries. Thomas Kirk presents just such a contingency model in his article, "Collection Development Programs in College Libraries: A Contingency Perspective." Using the contingency approach to organizational structure and behavior (a recent development in management theory), Kirk shows that it is possible to determine the characteristics of the various parts of collection development and identify possible models for the organization of collection development in college libraries. The selection of the appropriate model for a particular library will depend on certain local features. Kirk argues that, because collection development is a diverse set of activities with varying requirements for technology, environments of operation, expertise among workers, and organizational structure, collection development should not be looked at as a single entity.

In his article "Ethics and Collection Development," William Hannaford holds that collection development is an ethical activity and not merely a matter of the taste of selectors. In a traditional philosophical manner, he divides all human activity into two categories: that which has little or no impact upon others and that which does. Actions in the first category are said to be in the private domain and to be matters of taste. Those in the second category are in the public domain and are ethical. Collection development, which falls into this second category, is an ethical activity, and as such its rightness or wrongness has nothing to do with whether any specific individual or group does it or whether it is done on the basis of publication or use. Hannaford further argues that the various codes of ethics produced by the American Library Association (ALA) are really only codes of etiquette and that it is time for librarians, including those in collection development, to start paying attention to the ethical implications of their behavior.

Ockham's Razor and Collection Development

by Thomas W. Leonhardt

Richard Popkin, writing for the *Academic American Encyclopedia,* explains Ockham's Razor thus: "The principle [Ockham's Razor] states that a person should not increase, beyond what is necessary, the number of entities required to explain anything, or that the person should not make more assumptions than the minimum needed."[1] In a word, simplify. This principle should be kept in mind anytime we write about collection development, anytime we write a collection development policy, anytime we write a collection development job description, or anytime we try to evaluate a collection development proposal, project, or program expansion.

The way we describe ourselves and the process of book selection and our preoccupation with trying to show that we are scientifically developing and managing our collections should alert us to the need to examine what we are doing. The RLG Conspectus epitomizes what is going on, and the amount written about it and its curative powers makes me wonder if we are not protesting too much. As anyone who has written job descriptions can tell you, it isn't always what someone does that gets a job reclassified upward, it is how you describe the job. We describe what we do well and in great detail, but we gloss over the results. Where's the beef? Who knows? No one is saying, but we are told time and again what a good job we are doing and we are told that we are scientifically analyzing collections and making it possible to share collections and even coordinate what we buy. There is much truth in these claims but I think the benefits are and should be limited. I also think that libraries can expend a great deal of energy in process without producing a product that justifies that expenditure and that does not necessarily benefit the library's users, our raison d'être, if we pause to remember.

We used to select books, acquire them, gather them, and so on. These are plain, forthright terms that said what we did. There was no felt need to embellish them, for acquisitions was noble work by definition. Some great collections were built in those days, collections that will never be matched again, primarily because of money but also because there are probably too many cooks nowadays, cooks who lack the vision and the bookishness of bygone days. This is not a reflection on the many fine selectors, both faculty and librarians, out there but more a comment on the specialization that has overtaken society. How great collections were built is another essay, but suffice it to say that those collections were built by one or two visionaries per institution who had many opportunities for receiving and buying collections ready made by bibliophiles and scholars in the broadest sense of the word.

Now we develop collections. *Development* is supposed to connote a process more scientific (more methodical, too?) than mere selection or gathering (what then is an approval plan if not a gathering plan for those with money enough to support the habit?). I am not convinced that we needed to change the name of what we do. That, too, is the subject of another essay, but part of the impetus for change was to differentiate the mechanical aspects of acquisitions from the selection of materials. That was simplistic and wrong but it prevailed, and here we are with descriptions of ourselves that are not as honest as they once were. I am not sure that the jobs themselves are as honest as they once were in that we do purport to be building collections scientifically. Our methods may be scientific but do they yield scientific results? I say no. We should use the terms that do not mislead us into thinking that a name change will help us choose books better or successfully make up for an inadequate budget. *Collection management* may be a good description of what we all do in libraries, but to corner its use and meaning for exclusive use by book selectors is both unfair to others in the library and self-serving. The argument put forward by some is that all aspects of the collection should be under the aegis of the collection development librarian. There are many problems to that approach and argument but, in summary, total responsibility belongs to the library director who oversees the efforts of many who work together for a common good. Pompous job titles can lead to pompous notions. We must all guard against elitist notions in our business. We need each other and no one person can know everything. We must remember, too, that those who know what they don't know and turn to others are intellectually honest and are appreciated by colleagues.

This development within the American Library Association and in libraries throughout the country reminds one of the fairy tale about the emperor's new clothes. We all know the story about the naked emperor. He knew he was naked, his courtiers knew he was naked, everyone knew he was naked, but no one was willing to say so lest he or she be taken for a fool. A simple child, too young to be vain, too honest to remain silent, shouted the truth. The fraudulent tailors profited from these new clothes, that we know, but did the emperor and his subjects gain anything from the experience? One can hope so, but it was only a fairy tale, meant to instruct the listener or reader, not the characters in the story.

Did we librarians, readers and hearers of the tale, learn the lesson? Apparently not, judging from the way we follow trends and accept them on faith rather than on empirical evidence. Apparently not, judging from the way we construct elaborate procedures, committees, and frameworks that are never finished or that never produce anything more than a structure. The cliché commonly heard in informal but heated discussions is "smoke and mirrors." Ockham also wrote that "matter is matter and form is form."[2] We should remember that in our discussion and add that "process is process" and "substance is substance." Process is not a substitute for substance. Process without substance is like the emperor's new clothes.

Related to this issue of overcomplication is Parkinson's Law, or the rising pyramid: "Work expands so as to fill the time available for its completion."[3] I first heard of this law from an army sergeant in charge of a detail on which I was privileged to serve. There were fourteen of us, with seven implements, assigned to beautify the lawn of the bachelor officers' quarters. We were given the entire day to complete the task and, by the end of the day, we were done. Even with double the number of tools and workers, it would have taken the same amount of time, because if we had finished the job early, the sergeant would have found us another detail—one that might not have been as easy as the lawn detail.

Quoting from Parkinson again: "Granted that work (and especially paperwork) is thus elastic in its demands on time, it is manifest that there be little or no relationship between the work to be done and the size of the staff to which it may be assigned. A lack of real activity does not, of necessity, result in leisure. A lack of occupation is not necessarily revealed by a manifest idleness. The thing to be done swells in importance and complexity in a direct ratio with the time to be spent."[4] His "explanation of the factors underlying the general tendency to which this law [Parkinson's] gives definition [is] (1) 'An official wants to multiply subordinates, not rivals' and (2) 'Officials make work for each other.' "[5]

In informal discussions I would not have to go any further to elicit nods of approval and example after example of what I am talking about. What is it that collection development officers do? I know that I am tarring many with the same brush, but I believe that there is a problem that is ignored in the literature. Two reasons for the widespread acceptance of the RLG Conspectus, for example, are that it helps justify the existence of many jobs in academic libraries and it provides justification for a collection development officer to do nothing but collection development. There are reasons why a collection development officer is needed, but in many (most?) academic libraries the responsibility for coordinating policy and gathering budget data, working with faculty, and so on can be delegated throughout the library. But will the latter arrangement be as effective? I counter with the question, will it *not* be as effective? How, after all, is the effectiveness of a collection development program or officer measured and evaluated? For the individual, staying power is measured more by interpersonal and political skills rather than by which titles were selected and how those titles were used by the faculty and students.

The literature contains many testimonials about the RLG Conspectus. Yet the Conspectus represents better than anything else what can happen when we blindly accept something, no matter how good it might be in certain settings for certain things, and then apply it indiscriminately. The archetype RLG Conspectus was meant to be used in a total university library context. Written as Stanford's collection development policy by Elmer Grieder and Pete Johnson, it was a thick, thorough document that helped me, as gift and exchange librarian, evaluate offers of gifts. It also offered me a chance to work with curators, branch librarians, reference librarians, and other selectors in learning how to apply the tenets of such a document. The document itself was lengthy but simple in style and format. The sophistication came from using it in working with the collection and its users. When a gift came in with scores of novels by women, from the eighteenth to the twentieth centuries, you knew that you had a tremendous resource. But the collection development guide did not say that women authors were a part of the collecting policy and there may not have been someone specializing in women authors. How did we know we were weak in that area? We searched the catalog. My point is that a collection development policy can be an invaluable selection tool. It isn't meant to have a life of its own and it isn't meant to substitute for intelligent, well-read librarians (and faculty) who are committed to building a strong collection through assiduous selection.

We need to simplify our approach to collection development and evaluation. There is nothing wrong with collection evaluation and there is nothing wrong with using the RLG Conspectus for that evaluation, but it should be used thoughtfully. Great detail should be avoided unless you are completely convinced that you need it. The more detailed we get, the more accurate we tend to think we are, and we in fact imply great accuracy by such detail just as we imply accuracy when we say we have 501,396 volumes instead of 500,000. Both numbers are probably wrong but at least one of them is honest. Sampling and statistics may be scientific but we still need to realize that if we sample, we are not getting a completely true picture of the universe—there is room for error. We must realize that the application of sampling techniques can be done badly, and that, even when done well, sampling is a quantitative, not a qualitative, measure. Yet in a very real sense, the more books you have, the more likely you are to have a good collection. Measurements do not tell us anything about the quality of the books and journals in our collections. That is sometimes mentioned, in passing, in articles extolling the virtues of the RLG Conspectus, and we are told that in conjunction with such measures we can also search against standard lists and bibliographies. Of course we can and we should, but in this day and age, although sampling has its place, we need not rely on it.

The National Shelflist Count is an example of overzealousness in sampling, although it is unclear why, in this digitized age, such an antiquated approach is still being tolerated and supported. LeRoy Ortopan discusses the limitations of the shelflist approach to collection assessment and mentions the possibility of more accurate machine counting.[6] Even so, he feels that the shelflist approach as a collection analysis tool has value and encourages others to join in the project. Ortopan offers no evidence that the project has yielded any positive results other than to tell libraries where their collections have grown, based on what they have cataloged, not on what they have bought.

Joseph Branin, David Farrell, and Mariann Tiblin conclude, not surprisingly, that the National Shelflist Count Project should be expanded and continued despite some serious problems and deficiencies. They argue that "it [the National Shelflist Count Project] is a valuable project for gathering compatible quantitative data on collection sizes by subject. It provides useful information for collection evaluation and description. To discontinue this project would weaken the efforts at establishing a national network of research library collections."[7] There is passing recognition that we live in an automated environment: "The professional organization assigned responsibility for the project should explore the possibility of automated title counts and make this option available to participants. RLG and OCLC may be able to assist with the effort."[8]

Thomas E. Nisonger describes a 1984 project conducted by the Association of Higher Education of North Texas (AHE) consortium using the RLG Conspectus and building on work done using the SUNY/OCLC approach. "In essence the AHE project represents a computerized shelflist measurement of multiple libraries employing the RLG Conspectus breakdown."[9] Nisonger also points out that "the level of specificity in the RLG Conspectus breakdown may be too detailed for libraries whose collections are smaller than the size of ARL institutions."[10]

Nisonger's article is an argument for simplifying the whole process of collection analysis and assessment by relying more on automation and less on the labor-intensive, subjective, and inaccurate efforts of collection development minions who want to find ways to justify their existence not as librarians but as collection development specialists.

David Farrell and Jutta Reed-Scott offer no empirical evidence that the North American Collections Inventory Project (NCIP) is actually working. The authors indicate that there are problems regarding NCIP's complexities and its labor intensiveness. But we are asked to accept *a priori* that the Conspectus, as described here, is the way to go in order to achieve sound collection analysis and to begin to practice cooperative collection development on an international basis. Amazingly, this article, while going beyond the research library in its recommendation of the Conspectus, makes no mention of automation other than to note that "the conspectus does not give item-level information, and the rapidly expanding bibliographic networks are better sources for known-item searches."[11] This makes OCLC, WLN, RLIN, and Utlas sound like emerging technologies. The authors make no mention of the SUNY, AHE, and Amigos projects that use Conspectus and shelflist techniques to study overlap of collections. No one outside of Illinois seems to care that the twenty-eight academic libraries there already have access to their collective collection through a common online catalog and circulation system.

The point of these criticisms of two national attempts to measure the strengths of library collections is not that such efforts are not needed—they are. Rather, the point is that they are labor-intensive, overly complex efforts that all but ignore the automated environment in which we live. They are complicated approaches that even when begun could have made greater progress through such efforts as those of SUNY, AMIGOS, AHE, and the state of Illinois. The benefits of the Conspectus that Farrell and Reed-Scott mention seem to be right out of Parkinson's Law of Collection Development—collection development librarians train other collection development librarians to spend their time in painstaking work that could be achieved more easily and more accurately through automated approaches.

The Pacific Northwest adoption of the Conspectus methodology has been hailed as an example of what can be done by small libraries and by regions. What is never mentioned in print is that many of the larger libraries in the area would have preferred to spend grant monies on retrospective conversion so that overlap comparisons could be made and so that for interlibrary lending, borrowing, and acquisitions, title-by-title searching could be done. There was no support for such an approach because it was not what was being sold at the time. So a partial database of strengths and weaknesses of Northwest collections is available but, for interlibrary cooperation, did any of those libraries discover anything that they did not really know before? Are the WLN libraries in the area better able to borrow from and lend to OCLC libraries in the region because of the Conspectus approach? Is any library not purchasing something because they know that another library with a stronger emphasis will buy it? We are told to accept on faith that the Pacific Northwest approach is good for everyone. The Pacific Northwest approach gets even more detailed than ARL libraries and makes such distinctions as:

1a = Minimal, uneven coverage
1b = Minimal, well chosen
2a = Basic information

2b = Augmented information
3a = Basic study (undergrad.)
3b = Intermediate study
3c = Advanced study
4 = Research level
5 = Comprehensive level.[12]

This detail is to be used by small public libraries and by large research libraries. Who out there will accurately distinguish between minimal, uneven coverage and minimal, well-chosen coverage and which two librarians will use those terms the same way? And who is going to admit to uneven coverage when "well-chosen" is more complimentary?

The Conspectus approach most definitely has value but that value seems limited and questionable. When we are asked to contribute scarce resources, can we justify the time spent by librarians when that time might be better used in direct services to our students and faculty? There is a need for more management data, but it must be collected as simply and accurately as possible. With an automated system such as Innovacq, we can now do our own analyses of what we buy, how much we spend, what our average costs are, and so on. Work done at the time of order, receipt, payment, and cataloging yields valuable data to use in looking at costs and additions to the collection by class (Library of Congress or Dewey), by requesting department, by requesting librarian or faculty member, by type of material, by type of acquisition, and so on.

We can collect similar data through the OCLC Interlibrary Loan Subsystem. We can send our OCLC or RLIN tapes to AMIGOS to have them analyzed. We can compare our machine-readable records with the third edition of *Books for College Libraries* and see where we converge with this standardized list and where we fall short. We should be seeking to get all such lists in machine-readable form for similar analysis. Instead, we insist on fostering manual processes that depend too much on human labor and judgment and that are done inconsistently even within the same library because of the reliance on opinion.

Certainly the college library and the small or medium-sized academic and research libraries should proceed with caution when considering either the RLG Conspectus or the National Shelflist Project as models to use in collection assessment. If either is decided upon, the adopting library should make every effort to simplify the standard and make it as easy and foolproof as possible. The more complicated the standard becomes, the greater the chance for failure or abandonment by those with not enough time to spend on the project and too much common sense. Let us get dressed now, and if you see one of your colleagues wearing that magical birthday suit made of questionable cloth, call him or her aside and make a sensible observation.

NOTES

1. *Academic American Encyclopedia* (Danbury, Conn.: Grolier, 1985), s.v. "Ockham's Razor."

2. Meyrick H. Carre, *Realists and Nominalists* (Oxford: Oxford Univ. Pr., 1967), 119.

3. C. Northcote Parkinson, *Parkinson's Law* (New York: Ballantine Books, 1969), 119.

4. Ibid., 15.

5. Ibid., 17.

6. LeRoy D. Ortopan, "National Shelflist Count: A Historical Introduction," *Library Resources and Technical Services* 29 (October–December 1985): 328–33.

7. Joseph J. Branin, David Farrell, and Mariann Tiblin, "The National Shelflist Count Project: Its History, Limitations, and Usefulness," *Library Resources and Technical Services* 29 (October–December 1985): 340.

8. Ibid.

9. Thomas E. Nisonger, "Editing the RLG Conspectus to Analyze the OCLC Archival Tapes of Seventeen Texas Libraries," *Library Resources and Technical Services* 29 (October–December 1985): 324.

10. Ibid., 323.

11. David Farrell and Jutta Reed-Scott, "The North American Collections Inventory Project: Implications for the Future of Coordinated Management of Research Collections," *Library Resources and Technical Services* 33 (January 1989): 23.

12. Peggy Forcier, "Building Collections Together: The Pacific Northwest Conspectus," *Library Journal* (April 15, 1988): 45.

Collection Development Programs in College Libraries: A Contingency Perspective

by Thomas G. Kirk, Jr.

The literature on collection development has been dominated by a focus on specific elements, such as collection development policy and methods of collection assessment.[1] Recently some attention has been given to the overall enhancement of collection development in college libraries.[2] The literature, however, has largely ignored the development of a conceptual context within which to view all of the activities that comprise collection development. The contingency theory of organization behavior and structure is such a conceptual context. In its most generalized, simple form, the theory suggests that everything depends on everything else. More concretely, the theory identifies elements of an organization and how they interact in the behavior of the organization. This paper provides a brief overview of the development of the theory and then applies it to college collection development programs.

CONTINGENCY THEORY

The contingency theory of organization behavior and structure and the coincident contingency perspective on management of organizations is the result of ninety years of study and research. The industrial revolution led to the development of complex organizations. As they developed, management practitioners, sociologists, psychologists, mathematicians, and other scholars proposed an array of theoretical explanations of organizations and their behavior. Often these theories and the research that supported them were cited in the development of principles or rules for successful management. Such principles were intended to change the way managers should function in order to make their organizations more effective.[3] But each principle tended to run the course of emerging from research findings and then, in the popular management literature, being elevated to a central, sometimes exclusive, position in determining management effectiveness. Subsequent research demonstrated deficiencies in the veracity of the principle. As each new theory proved inadequate a new one took its place, usually by replacing the previous theory rather than modifying or adding to it. This lack of any progress in understanding organizational phenomena left managers cynical about the relevance of organizational theory to practical management issues.[4]

The contingency theory of organizations has its beginnings in the context of fundamental shifts in social science research (e.g., open systems and modeling) and the dissatisfaction with previous one-dimensional management theories. Initially, three elements of an organization—structure, environment, and technology—were central to the contingency theory.[5] The early studies of Burns and Stalker looked at the relationship between the environment in which organizations function and their structure.[6] They found that organizations operating in uncertain environments were likely to be less structured while organizations operating in a stable environment were more structured. This lead to a model which suggested that management align an organization's structure with its operating environment in order to maximize efficiency and effectiveness.

At about the same time, Joan Woodward published a summation of studies which looked at the relationship between technology employed by organizations and the structures of organizations.[7] *Technology* refers to the methods used to carry out the tasks of the organization. The term does not refer specifically to automation or machinery, although they are part of the processes or methods. The results of these studies found that the complexity of the technology is inversely related to the degree of structure. Organizations that complete their tasks in a highly routine and programmed fashion use low technology, while those with varying and unprogrammed tasks use high technology. Organizations operating with low technology are more highly structured with formal communication mechanisms and formally transmitted procedures. Organizations operating with high technology are less structured with informal communication structures that operate with less formal procedures.

Some were not satisfied, however, with the "crude collective categories." These individuals generally viewed each characteristic of the environment or the structure of the organization as having two states: high and low.[8] In response, research during the 1970s was devoted to exploring finer differentiations in the states of the environment and the organization. In turn, an effort was made to show causal relationships between the more precisely defined characteristics and organization effectiveness.

Schoonhoven critiqued the status of the structural contingency theory and suggested that the theory as then understood suffered from (1) a lack of clarity, (2) the failure to recognize the causal relationship being assumed, (3) the failure to differentiate the specific forms of interaction between variables, and (4) the assumption that the relationships are linear and symmetrical (monotonic).[9] In short, the contingency theory had fallen into the trap of earlier theories by assuming that direct linear causal relationships existed that would predict what organization structure would be appropriate if the organization is to be successful in a given environment. The only difference from earlier principles of management was the multiple characteristics that were factored into the relationship.

Schoonhoven went on to propose solutions to the problems in the contingency theory. Her revision of the model suggests that while there may be causal relationships among organization characteristics, the characteristics cannot be considered separately. Rather, they form a complex, interacting system. Furthermore, the relationships—instead of being linear and symmetrical—are nonmonotonic (i.e., one in which an increase in the value of one characteristic will not have a direct linear effect on the situation). At a point in the range of values for a characteristic, the nature or degree of an effect will change.

CONTINGENCY THEORY AND COLLECTION DEVELOPMENT

Contemporary contingency theorists view organizations as open systems with five elements that are fundamental to their behavior: strategic position, structure, environment, technology, and staff. These elements interact over time and affect each other. Programs of collection development in college libraries, like other organizations, can be viewed from this perspective.

Strategic Position

Strategic position refers to the organization's posture within the environment. As it refers to collection development, the issues are:

1. The existence of and relationship with other libraries on campus, and the relationship to audiovisual services and computer services.
2. The collection objectives of the library. Will the library collect materials in all formats (e.g., microfilms, media, machine-readable files)? Will the library's collection development policy address faculty research needs as well as undergraduate curriculum needs? Will the library collect in a specialized subject area as part of special collection or other research-oriented collection? Will the library develop a collection of institutional records, or other archival research materials?
3. The internal and external impact of collecting posture. Bonita

Bryant has described three postures that a library might take toward collection development: acquisitions, selection, and management and control, each requiring different levels of staffing and library organization.[10] The *acquisitions* posture relies on outsiders, primarily faculty, for the selection of material. The *selection* posture retains decisions about selection within the library but depends heavily on input from user groups. Such a posture usually means the library has departmental liaisons and relies heavily on input from the reference department. The *management and control* posture reserves all collection development decisions to the library staff. Commonly, staff with specific subject expertise are assigned these responsibilities, which include not only item selection but also weeding, collection assessment, and management activities (e.g., budget analysis and allocation).

Strategic position, like the other four elements of an organization, has a number of possible states or conditions. The theory proposes that the appropriate choice for the organization depends on the condition or state of the other elements. Therefore, a very small library staff or a staff without the diverse subject knowledge needed for collection development could not effectively use the selection posture. Neither could a library use the acquisitions posture if the faculty are not attentive to collection development. A strategic position should not be selected in isolation; it should be developed out of a careful analysis of the characteristics of all elements of the library organization.

Organization Structure

Organization structure refers to the relationships of parts of an organization with one another and with the environment outside the organization. Traditionally, organization structure included the manager's span of control, the reporting hierarchy, and the assignment of decision-making responsibilities. In the contingency approach to organizations, organization structure also includes the relationships, both formal and informal, that parts of an organization have with other parts and with the environment outside the organization. Attention is given to the nature of the relationships and particularly to the flow of information among the parts of the organization and with the environment outside the organization. The latter is referred to as a boundary spanning or bridging function.

Library managers regularly assess the organization structure of collection development. From the contingency perspective, such assessment must include the other four elements of the organization: strategic position, environment, technology, and staff. For example, in designating who should be responsible for item selection decisions, four sets of questions, corresponding to the four elements, should be answered before making a decision. These questions include:

1. Strategic position: What strategic position does the library wish to possess? Is collection development part of the basic expectations of all professional positions? What role are teaching faculty to have in collection development? Are there other related collections on campus?
2. Environment: What relationships with teaching faculty exist? Are there cooperative collection development arrangements with nearby libraries? What is the reputation of the library in the community?
3. Technology: How complex and time consuming are the procedures for item selection? Do the criteria for selection require in-depth subject expertise?
4. Staff: What staff are available to make such decisions? What are their qualifications? What other responsibilities do they have? Do these responsibilities contribute to or detract from the item selection responsibilities?

The conditional nature of the contingency approach strongly suggests that the answers to these questions should reflect differences across the library organization and its environment. Therefore, the contingency approach encourages variation across the organization and in the interaction with the environment that is appropriate to the circumstances of either the individual staff member or subject area.

The contingency approach emphatically indicates that no one organizational structure is best for all college libraries. What is best for an individual library depends on the interplay of structure with the other elements of the organization. The manager must assess the organization and attempt to determine what structure will be most suitable.

Environment

Environment is the least concrete of the dimensions that affect organization performance and the one least susceptible to change by the library as an organization. The environment of an organization includes all those factors outside the organization that influence the activities of that organization. In collection development the environment includes other activities and programs of the library. For example, is there a bibliographic instruction or other program that can provide an important mechanism for boundary spanning activities in collection development? The environment also includes such groups as publishers, vendors, faculty, college administrators, and students. Events that have direct influence on the library are also part of the environment, including curriculum developments and changes in funding. Other, less direct influences include authors and the development of scholarship, review sources, regional accrediting bodies, government tax policy, inflation, foreign exchange rates, and the general and specific expectations for library services and collections.

Although there is little that an individual library can do about the environment, one issue should be considered by the manager when formulating the collection development program: the creation of mechanisms for maximizing the boundary bridging between the library and the other organizations in its environment. For example, a bridging activity with faculty and students on library use assignments or faculty research interests is often productive. The library's effort to seek adequate funding from the college administration provides further opportunities for boundary-spanning activities. Other bridging activities involve gathering information on vendor services, discounts, and payment plans, and the day-to-day communication between the library and vendors or faculty about individual orders.

Each of these boundary-spanning activities and its degree of development has an impact on and is affected by strategic position, organization structure, technology, environment, and staff. These activities are likely to be most influential in determining the attitudes of outsiders about the library's ability to function effectively. It is through the flow of information into and out of the organization that the organization is perceived as effective by its constituencies in the environment.

Technology

In her study of the organization of collection development in large academic research libraries, Elaine Sloan defined technology as the skills, materials, and techniques employed to carry out the task of collection development.[11] This includes the use or deployment of personnel, the order methods used (including the presence or absence of automation), and the extent and formality with which a collection development policy is used. The essential issues for the manager are the complexity and stability of these elements of the technology. If the elements are stable and simple, then the organization structure can be highly differentiated and work expectations of employees clearly articulated and differentiated. However, if the technology is complex, the organizational structure can be less complex and the work assignments will be more complex and less clearly differentiated. The manager's goal is to identify the procedures and processes (technology) that are appropriate to the nature of the other four elements of the organization.

Staff

The staff is obviously a pervasive element of organization behavior because by definition the organization does not exist without people. Organizations are collections of people ostensibly associated to accomplish goals that individuals alone cannot achieve. In the narrower sense, as an element of organization behavior, *staff* refers to the behavior of the individuals who are part of the organization. This includes behavior directly related to the completion of job responsibilities as well as behavior of a more general nature that is indirectly related to completion of job responsibilities or interactions with other members of the organization. In the contingency theory of organizational behavior, the elements of staff center on personnel questions, such as motivation, productivity, satisfaction, leadership, and performance. These elements are common to other parts of the library's program but perhaps are most difficult to assess relative to a collection development program and therefore are often overlooked.

If the other four elements of the organization are to be designed to enhance staff performance, then more attention must be given to ways of assessing staff performance in collection development. This is one of the most underdeveloped areas of library personnel management.

EFFECTIVENESS

Five interacting elements of organizations are postulated by the contingency theory as determining the operation of the organization. The effectiveness achieved by the organization, however, is not inherent to some particular combination of characteristics of the five elements. Instead, effectiveness is a result of judgments made about the operations from the perspective of some observer: library managers and staff (internal constituencies), and faculty, students, college administrators, alumni, and off-campus communities (external constituencies).

A series of critiques of the literature has suggested a new paradigm for organization effectiveness.[12] Cameron and Whetten claim that universal propositions linking a set of independent variables (organizational characteristics) to effectiveness can never be known because the meaning of the dependent variable (i.e., effectiveness) continually changes. Instead, they describe organization effectiveness as a construct and define constructs as

> abstractions that exist in the heads of people, but have no objective reality. They are mental abstractions designed to give meaning to ideas or interpretations. One difference between constructs and concepts is that concepts can be defined and exactly specified by observing objective events. Constructs cannot be so specified. Their boundaries are not precisely drawn.[13]

Cameron and Whetten suggest a need for clarification of the models of effectiveness. Furthermore, when students of organizations explore the construct, effectiveness should be studied in relationship to multiple perspectives. To accomplish this, Cameron and Whetten suggest answering seven questions that outline the dimensions of the multiple perspectives they have gleaned from their review of the literature:

1. What is the purpose of judging effectiveness?
2. What level of analysis is being used?
3. What span of time is being studied?
4. What type of data are being used for judgment of effectiveness?
5. What is the referent against which effectiveness is judged?
6. On what domain of activity is the judgment focused?
7. From whose perspective is effectiveness being judged?[14]

Cameron's multiple perspectives view of organization effectiveness is another part of the contingency view of organizations. It therefore is another element for library managers to consider in the management of collection development. By incorporating the multiple perspectives of effectiveness into collection development programs, the reality of competing demands within the environment are acknowledged.

CONCLUSION

A full accounting for all the specific factors relevant to making decisions about a college library's collection development program is not possible here. Instead, the emphasis has been on developing the contingency perspective on organization behavior as a framework within which to examine a collection development program and make decisions about its modification. The contingency perspective suggests that decisions be made in the context of an analysis of the relationships among the five elements of an organization: strategic position, structure, environment, technology, and staff. The perspective does not provide a set of rules or principles that direct the course of action. The responsibility of the manager is to anticipate the desired outcomes and set in motion changes in the five elements in order to achieve those outcomes.

There is no guarantee that the analysis and proposed changes will be the best ones. Organization theory can provide a reasonable *post facto* explanation but has very poor predictive values. Though the manager's most important tool is the ability to analyze the organization, fallibility creates great uncertainty. Organization effectiveness will ultimately be judged by the various constituencies.

Although its predictive power is limited, the contingency perspective does avoid the trap of assuming that there are principles of management that will solve an organization's problems or that a set of organization characteristics exists that will guarantee successful achievement of the organization's goals. The power of the contingency perspective is to focus attention on the functioning of the organization and whether that func-

Thomas G. Kirk, Jr.   53

tioning meets the expectations of the constituencies. The perspective clearly defines the manager's role as one of an active student who must understand the organization and develop strategies for its modification in order to maximize the community's view of that organization's effectiveness.

NOTES

1. William E. Hannaford, Jr., "Collection Development in College Libraries," in *Library Resources for College Scholars,* ed. Robert E. Danforth (Lexington, Va.: Washington and Lee University, 1980), 13–17; Theresa Taborsky and Patricia Lenowski, *Collection Development Policies for College Libraries* (Chicago: Association of College and Research Libraries, 1989); Blaine H. Hall, *Collection Assessment Manual for College and University Libraries* (Phoenix: Oryx, 1985).

2. Bonita Bryant, "The Organizational Structure of Collection Development," *Library Resources and Technical Services* 31 (April 1987): 111–22; Carol Cubberley, "Organization for Collection Development in Medium-sized Academic Libraries," *Library Acquisition: Practice & Theory* 11 (1987): 297–323; Lynne Gamble, "Assessing Collection Development Organization in a Small Academic Library," in *Energies in Transition,* ed. Danuta A. Nitecki (Chicago: Association of College and Research Libraries, 1986), 82–85.

3. Jay R. Galbraith, *Organization Design* (Reading, Mass.: Addison-Wesley, 1964); Claude S. George, *The History of Management Thought* (Englewood Cliffs, N.J.: Prentice-Hall, 1972); Harold Kootz, "The Management Theory Jungle Revisited," *Academy of Management Review* 5 (July 1980): 175–87; Harold R. Pollard, *Development in Management Thought* (New York: Crane, Russak, 1974).

4. See Richard De Gennaro, "Library Administration and New Management Systems," *Library Journal* 103 (December 15, 1978): 2477–82 for one library manager's expression of skepticism.

5. Johannes M. Pennings, "The Relevance of the Structural Contingency Model for Organizational Effectiveness," *Administrative Science Quarterly* 20 (September 1975): 393–410.

6. Tom Burns and George Macpherson Stalker, *The Management of Innovation* (London: Tavistock, 1961).

7. Joan Woodward, *Industrial Organization: Theory and Practice* (London: Oxford Univ. Pr., 1965).

8. Lawrence B. Mohr, "Organizational Technology and Organizational Structure," *Administrative Science Quarterly* 16 (December 1971): 444–59.

9. Claudia Bird Schoonhoven, "Problems with Contingency Theory: Testing Assumptions Hidden Within the Language of Contingency 'Theory,' " *Administrative Science Quarterly* 26 (September 1981): 349–77.

10. Bryant, "The Organizational Structure of Collection Development."

11. Elaine Carol Frank Sloan, "The Organization of Collection Development in Large Research Libraries" (Ph.D. diss., Univ. of Maryland, 1973).

12. Kim Cameron, "Measuring Organizational Effectiveness in Institutions of Higher Education," *Administrative Science Quarterly* 23 (December 1978): 604–34; Kim Cameron, "Critical Questions in Assessing Organizational Effectiveness,"

Organizational Dynamics 9 (Summer 1980): 66–80; Kim Cameron and David A. Whetten, "Organizational Effectiveness: One Model or Several?" in *Organizational Effectiveness: A Comparison of Multiple Models*, ed. Kim S. Cameron and David A. Whetten (Orlando, Fla.: Academic Press, 1983), 1–24; Kim Cameron and David A. Whetten, "Some Conclusions about Organizational Effectiveness," ibid., 261–77.

13. Cameron and Whetten, "Organizational Effectiveness: One Model or Several?" p. 7.

14. Cameron and Whetten, "Some Conclusions about Organizational Effectiveness," 261–77.

Ethics and Collection Development

by William E. Hannaford, Jr.

After a decade or two in hiding, ethics again seems to have come to the forefront in America during the past several years. Possibly this is because so much seems to have gone wrong so quickly. Some of this heightened interest is beginning to affect librarians. Talks are being given at conferences, books are being published, and institutes held that focus on the ethics of librarianship.[1]

The topic of professional ethics has been discussed by librarians for almost as long as the profession has existed.[2] There have been and continue to be various committees and task forces put in place to propose or to examine various codes of ethics.[3] Most of the historical codes, though, were more like codes of etiquette than codes of ethics.

> For the most part, the earliest of these discussions emphasized the responsibility of the librarian to employer and patrons and raised the issue of the librarian's deportment, frequently offering hortatory instruction as to appropriate dress and demeanor. Ethics and etiquette not being sharply distinguished, these treatises were the equivalent of instructions to physicians on their "bedside manners."[4]

It could be argued without much difficulty that the 1981 American Library Association "Statement on Professional Ethics" also falls into the category of etiquette rather than ethics, though it is a bit more sophisticated.[5] Though this present code is described as "the principles which guide librarians in action," it is, in fact, a list of six rules governing behavior. While earlier codes instructed a librarian not to "carelessly choose his company, nor indulge in habits and taste that offend the social or moral sense,"[6] the latest code instructs librarians to "provide the highest level of service through . . . courteous responses."[7] In effect the earlier and later codes do not differ much.

The fact that most professional codes of ethics were and are merely prescriptions of comportment, coupled with an increased awareness of global problems (e.g., nuclear annihilation, AIDS, and atmospheric contamination), make the discussion of ethics as it relates to various professions all the more pressing. This paper presents a foray into the ethics of library and information professionals as it relates specifically to collection development; it does not pretend to be a set of prescriptions about how collection development ought to be done.

THE ETHICAL VERSUS THE EXPEDIENT

> Crito: But, O my good Socrates, I beg you for the last time to listen to me and save yourself. For to me your death will be more than a single disaster. . . . The public will never believe that we were anxious to save you, but that you yourself refused to escape. . . .
>
> Socrates: Then, my good friend, we must not think so much of what the many will say . . . ; we must think of what the one . . . who understands . . . will say of us. And so you are mistaken, to begin with, when you invite us to regard the opinion of the multitude.[8]

The issue at stake in the dialogue between Crito and Socrates is whether Socrates ought to escape or stay in prison and go to his death. That is, should Socrates behave expediently and out of self-interest or should he behave ethically? Crito argues that Socrates ought to escape because, in effect, that is how the multitude, how etiquette, would have him behave. Socrates goes to his death, and the rest is history.

Most ethical theorists have argued that all deliberate human activity can be divided into two categories: the expedient and the ethical.[9] In other words, it has been held that there are two points of view that can be taken by human beings regarding their purposeful actions—the prudential point of view and the ethical, or moral, point of view. "The two points of view are conceived as polar opposites and, together with hybrid perspectives in between, are so conceived as to cover all that is relevant for the evaluation of deliberate behavior."[10]

The ethical, or moral, point of view differs from that which is merely expedient or prudential in that the former involves the public trust.

> In morality as I see it, we make judgements of rightness, wrongness, goodness, badness, etc., about actions, persons, character traits, motives and the like, and we do so, I believe, because these actions, agents, etc., have, are intended to have, or are thought to have certain kinds of effects on the lives of persons and/or sentient beings as such. Moreover, we take into consideration not only the effects on ourselves or on the agent in question (always a person or group of persons) but also and perhaps primarily the

effects on others who are or are likely to be affected. This consideration of others when they are affected may be direct or indirect, but it must be ultimate or for its own sake, not prudential or instrumental.[11]

The two categories above give rise to the two realms of human behavior, the private and the public. In the former, almost anything goes because such activity is said not to infringe, in any significant or interesting way, upon the rights of others. In the latter, where such infringement does occur, human activity is usually circumscribed by certain rules or laws. Thus, the private realm is often said to be governed by expediency, including etiquette, and the public realm by ethical codes or moral laws.

In the private realm, where the prudential point of view holds sway, deliberate action is most often described as self-interested. Examples abound. Choosing the flavor of an ice cream cone or which rules of etiquette to follow or the style of clothes to wear are as good as any. The public realm is the realm of the moral point of view; in it, deliberate activity is disinterested and covered by some moral or ethical principle. Examples also abound here. How one treats others is the classical case.

From this brief discussion it can be seen that the ethical point of view has at least two necessary conditions. First, an action must be deliberate, intentional, or purposeful. It cannot be accidental or unintentional. The action must have or be intended to have certain effects. Second, the action must have these effects, or at least possibly have these effects, not only on the agent but also on others. That is, the moral point of view requires that others be taken into account because the action affects them in a significant way.

COLLECTION DEVELOPMENT: ETHICAL OR EXPEDIENT?

Before it can be determined whether collection development is an ethical or an expedient matter, the nature of collection development must be explored briefly. Collection development may be defined as "the overall molding or development of a collection for a purpose to suit a group of users."[12] Put another way, it is "the intentional and systematic building of a library collection" with a certain end in mind.[13] It is intended here that the word *collection* take into account access to information in the broadest sense.

Should collection development be counted as an ethical or a nonethical activity? What is it that might make collection development ethical rather than merely expedient? Simply put, can collection development be morally right or wrong? These questions can now be answered.

If the definition given above is adequate, then it is obvious that collection development is an activity that satisfies the two requisite conditions of moral activity. That is, collection development is a purposeful activity, and it is intended to have certain effects on others, in this case a group of library users. In the college library, for example, collection development primarily affects undergraduates and faculty. It appears, then, that collection development can be counted as an ethical activity, that it can, in effect, be morally right or wrong.

COLLECTION DEVELOPMENT AND NORMATIVE ETHICS

Philosophers generally divide the study of ethics or moral philosophy into several categories, among them normative ethics and metaethics. The main task of normative ethics is to discover criteria with which moral judgments can be made. That is, normative ethics has to make clear just what norm or standard is being used when an action is judged right or a person good. Metaethics, on the other hand, is not concerned with norms or standards; it is concerned with issues that lie beyond traditional normative ethics. Metaethical issues include, for example, the meaning of the words *right* and *good* and the distinction between facts and values.[14]

Clearly, then, collection development falls in the ethical realm, and normative ethics is that part of ethics which is of primary interest. What remains to be done is to explore normative ethics a bit and to give a few examples of just how collection development might be counted an ethical activity.

Normative ethics, then, is concerned with the principles or laws that govern ethical behavior or action. It has been argued by many, if not most, modern moral philosophers that these moral principles are, in turn, either deontological or consequentialist (i.e., teleological) in nature.

> A deontological principle is one that states that the rightness or wrongness of an action is not entirely or at all determined by the consequences of the action, whereas a consequentialist principle states that the rightness or wrongness of an action is determined by the consequences of the action.[15]

Deontologists, such as Immanuel Kant, maintain that actions are right if they are done with good intentions.[16] Consequentialists (John Stuart Mill is a good example of one) might argue that an action is right if it produces good consequences.[17] Wrong actions, on the other hand, are the result of bad intentions or bad consequences. Though neither theory is quite as simple as I have made it out to be, this brief description will be sufficient to demonstrate just how collection development might be said to be an ethical activity or to be right or wrong.

Rather than take all of collection development in its richness, including weeding, budgeting, selection, management, and the like, let us look at one of the most important aspects of shaping a library collection for a college library—the selection of books. How, then, can the selection of books be ethical?

If we are deontologists, we ought to select books intending them to be the kinds of books we would have others select if they were selectors and we were readers. If we are consequentialists, on the other hand, we ought to select books that we think would produce good consequences or the greatest amount of good for the greatest number of users. Is this really the way librarians do collection development?

CONCLUSION

It is often argued by librarians that there are only two ways to build a collection—either on the basis of publication or on the basis of use.[18] University libraries are said to build collections the former way and college libraries the latter. One way to build is to select books that appear on certain lists, whether they are national bibliographies or publisher lists; the other is to buy books that one thinks will be used. Both of these are merely expedient; neither is ethical.

The appearance of a book on a list or the consideration of whether it is going to be used have little, in and of themselves, to do with ethical activity. Both kinds of normative ethical theorists discussed above, deontologists and teleologists, would argue that a book must be selected according to certain principles. Again, the former might argue that a variation of the golden rule must be applied to book selection; the latter, that the selection of a book must produce good consequences. Both would agree that collection development must be intentional, that a principle must be operative, and that the user must be kept in mind. Though just how ethical theories might apply specifically to the rich gamut of activities that make up collection development needs to be made clearer at another time and in another place, it has certainly been shown here that collection development is an ethical activity.

Collection developers, it seems, often select books on the basis of expediency, and do not treat collection development as the ethical activity that it is. The reason for this may well be that collection developers are often administrators eager to avoid confrontation and please other administrators while at the same time ignoring faculty and students. Maybe Oscar Handlin was correct when he said of librarians that "libraries are too important to leave to them," implying that librarians, for whatever reasons, often do not have the best interests of the user in mind when building collections.[19]

It is time for librarians involved in collection development to begin to explore the complicated relationship between ethics and collection development and to begin to build library collections in ways that are not merely expedient or products of self-interest. Collection development, like any other branch of librarianship, requires that librarians act as professionals and that they act ethically.

NOTES

1. There are many recent examples. Fred Friendly gave a talk on ethics at the 1989 American Library Association Conference in Dallas; two relevant books have appeared: *Ethical Challenges in Librarianship* by Robert Hauptman (Phoenix: Oryx, 1988) and *Professional Ethics and Librarianship* by Jonathan A. Lindsey and Ann E. Prentice (Phoenix: Oryx, 1985); and the 1989 Allerton Institute focused on "Ethics and the Librarian."

2. Lawson Crowe and Susan H. Anthes, "The Academic Librarian and Information Technology: Ethical Issues," *College and Research Libraries* 49 (March 1988): 123–30.

3. See Hauptman, *Ethical Challenges in Librarianship* and Lindsey and Prentice, *Professional Ethics and Librarians*.

4. Crowe and Anthes, "The Academic Librarian and Information Technology," 123.

5. American Library Association, "Statement on Professional Ethics" (Chicago: ALA, 1981).

6. Lindsey and Prentice, *Professional Ethics and Librarians*, 33.

7. American Library Association, "Statement."

8. Plato, *Euthyphro, Apology, Crito* (Indianapolis: Bobbs-Merrill, 1956), 52–57.

9. H. Gene Blocker and William Hannaford, *Introduction to Philosophy* (New York: Van Nostrand, 1974), 225–26.

10. John Kultgen, *Ethics and Professionalism* (Philadelphia: Univ. of Pennsylvania, 1988), 33.

11. William K. Frankena, *Thinking About Morality* (Ann Arbor: Univ. of Michigan, 1980), 25.

12. William E. Hannaford, Jr., "Toward a Theory of Collection Development," in *Collection Development in Libraries: A Treatise*, ed. Robert Steuart and George Miller (Greenwich, Conn.: JAI, 1980), 573–83.

13. William E. Hannaford, Jr., "Collection Development in College Libraries," in *Library Resources for College Scholars*, ed. Robert E. Danforth (Lexington, Va.: Washington and Lee Univ., 1980), 13–17.

14. Blocker and Hannaford, *Introduction to Philosophy*, 201.

15. Mark S. Halfon, *Integrity: A Philosophical Inquiry* (Philadelphia: Temple Univ., 1989), 171.

16. Immanuel Kant, *Foundations of the Metaphysics of Morals* (Indianapolis: Bobbs-Merrill, 1959).

17. John Stuart Mill, *Utilitarianism* (Indianapolis: Bobbs-Merrill, 1957).

18. Ross Atkinson, "Old Forms, New Forms: The Challenge of Collection Development," *College and Research Libraries* 50 (September 1989): 507–20.

19. Oscar Handlin, "Libraries and Learning," *The American Scholar* 56 (Spring 1987): 205–18.

Part 3

Effective Collection Development

Collection development is one of the most difficult and most important activities undertaken by a college library. Often it is more complicated for college libraries than for university libraries because college libraries usually are constrained by limited funding. University libraries, on the other hand, can develop their collections on a grander scale.

If "collection development" means a set of activities—including evaluation, budgeting, selection, deselection, storage, preservation, and management—that results in the intentional and systematic building of a library collection, then it is clear that collection development is an umbrella for much of what goes on in libraries. The five papers in this section address some of those activities and some effective ways that they can be accomplished in the college library.

Evan Farber's paper concerns the relationship between bibliographic instruction and collection development. He argues that collection development in the college library differs significantly from that in the university library. Limited funds and changeable course offerings dictate that the college library collection focus on undergraduate rather than research materials. The collection must be tailored to users' needs—those of faculty, to be sure, but more important, those of students. And these needs become known through an effective bibliographic instruction program.

Farber defines an "effective" bibliographic instruction program and explores its potential contribution to the college library collection development effort. For example, he argues that effective bibliographic instruction for collection development means not only lecturing to classes but taking a proactive role in helping faculty design assignments that require students to make better use of library materials.

Many college libraries are newly engaged in using allocation formulas for materials budgets, and, in his paper, Michael S. Freeman critically examines components of several book allocation formulas. While the allocation of materials budgets may have a certain utility and serve effectively the library's political environment, specific variables employed in formulas often have little applicability to the major objective: to produce fair and intellectually sound apportioning of funds.

Freeman argues that allocation formulas taken by themselves may be neat and tidy, and they may bake some political bread. On the other hand, such formulas, when not closely connected to or part of a comprehensive collection policy, may reduce the expectations of active library constituents. Obviously, this can affect a library's long-term financial support. In short, Freeman is arguing that formulas may not be the panacea that many librarians thought them to be.

In "New Faculty, New Courses, New Programs," Willis E. Bridegam maintains that faculty turnover and the introduction of new academic courses and programs place continuing pressure on librarians concerned with collection development. Administrative decisions to hire new faculty or to begin new academic programs should be supported by firm commitments to provide the necessary library funding. Further, he argues, librarians should be prepared to give candidates for faculty positions a frank appraisal of the strengths and weaknesses of the collection in their areas of interest. New faculty members and librarians must share the responsibility for developing the collection to the agreed-upon level.

Bridegam discusses other factors that affect a library's collection (e.g., decisions by faculty to offer new courses or to pursue new areas of research), and proposes various techniques for assessing and improving the collection.

It is fashionable in the literature of librarianship to view with disdain the so-called "how I did it good" pieces, or accounts of innovations in particular libraries. Richard Werking argues, on the other hand, that such accounts are often valuable, at least as valuable as the higher-status pieces devoted to theorizing and philosophizing. Werking's "Return to Alexandria" is one of the more exemplary "how I did it good" papers, by virtue of both the magnitude of the task addressed and the measure of success realized in accomplishing it.

In the late 1970s, Trinity University's trustees, administrators, and library staff came together to begin a collection development effort that was to be highly unusual, if not unique, among U.S. colleges. The Trinity library administration hired its first collection development officer, received considerable funding, and undertook several projects to increase rapidly the size of the collection. In only eight years, the library doubled its collection of books and bound periodicals to more than 600,000 volumes. Although the Trinity experience may be unique, this paper is valuable because it shows how numerous collection development programs, usually employed over a long period, can be compressed into a relatively short period.

There has been, over the years, a debate about what to call the set of activities alluded to earlier in this introduction. For many, including the co-editors of this book, the older and better-known term *collection development* is more than adequate; for others, the newer *collection management* is preferred. Herbert Safford and Katherine Martin argue that collection development should be distinguished from collection management. They claim that the older nomenclature emphasizes selection and acquisition through purchase of library materials, whereas the newer term focuses on a broader but still coherent set of activities that includes selection and acquisition but emphasizes as well faculty liaison, collection analysis, resource sharing, gifts programs, preservation, deselection, inventory and materials replacement, stack maintenance, and so forth.

Those who think that language is unimportant may argue that such a debate is only a matter of semantics, yet such debates often clearly delineate the salient issues at hand. Safford and Martin contend that contemporary library practice calls for adherence to the terminology of collection management to describe professional tasks centering on evaluating and enhancing the collection of library materials. Collection development in their view is an attenuated concept that by now should have been superseded by the more encompassing notion of collection management.

Bibliographic Instruction and Collection Development in the College Library

by Evan Ira Farber

In discussing the relationship of collection development and bibliographic instruction, it's appropriate to begin with some basic working statements. My concept of what a college library collection should be really first occurred to me shortly after I came to Earlham College in 1962 and began to see how different the purposes of a university library, from which I had just come, were from those of a college library, to which I had recently arrived. Those differences in purpose and their implications for administration and services, and especially for the collection, became increasingly obvious to me over the next few years; a decade or so later, that concept of a college library collection had taken shape, and in 1975 I wrote,

> the needs of college undergraduates have to be determined by different criteria than those used for university students. A college library must have, first of all, a collection of cultural and recreational materials that can expand students' horizons; second, a good basic collection that will meet their curricular needs; and, third, a good reference collection that will serve as a key to the immediate library, and to resources elsewhere. Only after these three needs are met should we think about a collection to fill the occasional research need.[1]

I still feel those are the basic criteria by which college libraries should be guided and I will use that concept of a collection in this discussion.

When I refer to bibliographic instruction, I have in mind only course-related (or, even better, course-integrated) instruction. The other method of teaching use of the library (as a separate course) is used in a number of institutions, but is not nearly as widespread in practice as course-related instruction. While a few of the points below are somewhat applicable to the separate course approach, that approach has much less relevance for collection development. The reasons for that should become apparent.

64

The first of the criteria in my 1975 statement—that a college library must have "a collection of cultural and recreational materials that can expand students' horizons"—is one that is probably affected only minimally by the presence or absence of a bibliographic instruction program. That is, no matter what the curriculum, a respectable college library should have certain standard works representing the ideas and work that constitute our cultural and intellectual heritage. Of course, the definition of what is included in that rather nebulous concept will change over time. Such a collection should now certainly include works, for example, by certain significant Asian and African writers, whereas some years ago those authors would be found in only the more sophisticated college library collections, if even there. The nature of that conceptual change, however, will be shaped almost as much by the content of higher education in general as by the context of an individual institution. Insofar as recreational reading materials are concerned, their selection will be affected somewhat by the existence of a bibliographic instruction program for reasons that I believe will become apparent later.

How the second criterion of an undergraduate collection—the support of curricular needs—helps shape that collection is subject to wide variation from library to library. Yet there is no doubt that it is the criterion most central to our discussion. Any particular curriculum, after all, is simply a structure, a framework, sometimes logical, more often—and more cynically—an accretion of courses established by tradition, by faculty politics, by administrative fiat, by student demand, by departmental need, or by individual faculty preference—or by any combination of these. What we are interested in, however, are those activities that add substance to the structure, form to the framework, and permit that conformation to result in an effective undergraduate education. They are the activities that constitute the teaching/learning process, and librarians are interested in them here because of that second criterion, support of the curriculum. If the basic purpose of building a library collection is to support the curriculum or the teaching/learning process, and the primary purpose of bibliographic instruction is to enhance that process, then the relationship between the two should result in a symbiosis, in which both not only support and enhance the teaching/learning process but also reinforce each other. It is my contention—my major premise, really—that a bibliographic instruction program, by promoting closer working relationships between librarians and classroom teachers, and between librarians and students, makes the job of developing the collection easier and results in a collection that better meets the needs of students and teachers.

"Closer ties" is the key. Let us first discuss those ties with the faculty. Cooperation between teaching faculty and librarians is a hallmark of practically any bibliographic instruction program and, simply as a factor of cause and effect, results in closer ties. Cooperation takes place at several points during the process. It takes place first at the initial contact, when an instructor decides to have library instruction in conjunction with an assignment. It occurs next when the teacher and the librarian talk over the instruction. Third, cooperation takes place during the instruction itself, which usually is given in the classroom or in the library, and, finally, it occurs during the follow-up, either immediately following the session or later on, in planning a repeat session. Each of those steps entails working together, at times briefly, at other times, more extensively. The first step, the initial contact, is simply based on acquaintance: on the teacher's part, acquaintance with the purposes of bibliographic instruction and, to some extent, the procedures; and on the librarian's part, acquaintance with the course and, just as important, with the teacher's academic interests and working style. The second step, planning the instruction, incorporates and builds on some of the interactions of the first, and involves detailing the assignment—its purpose, content, and timing, and the instructions to students. This stage of the process provides the best opportunity for establishing closer ties. Classroom teaching is for the most part an autonomous affair, and it can be a lonely one. Instructors often do not have (or don't choose to take) the opportunity to talk over with colleagues their class assignments, even though those assignments are central to what concerns them most—being successful teachers.[2] Having someone to talk with about the assignment, especially someone who's interested in helping make it a success and, moreover, someone who poses no threat (as a department head or even another instructor might), can be very welcome, and on such an occasion the librarian can take the opportunity to become more familiar with the instructor's academic and other interests. In the third step, implementation, the students see the librarian and the instructor working together, and that's important for students' perceptions of the librarian's main role—helping them fulfill their assignments. The final step, follow-up, or evaluation, builds on and can strengthen the ties already established.

The reason for describing this process in somewhat more detail than may seem necessary is simply to show the working relationship between the librarian and the instructor, a working relationship that enlightens the librarian about the content and purpose of the instructor's courses, and at the same time increases the instructor's awareness of the librarian's role in the teaching/learning process, and how that role can help the instructor achieve his or her course objectives.

Now, how does that working relationship, those closer ties, affect collection development? As noted earlier, those ties make the job of developing the collection easier and thus result in a better collection that meets the needs of students and faculty. A lot has been written about that job, and, while commentators have differed on how much weight should be given to the faculty or to the librarians for developing the collection, the importance of cooperation in carrying out that responsibility has been recognized by all. Yet most of us have seen or at least heard of situations where there was a certain amount of rancor over book selection. Those situations, it seems to me, mostly stem from an adversarial relationship, a "we-they" feeling between the two groups, a feeling that might have been obviated or certainly ameliorated if the individuals had worked together in planning instruction. That process of working together in planning bibliographic instruction provides the ideal opportunity for appreciating each other's contribution.

A colleague has characterized bibliographic instruction in this regard as a "political lubricant." Not a very subtle term, to be sure, nor, as far as I know, one generally used in academe; it is, however, apt. Let's face it—administrative decisions and curricular policies *are* often determined by "political" relationships and considerations. Budgetary allocations and personnel decisions, both of which directly affect the library's ability to build and/or maintain a collection, are, if not shaped, certainly affected by such political considerations. There are, of course, many other activities, devices, and actions that also help promote more cordial relationships between teaching faculty and librarians. Any of these—receptions, parties, social occasions—can work to the library's political advantage, but as effective as any one might be at a particular time, none of them makes an inherent contribution to the educational process.

Working closely with faculty in planning instruction can create another opportunity for enhancing personal relationships. As noted previously, early in the planning process the librarian should become acquainted with the instructor's academic interests. That is, to be sure, most important for the instruction itself, but it can also be helpful in book selection and useful in informing the instructor about items (articles, publication announcements, etc.) that may lead to book requests. Even if the items are not of immediate use or significance, the librarian's thoughtfulness will be recognized and appreciated. Having a book on order or, even better, on the shelf when a faculty member sees a review can do marvelous things for improving relationships. There are few better ways of knowing what faculty members want or need than by talking to them about their courses. My observation that teaching is at times a lonely affair is not, I think, fully appreciated by librarians. This is particularly true in colleges, where individual faculty members may be the only ones in their specialties and so have no colleagues or even graduate students with whom to share their interests. Thus, when a librarian anticipates a need or sends an item reflecting that interest, it is particularly appreciated.

The preceding has emphasized the importance for collection development of close librarian–faculty working relationships. Those relationships tend to create a favorable political environment that gives librarians more freedom to develop the collection than they otherwise might have. Equally as important is the knowledge librarians gain about the content of courses, about the topics on which students will be writing papers, even about the subject matter and the discipline itself, which may go far beyond the course. That knowledge permits and even encourages librarians to look for and add to the collection materials that will support the courses and assignments. Combined with the freedom created by the favorable political climate, this knowledge can lead to active and effective collection development.[3]

So far, we've not really discussed the students' contribution to the bibliographic instruction–collection development equation, except insofar as they are the ones being taught or helped. Although that role is important, my assumption here is that, when students receive bibliographic instruction, their perception of the librarian changes: The librarian is now seen as a *colleague* of the teacher, someone who knows the course, the assignment, and ways to find information for that assignment. In other words, the librarian can help shape the topic as well as find information on it. Because of that consultative relationship, students and librarians work together more closely, more candidly; librarians come to know students' interests and needs much better, thus enhancing their ability to select appropriate items for the collection.

If there were such a thing as a perfect job of collection development, it would mean meeting every user's need or demand with the items on hand, by either having added them to the collection or having already borrowed them from elsewhere. Librarians are not clairvoyant, however, and can base their book selection only on what they anticipate will be needed. The standard advice for college library collection development officers is simple and straightforward: As Guy Lyle put it many years ago, the "most important influence upon the book stock of the college library will be the nature of the curriculum."[4] That's basic, sound advice, but it provides only general guidance. We can anticipate the needs of students and faculty more accurately, more precisely, by working closely with them through bibliographic instruction than by simply knowing the curriculum, no matter how accurate or thorough that knowledge is.

Knowing students' interests and needs more intimately may have another effect on collection development. Librarians, along with most faculty members, tend to be traditional in their ideas of curriculum content and other academic matters. Book selection for most libraries is based primarily on reviews in scholarly or other mainstream journals, or on *Choice*, or on publishers' mailings, or on other standard sources. These sources, however, may not reflect changes in student attitudes and styles (e.g., the recent growth of interest in Central America, in South Africa, in animal rights, in the Palestinians' cause, in homophobia). Some of those interests, such as the Palestinians' cause, were created as a result of particular courses or programs at this college and we might have predicted the demand for materials in those areas. It's not likely, however, that we would have predicted the enduring strength of those intestests or the sudden interest in such topics as animal rights. Although we could meet almost any student's need with some adequacy, we were able to respond in greater depth because students felt comfortable enough to talk with the librarians about their interests and to request materials.

Even with all the prescience humanly possible, however, even with the best possible working relationships with faculty and students, no library can hope to meet all student and/or faculty needs, and it must depend on filling those needs with materials from other libraries. Richard Werking has described interlibrary borrowing as a function of collection development when a library's administrative viewpoint shifts from being "collection-centered" to being "client-centered." When that shift occurs, interlibrary borrowing "becomes an important part of a library's collection development and acquisition processes, one that is undertaken in response to a demand that is expressed rather than presumed."[5] It is appropriate, then, to discuss briefly the relationship between bibliographic instruction and interlibrary lending.

The most obvious relationship in a small library is a simple quantitative one: Teaching students how to find materials will result in an increased demand for materials outside the library. That then raises an important policy question: How much of the library's (probably limited) resources should be given to meeting that demand? The only valid response is "as much as is needed." One really can't (or shouldn't) teach students how to use the library effectively, how to find information they can use for their papers and reports, and then say to them, "Sorry, but we don't have any of those items." In principle, that seems wrong, but aside from that, it will simply frustrate students and be counterproductive to the success of the bibliographic instruction program.

If, then, we agree to provide as many resources for interlibrary lending as are needed, those resources have to come from somewhere, and unless the college administration is willing to supplement the library's budget accordingly, they will have to come from a redistribution of the library's existing budget—very possibly from acquisitions. Such a redistribution, unless it cuts into the heart of the collection program, that is, into really essential items, is justifiable—improving interlibrary lending service will increase the availability of materials much more than would a limited number of added volumes.

Previously, I discussed the contribution of bibliographic instruction to librarians' increased knowledge of students' interests and needs. An expanded interlibrary lending service can also contribute to that knowledge. Materials requested from other libraries can provide clues to students' interests and needs; likewise, records of periodicals from which articles are requested can pinpoint titles that the library should acquire.

Finally, the process of providing support for curricular needs very much affects the processes of building a collection of cultural and recreational materials and a good reference collection. That is, by participating in bibliographic instruction, librarians can have a better reading of, a better feeling for, student and faculty needs and interests. In turn, this should help librarians build collections that reflect those needs and interests. Similarly, those same librarians should have a better sense of faculty and student interests in recreational reading materials as well as a better sense of the reference works needed. All areas of building a college library's collection, then, can benefit from the library staff's involvement in bibliographic instruction.

NOTES

1. Evan Ira Farber, "Limiting College Library Growth: Bane or Boon?" in *Farewell to Alexandria: Solutions to Space, Growth, and Performance Problems of Libraries*, ed. Daniel Gore (Westport, Conn.: Greenwood Press, 1976), 39.

2. "Colleagues don't talk much to each other about teaching. In 1978, Jerry Gaff surveyed 1,680 faculty at 145 institutions and found that 42% of them said that *never* during their entire career had anyone talked with [them] in detail about [their] teaching and helped [them] clarify course objectives, devise effective student evaluation, or develop a more effective approach for certain kinds of students. Only 25% said that discussions on these topics had taken place more than once. . . . To talk openly about teaching at many of our institutions implies one has a problem. One talks because things aren't going well. But if one knows the content well enough, one can teach it. . . . The reasons why dialogue about teaching does not occur are less important than the reasons why it should. *Colleagues could be better teachers if they talked to each other about what they do and why they do it.*" See *The Teaching Professor* 1 (July 1987): 1.

3. At various times during the writing of this paper, I went through several current issues of *Publishers Weekly*, selecting items in the Forecasts section for ordering. I do this regularly, but with these particular issues I tried to be aware of which items I selected because of our bibliographic instruction program—that is, because I had given instruction in certain courses. Of course, I have to ask myself, would I have chosen those same items simply because I knew our curriculum and collection, or did I choose them because I worked with certain instructors and students? Certainly, it's not easy to ascribe any single action to a particular experience. I do know, however, that I felt much more certain about my selections because of my contact with the instructors and their students. Indeed, there were several items I would have overlooked were it not for that contact.

4. Guy R. Lyle, *The Administration of the College Library*, 3d ed. (New York: H. W. Wilson, 1961), 234.

5. Richard Hume Werking, "Some Thoughts on Interlibrary Sending and a Resource-Sharing System for Academic Libraries in Texas," a memorandum distributed to the members of the AMIGOS Interlibrary Loan Policy Review Committee, December 13, 1988, 1–2. Werking prefers the phrase "interlibrary sending" to "interlibrary lending" or "interlibrary borrowing" since most transactions are not loans or borrowings but one-way transmissions of reproduced items.

Allocation Formulas as Management Tools in College Libraries: Useful or Misapplied?

by Michael S. Freeman

Library budgets have many different components and are scrutinized in various ways. Personnel and operations lines, large and complex aggregates, are administrative in character and subject to comparison with other campus centers having similar line items. Library directors must defend their appropriation as necessary to the enterprise and reasonable in relation to available resources, presenting data ranging from local wage comparisons to the value of the dollar on international money markets.

By contrast, the library materials budget is completely academic in nature. Classed as "instructional support," these lines carry a special meaning for faculty, who often will regard these funds as being held in trust for their own use. They agree that the educational mission of the library is to foster independent inquiry and the discovery of ideas; yet when the question of book and journal budgets is raised, the debate will often move to actual allocation of funds to each department.

The rivalries over materials budget allocations, so well documented in the literature, are emblematic of the profession's own insecurity vis-à-vis the rest of academia. Librarians will cite their faculty status as befitting them to control academic monies, though evidence that such status lessens the debate or bolsters the library with sufficient respect is not strong.[1] Resource allocation mechanisms abound, including a number of formula-based systems that have appeared in numerous articles in library journals. Librarians serving colleges are in a position to avoid impersonal approaches to budget management, and this paper will attempt to outline the problems with and present alternatives to a formula-based approach to the materials budget.

Most budget allocation schemes are not the result of careful research but are consensual documents designed to fulfill particular needs. Shirk is more graphic, describing published formulas as "notationally simplified expressions of arbitrary procedures."[2] Libraries of all sizes use formulas and other "scientific" budget apportionment systems to help them effectively interact with the environment and control their own future. Formulas insulate librarians from charges of unfairness and, though an illusion at best, are thought to ensure a certain degree of budget autonomy.[3] They also facilitate reporting to governing bodies and accrediting agencies, serving to demonstrate that the library is engaged in "systematic modeling" of its materials budget. These schemes are sometimes inherited from past administrations, and, when newly adopted, a major objective, often unstated, is to eliminate power struggles between librarians and faculty or competition among faculty departments.

Objective allocation systems are not unpopular. A survey in 1989 found that 43 of 102 college libraries used a formula in budgeting for library purchases.[4] Baughman found that 91 percent of faculty and almost three out of four college administrators favored allocation by formula.[5] But are automatic systems good in the long run for the profession or for the institution? Should librarians set up equations to simplify the collection development process? Librarians are certainly not of one mind; Baughman found that less than half the library directors were sanguine toward such apportionment systems.

Werking notes that many of these formulas are based on "head-count factors."[6] Originating in the 1930s, the formula, with principal factors assigned suitable weights, was given a tremendous boost in 1965 with the publication of a highly influential article by Verner Clapp and Robert Jordan.[7]

The so-called Clapp-Jordan formula was actually not a budget allocation device but an attempt to determine the minimum adequacy of library collections by interrelating a small number of objective components. The arguments were appealing and carried greater weight because both authors were associated with a major library funding agency, the Council on Library Resources. Moreover, the formula was tailor-made for colleges, and the authors used prestigious college libraries as test examples in their article.

The Clapp-Jordan formula is hard to apply, and the authors clearly recognized its limitations. Clapp and Jordan included both objective and subjective factors in proposing the formula, but they recognized the difficulty inherent in consistently applying nonquantifiable criteria, such as instructional methods, intellectual climate, or campus geography. So they simply ignored what could not be "easily and meaningfully measured." The result was an instrument the authors regarded as incomplete but which they did not hesitate to apply in its truncated form.

Clapp and Jordan introduced the concept of "weighting," a key element in nearly all later formulas.[8] They assigned weights to faculty members, undergraduates, graduate students, number of majors, and graduate concentrations. Their judgment here could be endlessly debated, but conceptually, few have questioned the implications of their approach. What librarians have done, in applying Clapp-Jordan, is to extend the number of variables or adjust the weighting for local purposes. For college librarians, the weighting system and the variables have become canon; the *Standards for College Libraries* for both 1975 and 1986 use criteria from Clapp-Jordan in dealing with collections.

In addition to the objective Clapp-Jordan variables, most formulas used by librarians include some of the following:

1. Enrollment (undergraduate, graduate, etc.)
2. Faculty size and faculty load
3. Courses and credit hours
4. Number of majors (undergraduate, master's, doctoral)
5. Circulation
6. Number of books published (often using some standard, such as *Choice*)
7. Library depth in particular disciplines
8. Interlibrary loans
9. Average cost per volume
10. Faculty publishing or research activity
11. Library staff size (sometimes broken down by area)[9]

Here are some formulas suggested by college librarians in the past five years:

Simple Formulas

Lynchburg College
   Uses four equal criteria (no weighting):

1. *Choice* titles per discipline
2. Cost
3. Enrollment by department
4. Potential use by department[10]

Maryville College
   Uses four criteria with circulation counted twice:

1. Circulation
2. Declared majors
3. Number of students
4. Average cost per title[11]

More Complex Formulas

Western Illinois University
   Uses four weighted variables:

1. Student credit hours
2. FTE faculty
3. Course credit hours
4. Book and periodical costs[12]

Youngstown State University
Uses six weighted variables and suggests an additional option:

1. Number of courses
2. Number of faculty
3. Number of undergraduate student majors
4. Books circulated
5. Interlibrary loans
6. Student credit hours

Option: Cost and productivity of books and serials by discipline compared to all disciplines. [13]

Formulas are often produced by committees of librarians and faculty who search, quite intuitively, for consensus. The criteria used vary widely from library to library, but two principles are always followed: criteria must be quantitative and easily compiled each year. Formulas are considered more successful when allocation changes from year to year are relatively small. Nearly all approaches mute the question of departmental contributions, in which allocations are considered more in terms of output and productivity with departments provided resources to the extent they serve the mission of the institution. [14] The preceding four allocation schemes deal primarily with inputs, a response found generally in higher education to the problem of scarcity.

Success is measured partly by ease of formula application, which is why most formulas with a strong theoretical mathematical base are rejected, and partly by how well the formula is received by faculty. Here are typical testimonials:

[The formula] increases faculty awareness of library needs. [15]

Of significance is the lack of dissatisfaction in the system in its 11 years of use at Lynchburg College. [16]

Departments with reduced allocations accepted the formula with good grace. [17]

The formula is primarily a tool for responding to external pressures, but, while often effective in assuaging constituencies, it may also have longer-term negative effects on other things the library wishes to do. Its very neatness can be a serious problem. The formula is one of those constructs that works regardless of the size of the pie, and this is very dangerous for libraries. It may silence critics, but formulas do not raise expectations or communicate useful data. Formulas do not require collection development policies nor do they mandate that libraries interrelate collection management with library services. The formula may insulate the professional staff members, but it hardly inspires them to think in terms of the information needs of the community.

Allocation formulas sometimes find their way into larger collection development policies, in which case they are debated along with other collection development policy components, such as library mission statements, selection responsibility assignments, format information, and detailed discipline statements of collecting depth. An allocation formula may be included as a guideline rather than as a stricture in those situations where some reference to a formal budget division is required. This can also be the case in libraries where the collection development policy is of more recent origin than the allocation formula.

Both collection development policies and allocation formulas may be produced in response to external pressure. But good collection development policies are goal-setting, forward-looking documents that provide solid information about methods, constraints, and the environment of collection building. When formulas exist without strong collection development policies, they reduce expectations of formally active constituents, and this can, in the long run, affect a library's financial support. Formulas may be fair and neat, but do they inspire and inform stakeholders and college administrators?

Formulas assume a probable rather than an expressed need. But expressed needs are the byproduct of regular faculty-student-librarian interaction. It is precisely because these constituencies are small and contacts so frequent that college librarians can avoid the quick fix provided by the formula. Werking characterized the process as "artistic" rather than scientific, but this offers no guidance to librarians in the field.[18]

College librarians should replace formulas with good judgment achieved through (1) continuous discussions with every faculty member; (2) thorough analysis of course syllabi; (3) feedback from librarians conducting bibliographic instruction and from reference librarians handling reference questions; (4) systematic evaluation of faculty publications and research in progress; and (5) information about new courses, majors, and programs. Other factors to be considered include the strength of existing collections, the availability of resources at neighboring institutions, the efficiency of interlibrary loan services, and the relative value of older material versus newer sources for users within the discipline.

College librarians should consider budget allocations as part of the larger collection development picture. In addition to collecting principles contained in formal collection development policies, specific goals to be achieved in the current and later fiscal years should be formulated. Librarians should meet with all department members and program participants to map out collection development objectives. They may find that using some breakdown of the Library of Congress (LC) or Dewey classification provides a useful approach, and Oberg has shown how the RLG Conspectus, a collection evaluation instrument, can be adopted by college libraries with choices as to specificity.[19] Insofar as possible, objectives for subject categories should be expressed in terms of specific collecting tools, though any such list can never be complete. For current acquisitions, the major reviewing sources and the best book lists and publishers can be identified. For retrospective purchases, subject bibliographies can be specified. Acquisition limits (e.g., by language or type of source) may also be included. The specific responsibilities of librarians and individual faculty for building collections should be delineated.

For newly published material, data on literature size will be useful in arriving at estimates of likely costs. These can be acquired using *Choice* (which now provides listings by call number) or from vendors (Baker & Taylor publishes a monthly bibliography of approval plan titles). Annual costs for older titles can also be estimated by sampling and comparing current holdings against bibliographies and deciding how many years it will take to reach a stated objective. Money decisions should be based on need and demand, not on the relative position of one department versus another. The important point is to match dollars (admittedly through estimates) with goals. The one-year estimate, when all departments and programs are added together, will surely exceed the materials budget for many college libraries. However, if realistically determined, these large figures, when pared down, can provide the basis for an annual budget allocation.

Although careful budget tracking and frequent fine-tuning are necessary, there are many advantages to this approach. Faculty will have a clear idea of objectives and be collaborators in both their formulation and implementation. Progress can be more easily charted, and funding administrators can determine the specific impact of increases or decreases in library acquisitions dollars. The system does not eliminate the political side of acquisitions, but it shifts the discussion from formula components to objectives that actually relate to the business of the library, the department, and the curriculum. Some might say that the plan may unduly raise the expectations of faculty members, yet it can also be argued that faculty with high expectations serve the acquisitions process best. They challenge librarians to provide what is needed, and they are the best allies when defending a materials budget.

The argument in this essay is not meant to reject technical methods. The construction of formulas represents a behavioral approach to the library budget process, but the criteria that drive the equation are applied unreflectively and without clear understanding of the ways in which they relate to the main question: How can limited funds be used to build collections most effectively? The remedy is to take an empirical approach and systematically address the problem in terms of the real strength of college libraries: the close relationship between librarians and library users.

NOTES

1. Mary Biggs, "Sources of Tension and Conflict Between Librarians and Faculty," *Journal of Higher Education* 52 (March–April 1981): 186–91.

2. Gary M. Shirk, "Allocating Formulas for Budgeting Library Materials: Science or Procedure?" *Collection Management* 6 (Fall/Winter 1984): 38.

3. For a case study on the political problems associated with allocation formulas, see K. Suzanne Johnson and Joel S. Rutstein, "The Politics of Book Fund Allocations: A Case Study," in *New Horizons for Academic Libraries*, ed. Robert D. Stueart and Richard D. Johnson (New York: K. G. Saur, 1979), 330–40.

4. Theresa Taborsky and Patricia Lenkowski (comps.), *Collection Development Policies for College Libraries* (Chicago: Association of College and Research Libraries, 1989), 12.

5. James Baughman and others, "A Survey of Attitudes Toward Collection Development," in *Collection Development in Libraries: A Treatise* (Part A), ed. Robert D. Stueart and George Miller (Greenwich, Conn.: JAI Press, 1980), 89–138.

6. Richard Hume Werking, "Allocating the Academic Library's Book Budget: Historical Perspectives and Current Reflections," *Journal of Academic Librarianship* 14 (July 1988): 141–42.

7. Verner W. Clapp and Robert T. Jordan, "Quantitative Criteria for Adequacy of Academic Library Collections," *College and Research Libraries* 26 (September 1965): 371–80.

8. Robert E. Burton, "Formula Budgeting: An Example," *Special Libraries* 66 (February 1975): 62.

9. William E. McGrath and others, "An Allocation Formula Derived from a Factor Analysis of Academic Departments," *College and Research Libraries* 30 (January 1969): 51–55; Donna Packer, "Acquisitions Allocations: Equity, Politics, and Formulas," *Journal of Academic Librarianship* 14 (November 1988): 278.

10. Mary C. Scudder, "Using *Choice* in an Allocation Formula in a Small Academic Library," *Choice* 24 (June 1987): 1506–11.

11. Joan H. Worley, "Collection Development in the Small College Library: Can Less Be More?" *Choice* 25 (June 1988): 1512–17.

12. Donna M. Goehner, "Allocating by Formula: The Rationale from an Institutional Perspective," *Collection Management* 5 (Fall/Winter 1983): 161–73.

13. David C. Genaway, "The Q Formula: The Flexible Formula for Library Acquisitions in Relation to the FTE Driven Formula," *Library Acquisitions: Practice and Theory* 10 (1986): 293–306.

14. Jasper G. Shad, "Fairness in Book Fund Allocation," *College and Research Libraries* 48 (November 1987): 482.

15. Genaway, "The Q Formula," 306.

16. Scudder, "Using *Choice* in an Allocation Formula in a Small Academic Library," 1509.

17. Worley, "Collection Development in the Small College Library," 1516.

18. Werking, "Allocating the Academic Library's Book Budget," 143.

19. Larry R. Oberg, "Evaluating the Conspectus Approach for Smaller Library Collections," *College and Research Libraries* 49 (May 1988): 187–96; Anthony W. Ferguson, Joan Grant, and Joel S. Rutstein, "The RLG Conspectus: Its Uses and Benefits," *College and Research Libraries* 49 (May 1988): 203.

New Faculty, New Courses, New Programs

by Willis E. Bridegam

One of the most difficult problems college librarians face is that of antici-
pating and responding to academic initiatives that require significant library support. In some institutions new faculty appear unexpectedly with
booklists in hand; new courses come to the librarians' attention when
they are announced in a faculty meeting or in the college catalog; and new
programs seem to become evident only after they have become inevitable.
These problems are surprisingly common in many colleges, but there is a
solution: involvement of the librarians in planning for changes in the
academic program of the college.

College librarians have the important responsibility of knowing the
information needs of the faculty and students. Robert Broadus mentions
the sense of community that often exists at college libraries, making it
possible for the librarians to know the personal interests of faculty as well
as students.[1] This knowledge is not available to the librarians who seques-
ter themselves in their offices. It comes from regular interaction with
faculty and students, in the library, at lunch, or whenever communication
can take place. The librarians must be an integral part of the academic
community.

Some colleges carry out long-term academic planning through educational policies or academic priority committees. If librarians are not on
these committees, they should at least be aware of their agendas and
reports. Very often, however, these committees review and comment on
proposals that have reached maturity in earlier discussions.

Because of their size, many colleges have a thin layer of administration.
For this reason, presidents and deans of faculty often make academic
decisions that have profound effects on the library. The successful librarian will communicate regularly with administrators about changes in academic programs and counsel those who have the power to make academic
policy changes, emphasizing, before final decisions are made, the effects
of those decisions on the library.

Most academic program initiatives come from academic departments. It is there that someone realizes that consistently large enrollments will support a request for another faculty member, or that a grant opportunity will enable the college to begin instruction in a new subject area. It is the departments that must gather the statistics and the intellectual arguments to support their requests to the dean and president. And, in the case of interdisciplinary enterprises, the departments must conduct negotiations with each other.

The astute college librarian will learn of departmental ambitions at an early stage when it is still possible to comment on and perhaps influence the nature of the proposals. If a department is proposing the addition of a faculty member in a field that is poorly represented in the library collection, an estimate of the cost of providing adequate support in that area may cause the department or the administration to think twice about pursuing the idea. If a new course requires the purchase of books in a foreign language, it is essential that the library have a cataloger who is capable of cataloging books in that language. If a new course requires special equipment, space, or staffing, it is important that these factors be considered as early as possible.

COLLECTION ASSESSMENT

With the early warning that a new academic initiative is likely, the college librarian will want to consider an assessment of the affected portion of the collection. This assessment may take the form of a formal study or simply a rough appraisal of the collection's strengths and weaknesses. Before undertaking the collection assessment, the librarian should have a clear understanding of the department's motives or goals. This may require a formal meeting with the department or a series of informal conversations with its faculty.

The collection assessment should begin with a review of the pertinent portion of the collection and related subject areas. The collection development policy should also be consulted. Within the new subject area, the librarian must estimate the strengths and weaknesses of the current serials, media, and book collections, the need for retrospective collection building, the utility of special collections and archives, and the accessibility of remote databases.

Serials

Because serials commitments are usually ongoing and expensive, the librarian most likely will want to construct a serials list with the titles in priority order. If foreign newspapers will be required, airmail costs should be included. The librarian must consider how difficult it will be to place standing orders for certain foreign serials. The principal journals and annuals in the field should be listed, with an indication of recent price increases for a representative few. If the serials are published abroad, the current stability of the dollar may also be worth considering since its devaluation can result in sharp and unexpected price increases.

Current Books

Understanding the need for current books to support a new area of study is vital. Recent book purchases in related fields can be examined, and a check of reviewing publications can give the librarian a sense of how many worthwhile books are available in the field. The need for duplication must be considered as well.

Retrospective Collection

In some disciplines the strength of the retrospective collection will be critical. Improving this portion of the collection rapidly will be one of the most difficult problems facing the librarian. The librarian can make a quick assessment by spot-checking the collection against relevant subject bibliographies. The physical condition of older materials should also be considered. Faculty members who are knowledgeable in the field should be asked for their opinions on the major weaknesses of the collection and the approximate cost of filling the gaps. A local specialist book dealer might also be helpful in providing a quick evaluation and information on the likelihood of finding the required books and periodical runs. The availability of reprints and facsimile editions should be considered, as should microtext copies of needed material. The strengths of nearby collections should also be considered.

Media Materials and Remote Database Access

Requirements for media materials, such as microtext, sound recordings, photographic slides, film, and videotape, must be analyzed. Improving the media collection usually requires further investment in special equipment and regular maintenance of that equipment. In most cases, the equipment must be secured and its use monitored. The cataloging of media material demands the services of a cataloger with training in these special formats. Remote database access will require a sizable budgetary commitment for the necessary staff and computer search time.

Special Collections and Archives Material

Fields that emphasize research requiring primary source material may depend in part on the library's special collections and archives departments.

The strength of these collections, the available level of staffing, and the accommodations for users in these departments should be considered. The likelihood of expanding the special collections through gifts is a further important consideration.

COST ESTIMATES

When the new library requirements have been analyzed fully, it is important to try to place a price tag on the overall request. For current material, the *Bowker Annual* reports recent average volume costs for major subject areas, and approval plan vendors may be able to supply more timely data. The costs of microtext sets and reprints are readily available. Unless the librarian is aware of a previously assembled retrospective book collection in the desired subject area, it is likely that the cost of building the retrospective book collection will have to be amortized over a number of years. Anticipated incremental staff and equipment expenses should also be included. The librarian should be prepared to answer the following questions: What will it cost to improve the collection to the point where it supports teaching in the new area? What additional costs would be incurred to develop the collection to the point where it will support honors theses? How much more will it cost to bring the collection up to a level where it will support faculty research in the new field? The result should be a comprehensive statement of estimated library costs for the change in the academic program—a library budget impact statement.

POLITICAL CONSIDERATIONS

When the library budget impact statement, including the cost estimate, is finished, it is important to discuss the statement with the department or with key faculty members before forwarding it to administrators. The cold realization of the incremental library cost to support a new faculty member or course may discourage the department from proceeding. More likely, faculty members will simply review the statement and offer their comments. To omit consulting the department or its representatives at this critical juncture could be a major mistake since it is through such consultation that understanding is achieved and departmental support is won.

No matter how proposals for change in college academic programs are considered, evaluated, and acted upon, it is important that administrators who have the power to approve or disapprove these proposals take into consideration the library budget impact statement. With this information, which is so vital in a small institution where resources are scarce, administrators will be in a much better position to make the best decision.

NEW FACULTY

If the curriculum change involves a new faculty member, the participation of the librarian in the interview process may be helpful. New faculty whose teaching and research depend heavily on the holdings and services of the library should be given an opportunity to talk with the librarian about the strengths and weaknesses of the collection in their subject specialty. A review of the appropriate portion of the collection development policy, if one exists, could be revealing. Visits to the pertinent portion of the reference collection and stacks can reinforce generalizations about the strength of the collection.

The librarian can collect useful information about the library expectations of each candidate. During the interviews, the librarian can learn how much additional development candidates believe will be necessary to bring the collection up to an appropriate level; how willing they are to rely on the resources of other libraries in the area; and the extent of their special needs, such as access to currently unavailable databases, primary source material, or media requiring special equipment for viewing or listening. During these interviews, the librarian has a responsibility to be candid about the weaknesses of the collection and frank about the possibilities of obtaining additional funds to improve the collection. It is a time for reality and candor, not rose-colored glasses and false promises.

IMPLEMENTATION

Once an institutional commitment has been made to a new faculty member or new academic program, the librarian has the obligation to make effective plans to support that commitment. If the commitment is made to a new faculty member, a good place to begin is with the person's résumé. Information of particular interest will be the appointee's publication record, courses previously taught, and grants received. The librarian should try to meet with the new faculty member to discuss plans for development of the collection. At that meeting the librarian can emphasize the need to receive reserve requests well before the beginning of the next semester. The librarian should also reiterate and/or clarify the library's commitment to the new faculty member and, if possible, obtain the faculty member's promise to help build the collection. It is also important at this early date to establish the understanding that collection development will be a continuing responsibility requiring close cooperation between the librarian and the faculty member in the years to come.

New course decriptions and syllabi for those courses provide valuable information about collection needs. The library's support of a new program will require extensive consultation with the faculty who have proposed it and with the dean of faculty. In the case of a new program, the head librarian will probably want to assign specific responsibility to a librarian for coordinating collection development in the new discipline. The head librarian should also make clear the extent of the library's commitment to the new program.

When there is doubt about how to proceed with improvement of the collection in support of the academic initiative, the librarian may wish to visit a nearby library that is known to provide excellent support in that subject area. A discussion of such matters as specialist book and periodical dealers, sources of out-of-print books, and tips on obtaining foreign government documents can often save a considerable amount of staff time and lead to more effective collection development.

The task of assessing the current collection and selecting additional materials to strengthen it varies with each discipline. In the sciences, it is important to consider the need for current information, the high cost of science periodicals, and the need for remote database services. In the social sciences, the special needs may be for domestic or foreign government documents, maps, or access to census information. In the humanities, development of the retrospective collection may have a high priority. The support of new subdisciplines within music, fine arts, film study, and language instruction may require substantial investments in media and playback equipment. An expanded language instruction program could even demand installation of a satellite antenna to receive foreign television programming. New area studies programs may present the problem of obtaining relevant materials from abroad.

While making plans for the expansion of the general collection, it is important not to overlook the need to develop the reference collection. This step is critical in smaller libraries where librarians do not have the resources to develop vast general collections.

Selective bibliographies can be of considerable use, but the demand for currency in some disciplines may lessen the value of older bibliographies. When using bibliographies for selection purposes, remember that someone else's selections may not be the best books for your library. There is no substitute for knowing and understanding the precise needs of your faculty and students.

Gifts-in-kind can help substantially in developing the collection in a new area. By publishing a call for donations of books to support a new academic program in the Friends of the Library newsletter, the librarian may be able to obtain a number of useful volumes, or even whole collections. Gifts, however, can be problematic unless there is a clear understanding that the library has the right to dispose of them as the library sees fit. Only those volumes that serve a useful purpose should be added to the collection.

The holdings of nearby libraries should influence the selection of material to be added to the library. The degree to which bibliographic information is readily available about the holdings of local libraries should, of course, influence the selection process. If there is a union list of serials for the area or region, and if there is a shared online catalog, the holdings of nearby libraries will be more apparent to users and more accessible. A book delivery system serving the libraries will encourage sharing of resources. But the necessity for considerable duplication among the library collections must be kept in mind since each library will require the basic books and periodicals needed to support teaching. Cooperative collection development is most desirable in the area of little-used materials.

FUND-RAISING

When an institution makes a commitment to change or expand its academic program, the college librarian is sometimes asked to support that commitment by applying for foundation or government grants, or by soliciting funds from individuals identified by the development office. Faculty cooperation is essential if this effort is to be successful. The librarian and appropriate faculty members must develop carefully thought out and well-argued proposals. In all cases, it is important that the primary justification is direct support of the new or changed academic program. It is also important to consider including the staff costs for acquiring and cataloging the new material for the library.

DISCONTINUED ACADEMIC PROGRAMS

It is the librarian's responsibility to respond not only to the creation of academic programs but also to the discontinuation of them. Too often librarians become so preoccupied with responding to academic initiatives that they lose track of the departure of faculty whose specialties are not replaced or the removal of some courses from the curriculum. An annual departmental review of current serials encourages the removal of subscriptions that are no longer needed. When a professor is leaving the college, the librarian should think not only of recovering all of the books the professor has borrowed but also of revising the collection development statement for that area. Courses dropped from the curriculum should prompt a similar reaction. Again, college librarians have a good chance of obtaining this information since their academic community is usually relatively small.

CONCLUSION

College librarians have an obligation to keep themselves informed of academic planning that will affect their libraries. By contributing a library perspective to academic planning in its earliest stages, librarians can influence the direction of these programs. By informing administrators of the library costs of academic initiatives before commitments or decisions are made, librarians can help their institutions to budget accurately and realistically. By working closely with teaching faculty to develop library collections in accordance with changing academic needs, college librarians can provide meaningful support for the development of the curriculum.

NOTE

1. Robert N. Broadus, *Selecting Materials for Libraries*, 2d ed. (New York: H. W. Wilson, 1981), 18.

Return to Alexandria

by Richard Hume Werking

In 1976, Daniel Gore edited *Farewell to Alexandria*, which concluded with his own essay of the same title. In it Gore predicted that the watchword for college libraries in the future would be the "no-growth collection," a steady state in which the number of volumes remained constant, as colleges eschewed the amassing of books and a mindless, futile pursuit of a comprehensive Alexandrian collection.[1] Although I know of no academic library, including Macalester and Lewis and Clark colleges during Gore's directorships, that has in fact adopted Gore's no-growth model, it is an idea that has a certain appeal in some quarters (not just among fiscal vice presidents), and that one hears discussed wistfully from time to time.

This paper recounts how the library collection at Trinity University in San Antonio behaved very differently from the no-growth model, in fact doubling between 1980 and 1988. Readers are hereby warned explicitly: What follows is an example of the "how we did it in our library" genre. As virtually all readers know, it is fashionable in the literature of librarianship to view with disdain accounts of innovations in a particular library. For my part, I have often found them to be valuable and as a group considerably more valuable than the higher-status, but all too frequently vaporous, pieces devoted at length to philosophizing about one thing or another. There are exceptions both ways, of course, but I hope that the following account of Trinity's accelerated collection development program is not among them.

Compared to many colleges and universities, and certainly compared to most of those which today can be legitimately viewed as its peer institutions, this Trinity University has had a relatively nomadic past.[2] Founded

in 1869 by the merger of three struggling Presbyterian colleges in postbel-
lum Texas, the university remained at its original campus in Tehuacana,
Texas, until 1902. Beset by financial difficulties, Trinity moved in that
year seventy-five miles northwest to Waxahachie, just south of Dallas
(and famous in the 1980s as a film-making site, e.g., *Tender Mercies,
Places in the Heart, 1918*). Forty years later, continuing to face financial
problems, the school was brought to San Antonio by several prominent
members of the city's business community, and in 1952 moved to its
present site on "Trinity Hill" atop an old granite quarry three miles north
of the downtown area. From the 1950s to the late 1970s, the University
prospered and grew in numbers of students and programs; by 1979 it was
enrolling 3,200 students (2,600 undergraduates and 600 graduate students) and offering master's degrees in eighteen disciplines, including
English and History.

In 1979, Trinity's current president, an energetic forty-two-year-old
economist who had risen from assistant professor to Vice President for
Academic Affairs at the University of Kansas, assumed his new position.
Strongly supported by the Board of Trustees, Ronald Calgaard was determined to see Trinity become one of the outstanding undergraduate liberal
arts institutions in the country. Hence, he quickly began paring the number of graduate programs until, by the fall of 1989, only three remained,
all professional programs. With the initiative coming from several prominent trustees as well as from the university's administration, the university
library was intended to play an important role in this transformation. As
President Calgaard put it a few years later, "If you want to build an
academic community with a reputation for excellence, a library is a major
component."[3]

The University Library, begun in 1869 as the 250-volume collection
of President W. E. Beeson, had grown slowly, reflecting the school's
economic difficulties. By the time of the university's final relocation in
1952, the library held about 50,000 cataloged volumes, and a majority of
the 2,386 volumes added in 1951–52 were gifts. In 1965, Robert A.
Houze, library director at Texas A&M, came to Trinity, succeeding James
Govan, who had assumed the directorship at Swarthmore. The achieve-
ments of Houze's directorship included conversion from Dewey to Library
of Congress by 1966; transformation of the card catalog into a COM
catalog by 1976, with virtually all bibliographic records for books con-
verted into machine-readable form; and a new building, which, when it
opened in 1979, combined into one location two major library sites and
two additional branches. The top two floors were occupied in 1979, and
one of the lower levels was opened in 1983; the lowest floor remains in
unfinished condition for future expansion. Other developments that
would bear directly on the collection's growth in the 1980s included the
adoption in 1976 of a liaison program, linking each reference librarian
with a group of academic departments, and the initiation in 1979 of a

fairly comprehensive approval plan with a leading book jobber. The approval plan provided the librarians with the opportunity for systematic participation in book selection. Consequently, by the end of the 1970s, an infrastructure was in place that would enable the library to embark on an ambitious program of collection development.

The trustees and university administration felt that if Trinity was to attain recognition and credibility at the national level as a distinguished liberal arts, predominantly undergraduate institution, its library collection would have to grow dramatically. Oberlin, in particular, and also Amherst, Swarthmore, Wesleyan, and Trinity College in Connecticut were those institutions most frequently held up as the appropriate models of outstanding colleges with excellent library collections. Hence the University adopted the goal of significantly increasing the collection's size as quickly as possible, a collection which in January 1980 numbered just under 300,000 volumes of books and bound periodicals.[4] Such a number was considered incompatible with academic distinction for a school of Trinity's size and diversity of academic programs. To demonstrate their seriousness of purpose, the trustees and university administration designated library acquisitions and expansion into an additional floor of the new building as significant elements in the new capital campaign to be launched in 1981.

In the meantime, in 1979 the new president made available special funds for acquisitions for two projects: buying titles that were included in *Books for College Libraries* (BCL) but that the library lacked, and replacing important titles that were found missing during a library inventory. The BCL project revealed that the library lacked about half the titles in that list, a result attributable largely to faculty control of the book budget before 1979. In addition to starting these two projects, the University in the fall of 1980 advertised for a collection development officer to lead its efforts. I accepted that position in March 1981, and assumed my new responsibilities in July.

By the time I arrived, the University had launched its capital campaign. Awaiting my attention was the first sum of money given to the campaign, a donation from the local Ewing Halsell Foundation. It was to be spent, and spent expeditiously, on buying "retrospective" books for the collection. These were to be titles that were not new imprints (and hence, obviously, not approval plan purchases), which ideally should have been bought in previous years, but because of funding shortages had not been. These and subsequent allotments of retrospective funds were limited to hardcopy books and bound periodicals; they were not normally to be spent for microforms or nonprint materials.

My first task was to establish an organizational structure that would select, acquire, and process this much larger number of books. As noted previously, a liaison librarian system involving most of the reference librarians was already in place. Even before I arrived they had begun some retrospective as well as approval plan and other current buying, using the larger budgets made available by the new president. In line with a similar system I had instituted at the University of Mississippi, I quickly dubbed these librarians "reference-bibliographers," and they have been absolutely essential to our success in buying both widely and wisely. The reference-bibliographers monitor the approval plan, identify other new titles for acquisition, generate orders for older titles, and review all order slips sent to the library by the faculty. Working closely with the faculty, we developed collection development statements for each academic department and program, which provided some very helpful scaffolding for our efforts.[5] In my second year, we added a reference-bibliographer position, bringing their number to five (which included the government documents librarian).

The other two areas that needed immediate attention were acquisitions and cataloging. New support staff positions were added in each department, doubling the size of acquisitions from five to ten FTE (full-time equivalent) positions and enlarging cataloging from eleven to eighteen. (Before 1984 we had a separate serials department, which handled both serials acquisitions and cataloging.) The paraprofessional who had been acting head of acquisitions for two years was made department head, and her position was upgraded to a professional, nonfaculty slot.

The summer and fall of 1981 were an especially busy time. Within six months we had encumbered the entire Halsell allotment of some $450,000, and additional funds were made available. In 1981/82, the library spent some $1,170,000 on materials (current and retrospective, and including binding), and in 1982/83, a bit over $1,500,000, an all-time high that we have not equalled since and probably will not for several more years.

Not surprising, such activity drew considerable attention from a number of book dealers, with many of whom we still do business today. One arrangement that did not materialize is worth recounting. In the fall of 1981 we received a visit from two representatives of a well-known book dealer. These gentlemen proposed an arrangement whereby they would find collections and purchase them on our behalf, and we would accept them, sight unseen. As I view it, and viewed it then, they wanted in effect a "letter of marque" to sail the high seas of the used-books world and haul in whatever they could. Needless to say, we demurred.

In January 1988 we added our 600,000th volume, reaching in eight years our goal of doubling the collection of books and bound periodicals. In other words, more than half the collection has been added in the past eight years. As a result, it is relatively up to date, since, in the process of buying many volumes, we made conscious decisions to reject even more that were outdated or otherwise inappropriate for our collection.

The two basic ways to acquire books, of course, are title-by-title and in collections. We have used both approaches with good results. For some of the title-by-title buying, we employed a technique of tape-matching that others may find interesting.

In 1981 we purchased from Stanford University several computer tapes that contained the bibliographic records for all titles (about 100,000) in their undergraduate library. We ran that database against our bibliographic records, produced a tape of the nonduplicates, and then printed the titles from that tape onto card stock in Library of Congress call number order. The cards were divided among the reference-bibliographers for review; those titles not selected were then forwarded to the academic departments for their consideration. Our operating assumption was that if a title were held by the Stanford undergraduate library, it was at least a likely, though by no means a certain, candidate for our collection and hence deserved our scrutiny. We eventually added about 6,000 books through this project.

We also employed the tape-matching technique in working with our approval plan vendor to conduct a retrospective run of our approval profile. Although this vendor's database of titles dated from the early 1970s, Trinity had not begun its approval program until 1979. We wished to identify titles that we would have received on approval (either as books or forms) if we had been on this bookseller's approval plan from the beginning. (I had encountered this idea at the University of Mississippi from then-director Calvin Boyer during a three-way conversation with the regional representative of the same vendor; within a few months the vendor was marketing this service at an American Library Association convention, with appropriate credit to Boyer.) Hence we received from the vendor a tape of eight or nine years' worth of retrospective titles that matched our current profile. We ran those tapes against our database to produce a tape of nonduplicates, and then ran that tape against the Stanford undergraduate library database. The remaining titles were printed out by subject catetgories and distributed to the liaison librarians. As a result, we added about 10,000 books.

Other title-by-title buying has involved us considerably with the traditional model of receiving order cards from faculty and acting on them. Faculty send cards to the appropriate reference-bibliographer (and occasionally to the wrong one, or to the acquisitions department, or to the library director), often with some indication of priority. In addition, reference-bibliographers have generated many orders after checking standard and specialized bibliographies. Titles that are out-of-print (o.p.) are ordered from o.p. book dealers or from the o.p. departments of book jobbers who are known primarily for supplying in-print titles.

One considerable advantage to having suddenly a much larger materials budget has been the freedom to dispense with formal allocations among academic departments. When I arrived at Trinity our acquisitions department, like many, had been keeping track meticulously of the encumbrances and expenditures against about thirty departmental lines. With enough funds to buy virtually any book requested by a faculty member, we stopped formal allocation.[6]

We found that, if the pie is large enough to accommodate normal appetites, there is no reason to spend a great deal of time devising a method to determine the precise size of the slice apportioned to each group of faculty. In the past couple of years, we have adopted a rough allocation scheme along divisional rather than departmental lines. As the budget gets tighter in the years ahead, and it surely will, we will likely have to return at least partly to a method of formal allocation among academic departments.[7]

In addition to titles we knew we wanted (from BCL, inventory follow-up, tape-matching, etc.), we have acquired on a title-by-title basis many thousands of books from book dealers who brought to our attention their catalogs, other lists, or photocopied title pages. We sent copies of our microfiche catalog to dealers whose stock seemed interesting, letting them check our holdings against their offerings after we gave them general guidelines about what sorts of things we were seeking. We gave a high priority to dealers who searched our lists accurately and whose stock was in good or better condition. For the most part we were seeking good, solid academic books in the liberal arts, not rarities or ephemeral items. At least one vendor preferred to pay a San Antonio rather than a New York wage rate to check our catalog against his, and through our good offices he hired one of our part-time employees for that purpose.

Another variation involved purchasing duplicates or discards from other libraries. We sent selected libraries a copy of our catalog, and they in turn sent us photocopies of title pages from books that were in good or better condition and not in our collection. These books became candidates for ordering and the title pages were dispatched to the reference-bibliographers for their evaluation; those not selected were usually forwarded to the appropriate academic department. For a time we even had an "approval plan" arrangement for duplicates with another Texas library, whose director is a friend who lacks neither energy nor good ideas. His library was managing a duplicates-exchange program for a considerable number of libraries within the state, and he was circulating lists of the available titles. After describing the sorts of works we were interested in, we sent him a copy of our catalog. His staff checked against it those titles that looked appropriate (primarily university press imprints) and were in good condition, and then sent us those books we apparently did not own. We returned the relatively few books that fell outside our collecting scope or were duplicates. For each title that we kept we paid a flat rate that was considerably cheaper than the book would have cost on the out-of-print market, even if it had been available and if we had known that we wanted it, but much more than the titles on the lists had been bringing from the other customers, who did their own checking and then ordered title-by-title. It was an inexpensive and worthwhile project, bringing us a number of titles we lacked, including (it is embarrassing to confess) Jonathan Kozol's *Death at an Early Age.*

Our approval plans for new books continue to account for about 10,000 titles added to the collection annually, a majority of our current acquisitions. Most are North American imprints, but we also bring in hundreds of British books, many French and German titles, and art exhibition catalogs through approval plans based on subject profiles and author lists. The vendors for our foreign-language plans even select a few titles that fall outside our profiles but deal with cultural issues, travel, biography, or social controversy.[8] The approval plans have freed acquisitions staff to devote the additional time needed to place firm orders for retrospective titles.

Periodic inventories of the collection over the past decade have identified missing books, incomplete multivolume sets, and volumes needing repair or replacement. Retrospective funds have been used to acquire needed materials identified in the inventory process. In addition, such funds are used to bind newly purchased serial backfiles, many paperbacks, and other new acquisitions needing preservation attention. In general, however, we have purchased materials in a condition that is ready for circulation.[9]

Many libraries are accustomed to using the expertise of faculty traveling abroad who are willing to devote some time to buying books for the collection. We have done this, and have also taken advantage of student interest and traveling. One of our political science students returned from Nicaragua not long ago with two boxes of interesting books, none of them duplicates.[10]

In addition to buying title-by-title, we have benefited considerably from purchasing book collections that belonged (often, though not always) to retired or deceased academics. The first and largest of these came to my attention when I was attending the 1981 ALA postconference institute on collection development at Stanford University. A book dealer was seeking a buyer for a 10,000-volume collection consisting of Latin American history and political science books, the property of retired Stanford political scientist Ronald Hilton. Professor Hilton's book catalog had been published by Scarecrow Press as an important collection of Latin Americana. After I assumed my new position at Trinity, I returned to Stanford and spent a couple of days going through every box of books to examine condition (which was excellent) and determined that the collection would be a good purchase for us, particularly given Trinity's interest in Latin America. Subsequent collections that we have purchased include the R. C. Stephenson collection of Russian literature; the Sir Henry Hardman collection of twentieth-century British economic, political, and social history; the Professor Benjamin Nelson (New School) collection, especially rich in historical sociology and intellectual history; and a substantial portion of the Eleanor Leacock (CCNY) collection of anthropology books. In all these instances we worked with vendors who had lists we could check for duplication; in one instance we helped a vendor create such a list. In every case we invited faculty to inspect the collection and suggest priority processing of certain titles as well as which duplicates we should keep as second copies.

Special collections have not been a very high priority for us, because we have sought to build a solid, general academic collection. Nevertheless we have benefited from the generosity of individuals who have donated some rare items, most notably an excellent copy of William Morris's Kelmscott Chaucer. We have also purchased selectively, using gift funds for a few examples of fine printing and for rare titles to commemorate the acquisition of our 400,000th, 500,000th, and 600,000th volumes. We have added many art, architecture, and archaeology volumes, especially those with loose plates, to Special Collections, as well as Texana and other Western Americana.

Emerging and changing priorities of the University had a direct impact on the collection's growth. New departments of art history and classical studies were added. Russian became a major within the Foreign Languages Department, and the Department of Sociology expanded to become the Department of Sociology and Anthropology. Also, the president created a number of "distinguished professor" positions and appointed to those named chairs (in art history, economics, geology, mathematics, education, English, philosophy, political science, business, chemistry, biology, classics, and computer science) individuals who often had definite expectations for the library's collections. Junior faculty appointed during the decade often worked in such subject areas as pre-Columbian archaeology, Pacific history, jazz, architecture history, women's studies, and volcanology, which had not been emphasized in the past at Trinity. Our buying of retrospective materials has taken these new interests into account.[11]

Readers probably will not be surprised to learn that these years of expansion were not exactly free of problems. Monies pledged to the capital campaign came in at only so many dollars a year, and the University administration was not always able to fund the retrospective acquisitions program as fully as we all would have wished. Hence, on two occasions, once for a few months and the other for over a year, we slowed our buying and shifted staff from acquisitions to cataloging in order to work down a 45,000-volume backlog accumulated in the early 1980s. As of fall 1989, the backlog was down to only three thousand or four thousand volumes. Moreover, like many other institutions, we have had to cut serials, effecting a major reduction in 1988 of 650 titles (430 periodicals and 220 other serials) worth just slightly under $100,000. Because of rising book prices, approval plan dollars purchase fewer books today. Although the university has diversified its financial base and become less dependent on the price of oil, the economic climate on Trinity Hill no longer reflects the boom years of the late 1970s and early 1980s.

The title of this chapter may be misleading. Obviously, no single library, much less the library of an undergraduate institution, can approach the Alexandrian ideal of a comprehensive collection. In fact, at a time when we have been doubling the collection, the number of items ordered for patrons through interlibrary loan has been increasing even more rapidly. Considering the growing academic intensity of the institution, this has been a phenomenon as appropriate and predictable as it is ironic.

Nevertheless, the title does seem appropriate as a juxtaposition to the no-growth library ideal, and one that captures some of the spirit of the Trinity library in the 1980s. Because of good fortune and because several factors came together ten years ago (most notably the generosity and commitment of a number of university trustees and the support of university administrators), Trinity committed itself to increasing the size of its library collection in order both to serve and to stimulate its academic intensity, and thereby to contribute to a more demanding climate of expectations on the campus. For instance, in 1982 and 1983, the average circulation per undergraduate per year was eleven books; by 1989 it had more than doubled, to twenty-seven. If America is, as one historian has suggested, a land of constantly "becoming" rather than simply "being," then Trinity in the past decade has been quintessentially American.[12]

During the past few years, it would have been tempting to become caught up in collection growth to the exclusion of virtually anything else, but we would have been shortchanging our patrons if we had done so. Hence we have emphasized service priorities, such as providing bibliographic instruction, arranging the entries in our subject catalog in reverse chronological order, providing access through the catalog to our backlog, promoting online database searching, and establishing table of contents services for faculty both for journals to which we subscribe and for those to which we do not.[13]

Our challenge in the future, one faced by almost all academic libraries, will be to continue collecting materials to store on site in anticipation of their use by patrons, while continuing to improve our patrons' access to materials that our library does not own in the traditional sense. Both are part of the acquisitions and collection development process. Access and storage mechanisms, both for the collections housed on our campuses and for those housed elsewhere, are not likely to become cheaper anytime soon. Consequently, the task of bringing our students and faculty into contact with the books, journal articles, and other materials they need for their scholarship will be at least as challenging in the coming decade at Trinity as it has been in the one just ended.

NOTES

1. Daniel Gore, "Farewell to Alexandria: The Theory of the No-Growth, High-Performance Library," in *Farewell to Alexandria: Solutions to Space, Growth, and Performance Problems of Libraries,* ed. D. Gore (Westport, Conn.: Greenwood Press, 1976), 164–80.

2. In addition to the venerable Trinitys in Dublin, Oxford, and Cambridge, all founded in the sixteenth century, *The World of Learning 1989* (London: Allen & Unwin, 1988, 1978) identifies three institutions in the United States with the name Trinity College: in Connecticut, Vermont, and Washington, D. C. Trinity in San Antonio is the only Trinity University listed (p. 1978).

3. Julie Catalano, "The Eyes of Texas Are upon It: Trinity University," *Wilson Library Bulletin* 62 (January 1988): 48.

4. There was some discussion about tripling the library's collection within a five-year period, as stated in the advertisement for the collection development officer. But this aspiration, over time, was scaled down to the more manageable goal of adding 40,000 volumes of books and bound periodicals each year until the size of the collection had doubled. See *College and Research Libraries News* 41 (December 1980): 23–24.

5. Examples of these collection development statements have been published in Theresa Taborsky and Patricia Lenkowski, comp., *Collection Development Policies for College Libraries,* CLIP Note #11 (Chicago: Association of College and Research Libraries, 1989), 128–42. Some of these statements owe much to, and were adapted from University of Texas at Austin, General Libraries, *Collection Development Policy* (1976).

6. I have made the point elsewhere that if libraries are buying books, allocation is in fact taking place, whether formally and systematically or not. "Allocating the Academic Library's Book Budget: Historical Perspectives and Current Reflections," *Journal of Academic Librarianship* 14 (July 1988): 140–41.

7. For readers interested in the issue of allocation, I offer citations to two of my own pieces: the *JAL* article cited above, and "Using *Choice* as a Mechanism for Allocating Book Funds in an Academic Library," *College and Research Libraries* 42 (March 1981): 134–38, with Charles M. Getchell, Jr. More recent than either of these is Donna Packer, "Acquisitions Allocations: Equity, Politics, and Formulas," *Journal of Academic Librarianship* 14 (November 1988): 276–86, which demonstrates the enduring attraction of applying mathematical formulas to the allocations process.

8. Craig S. Likness, "The Creative Use of Acquisitions Mechanisms in the College Library," in *Collection Development Issues in Medium-sized and Smaller*

Academic Libraries: Papers from the 1988 College Libraries Section Program, ed. Richard Hume Werking, in *Collection Management* 12, nos. 1–2 (1990): 3–9.

9. Craig S. Likness, Trinity's humanities librarian and head bibliographer, contributed this paragraph.

10. Likness, "The Creative Use of Acquisitions Mechanisms."

11. Another entire paragraph from Craig Likness.

12. Stephen E. Ambrose, *Crazy Horse and Custer: The Parallel Lives of Two American Warriors* (Garden City, N.Y.: Doubleday, 1976), 125.

13. For details about three of these initiatives, two of which are fairly uncommon in academic libraries, see articles in *College and Research Libraries News* 47 (January 1986): 7–9; 49 (January 1988): 12–15; 50 (February 1989): 142–43.

Collection Management: The Collection Development Alternative

by Herbert D. Safford and Katherine F. Martin

The evolution of the terminology of collection development is an important reflection of changes among college and university librarians in their attitudes and approaches to this activity. A focal point for understanding these changes in nomenclature, perspective, and practice is the question of the relationship between the concepts of "collection development" and "collection management." The editors and authors of these papers as well as others in the profession voice their sense that collection development and collection management are overlapping categories, or perhaps even variant expressions for the same set of activities.[1] Collection development or management, in this view, may be defined as "the activity that results in the intentional and systematic building of the library collection," as the editors of this book affirm. A second and more traditional view regards collection development as a superset of collection management, the latter consisting of the clerical and technical underpinnings of the intellectual activity known as collection development.

It is possible to argue a third case, however—that the expression *collection development* is an attenuated one and can be misleading if it is used to encompass the realm of activities necessary to make library materials available to users. This line of thinking, which is gaining some currency, would suggest that the designation *collection management* is probably better suited for such a task.[2] In this alternative view, collection management is a superset of collection development. This paper presents the view that collection management includes collection development as one, albeit very important, part of an integrated set of activities and that it is collection management writ large with which contemporary librarianship should be concerned.

Collection development is too often interpreted prima facie to mean the decisions that lead to adding various kinds of materials to the library's collections.[3] Too often, adding materials has meant collecting monographs. When we put it this way, we can see right away that anyone responsible for collection development must decide the range of materials to be selected and collected; certainly, in most libraries, these materials should include periodicals, compact disks, and nonprint materials of various sorts as well as books.[4] It is not at all clear that collection development officers (by whatever name) generally are charged with oversight of the complete library collection, though there would seem to be no particular logic in arguing that they should not be.[5] The decision to include responsibility for all library materials with their variant formats and machine-dependent characteristics under the umbrella of collection development is fundamental. Such a decision has broad intellectual, practical, and budgetary ramifications and presents great problems in that such a comprehensive responsibility crosses traditional departmental or organizational lines. Any expression of views on collection development that fails to encourage breadth of scope in addressing formats does a disservice to persons engaged in this work and to the nature of the collections they help to build.

If we accept the notion that collection development includes all library materials for all patrons, it should include all manner of ways of acquiring these materials. For example, it should include the library's gifts program. It should also include archives management. If it does not (and often it does not), the decision to exclude such activities from the responsibility of the collection development officer or team should be delineated and defended initially—not as an afterthought or because of tradition.

Again, if we accept collection development as inclusive of all manner of ways of *acquiring* all appropriate and affordable materials for all of our public, a better definition of collection development would include all manner of ways of making materials *available*. Putting aside the matter of bibliography, and specifically catalog construction, a number of noncataloging but technical activities other than getting materials into the library are suitably called collection development.[6]

A principal responsibility of persons charged with collection development is the analysis of current collections and trends in collection building.[7] This analysis does not in itself add one item to the collections but provides the foundation for decisions about what should be added to support the curriculum of the college or the mission of the parent institution.

Another aspect of collection development that does not directly add an item involves the various projects for sharing resources with other libraries.[8] Clearly the universal collection available to the user must be taken into account when one addresses the matter of what a patron may get from the library. The patron likely does not care whether the item is ready-to-hand or borrowed from another institution so long as it is made available in a timely fashion. Thus, collection development should be concerned as much with access as with the growth of the local collection.

Another apparently technical enterprise for making materials available to the public is preservation. If we choose to renew or sustain some materials, we are deciding to make those materials available but not those that will wear out and be discarded. Yet it is rare that collection development is seen to include preservation.[9] These are generally regarded as separate matters. But the decision to allocate a portion of the annual budget to binding and the rejuvenation of brittle books clearly implies that some money will *not* be spent on buying new materials. Thus, we are deciding to make available for a longer period materials we already own rather than to make available other materials that might be purchased. This is a straightforward instance of collection development— deciding what materials will be available to users, in what format, and in what condition.

Another activity central to collection development is weeding, or deselection. When librarians make the decision to allocate resources of time to identify materials to be withdrawn or placed in storage, they are deciding to allocate fewer resources to selecting new titles for purchase, evaluating gifts, reviewing exchange lists, and so on. In the process, however, they do build a valuable knowledge about the collection and its use that can be applied in the exercise of their selection responsibilities. A library director is responsible for the entire library budget, and there is no good reason that a collection development officer should not take a similar perspective since that individual's responsibilities include all of the materials the library holds. When an item is discarded, it is no longer available. Thus, weeding and discarding are in fact part of collection development.[10]

Conducting an inventory of the collection may also be considered a collection development activity. Collection development is, in essence, deciding what will be available to the public. Clearly, when we inventory, we should ensure that those materials represented in our catalogs are indeed available. If, after inventory, we simply deduct from the bibliographic record those items we fail to find, that in itself would be a type of collection development. We would be making clear to users that we have only some of the materials we originally claimed to own. Inventory is usually intended, however, not merely to clarify and correct the bibliographic record, which is perhaps a matter of collection interpretation rather than development, but also to lead us to replace items discovered to be missing. That is, we have to make decisions as to which materials we can do without and which we will need to replace because they are as important as or more important than new acquisitions. Thus, inventory becomes even more clearly a collection development activity.

A reader might observe at this point that surely all library activities have to do with making materials available to the user and thus with collection development in some broad sense. If this is true, calling the entire set of library activities *collection development* is not useful because all we have done is to suggest that all of librarianship is collection development, and we have made no appropriate distinctions. We can, however, distinguish collection development from a number of other broad areas of activity within libraries. For example, collection development is *not* the same as collection interpretation. Reference, bibliographic searching, and bibliographic instruction are *not* collection development activities, nor is the passing of materials to and from the user (circulation, or access services).

The fact is, however, that *much* of library activity *is* collection development. Stack maintenance, for example, is collection development since poor shelf reading precludes user access to materials and, therefore, effectively reduces the collection truly available to the public. Emphasis here has been on what is made available to the public sans collection interpretation because this is what distinguishes collection development as a set of activities. To define collection development too narrowly ignores the real purpose of this set of activities, that is, to make library materials available for use by patrons. Buying books, however astutely done, is only a small part of this process. Yet it is largely about buying books that collection development officers talk and write.

It is a basic error to emphasize such matters as whether one department or the whole library staff or the faculty or the vendor should select books, according to one formula or scheme or another, while ignoring the premise that what counts is the whole set of activities that make materials available to the public. Why should collection development officers be limited in their charge to selecting certain materials? Should not collection development officers, instead, look at, think about, and participate in the whole set of processes that have to do with making library materials available? If this were so, the charge to such persons would be significant indeed, perhaps overwhelmingly so.

It is arguable that, even putting collection interpretation and circulation aside, collection development as here described is too broad a range of activities to fall under one compass. Yet we do charge library directors with collection development from at least the budgetary perspective as well as with all other library activities. It is fatuous, therefore, to say that no one person can do all of what needs to be done. Rather, it is better to recognize the coherence of these various collection development activities and to organize staff to handle them in a fashion that recognizes the interconnectedness of these tasks. The alternative is to reduce collection development to "getting," something that acquisitions departments did reasonably well years before collection development came into vogue. If we mean something particular by collection development, we should mean that it is a principal, a focal set of library tasks that do have coherence but that are not concentrated on one narrow, albeit significant, activity.

And this is the reason that the expression *collection management* may be more illuminating than *collection development*. *Collection management* suggests that persons with this charge are responsible for managing a variety of resources to select, purchase, analyze, preserve, weed, inventory, and otherwise consider all library materials in such a manner as to maximize the likelihood that patrons will find in the collections what they are looking for. Indeed, collection management may be so broad a set of tasks that the entire library staff should be involved in this activity.[11] This approach, which is indeed a current posture in many larger libraries, would seem to suggest that another collection management activity is the management of collection management, something far removed from selecting books. The fact that large libraries have often given up on some of what is properly within the scope of collection management is no argument for this being a good thing. The larger the collection, the more difficult it is to practice bibliographic responsibility and to ensure the optimal use of resources available to the public. This is ironic since we are prone to believe that what is required to make materials available to the public is more money for more materials. If this were true, then the answer to all collection management difficulties would be to have bigger libraries, and there would be no need to emphasize the *management* of collections at all. On the contrary, librarians have a particular responsibility to manage their collections, and buying books is only part of that responsibility. Smaller libraries, with more limited resources, have an especially important job in managing their collections rather than merely making them grow statistically.

A loose analogy may serve to bring this line of argument to a conclusion. Every working day a bank must account for every penny of its resources. Every year a bank must audit its records to ensure accuracy and, thereby, availability of liquidity to its customers. If librarians took seriously their responsibility to make information resources available, they would not pursue the matter of having more dollars in the vault as an end in itself but would concentrate as well on ensuring that those dollars were responsibly managed. It is an important feature of small libraries that they can still do collection management. They can be bibliographically responsible, as banks must be fiscally responsible, if they decide that collection management is a coherent, fundable set of intellectual and practical activities that are client-centered. Collection management subsumes collection development as one of its parts and, far from being merely clerical, is essential to the definition of librarians engaged in the sets of activities just described.

The challenge to collection development officers is not whether to fund approval plans or to have the librarians or the faculty buy books under a particular allocation formula but rather to assume the burden of *managing* the collections. The expression *collection management*, which denotes the manner of allocating library resources of all kinds among a set of tasks intended to make library materials available, is a more dynamic and useful one than *collection development*, an attenuated expression at best. Can we stay in business if we martial resources to do all that collection management entails? A better question is, what business are we in if we do not do so?

NOTES

1. See, for example, Christopher Millson-Martula, "The Effectiveness of Book Selection Agents in a Small Academic Library," *College and Research Libraries* 46, no. 6 (November 1985); 504; David Farrell, "The NCIP Option for Coordinated Collection Management," *Library Resources and Technical Services* 30, no. 1 (January/March 1986): 48; and Paul H. Mosher and Marcia Pankake, "A Guide to Coordinated and Cooperative Collection Development," *Library Resources and Technical Services* 27, no. 4 (October/December 1983): 417–20.

2. *The ALA Yearbook of Library and Information Sciences,* first published in 1976, originally used the heading *collection development;* the term became *collection management* with the 1980 *Yearbook,* and in 1989 was changed to *collection building and management.* Although the nomenclature has varied, much of what is discussed each year has not. The content of each annual entry leads one to conclude, for example, that collection assessment and resource sharing remain perennial concerns.

3. Maureen L. Gleason, "Training Collection Development Librarians," *Collection Management* 4, no. 4 (Winter 1982): 1–8; William Miller and D. Stephen Rockwood, "Collection Development from a College Perspective," *College and Research Libraries* 40, no. 4 (July 1979): 318–24; Guy R. Lyle, *The Administration of the College Library,* 4th ed. (New York: H. W. Wilson, 1974), 170–99. Although Lyle does deal briefly with the significance of weeding and storage decisions in the collection-building process in the chapter entitled "Book Selection and Acquisition," he focuses on selection processes, factors affecting selection decisions, and the creation of collection development policies.

4. Richard K. Gardner, *Library Collections: Their Origin, Selection, and Development* (New York: McGraw-Hill, 1981), 179. Standard 2 of "Standards for College Libraries, 1986" stipulates that "the library's collections shall comprise all types of recorded information, including print materials in all formats, audio-visual materials, sound recordings, materials used with computers, graphics, and three-dimensional materials" (ACRL Ad Hoc College Library Standards Committee, "Standards for College Libraries, 1986," *College and Research Libraries News* 47, no. 3 (March 1986): 191). The published introduction to the Standards indicates that they are intended to apply to institutions offering bachelor's and master's degree programs.

5. Peggy Johnson, "Collection Development Officer, a Reality Check: A Personal View," *Library Resources and Technical Services* 33, no. 2 (April 1989): 153, 154; Elizabeth Futas, "Issues in Collection Development: Wanted: Collection Development Officer," *Collection Building* 4 (1982): 55–56.

6. Gardner, *Library Collections,* 179–268 passim; Mary J. Bostic, "A Written Collection Development Policy: To Have or Have Not," *Collection Management* 10, no. 3/4 (1988): 89, 91, 94; John Ryland, "Collection Development and

Selection: Who Should Do It?" *Library Acquisitions: Practice & Theory* 6, no. 1 (1982): 13.

7. Bonita Bryant, "Collection Management," *The ALA Yearbook of Library and Information Services* 13 (Chicago: American Library Association, 1988), 117; Bostic, "A Written Collection Development Policy," 91.

8. Mosher and Pankake, "A Guide to Coordinated and Cooperative Collection Development," 417–31; Richard M. Dougherty, "A Conceptual Framework for Organized Resource Sharing and Shared Collection Development Programs," *Journal of Academic Librarianship* 14, no. 5 (1988): 287–91. See also Bernard H. Holicky, "Collection Development vs. Resource Sharing: The View from the Small Academic Library," *Journal of Academic Librarianship* 10, no. 3 (July 1984): 146–47, for a discussion of the critical need for resource sharing on the part of the smaller academic library. Such cooperative programs are mandated by Standard 5.2.2 of "Standards for College Libraries," 1986.

9. For discussion of the connections between collection management and preservation, see Dan C. Hazen, "Collection Development, Collection Management, and Preservation," *Library Resources and Technical Services* 26, no. 1 (January/March 1982): 3–11; and Ross W. Atkinson, "Selection for Preservation: A Materialistic Approach," *Library Resources and Technical Services* 30, no. 4 (October/December 1986): 341–53.

10. Lyle, *The Administration of the College Library,* 198; Caroline D. Harnly, Cynthia Hall, and Lucinda Covert-Vail, "Weeding: One Answer to an Unreasonable Problem," *Technicalities* 5, no. 5 (May 1985): 3.

11. Mosher and Pankake, "A Guide to Coordinated and Cooperative Collection Development," 418.

Part 4

The Role of Faculty

The role of faculty in developing a library's collection may well have been discussed more than any other collection development issue. At the university level, collection development has long been the province of librarians, but in colleges this is newly won territory. There is a whole host of issues buried within the topic of the role of faculty in collection development in college libraries. This section will be able to discuss only a few of them.

It is obvious that college library collections are built to serve the needs of a specific group—students. The research needs of faculty have traditionally been sublimated, with librarians relying on interlibrary loans or neighboring university collections to provide more highly specialized materials. Librarians who manage larger collections, however, frequently find themselves in a compromising position, placing emphasis on student needs while attempting to meet at least a portion of research needs. Thus, how faculty do research and how scholarly communication works are important issues for collection development, especially for those colleges that make an attempt to support some faculty research.

The role of faculty in collection development at the college level is an especially pressing issue primarily because materials budgets are limited. It is the limited budget that gives rise to the perception that the college library can never purchase quite enough and thus cannot be a research library. Further, in this milieu, faculty are always acutely aware of what has been purchased and who made the selection.

All of this leads to concerns about how collection development is to be done, who should be doing it, and the clientele for whom it is being done. The stakes are high in collection development at the college level because so much is being asked of so little money.

Ronald Epp addresses the issues of faculty research and scholarly communication and how these impinge on collection development. In 1986, the American Council of Learned Societies published the preliminary results of a Survey of Scholars that was undertaken by its Office of Scholarly Communication and Technology. The Survey provides significant information on how well prepared faculty and academic libraries are to respond to the challenges created by new formats for scholarly communication. In describing and evaluating this data, however, the published response to this Survey has not addressed several important collection development implications. Epp's paper focuses on establishing the relevance of this Survey in forecasting faculty roles in the development of college library book collections.

Larry Oberg argues that college libraries must support faculty needs as well as those of students. He maintains that in a period of financial constraint, proliferation of information, and intensified resource sharing, college librarians have scaled down their expectations of the client activities that a college library collection ought to support. Today's collective wisdom is that librarians can no longer afford and no longer need to buy materials that relate only to individual faculty research interests. Instead, scarce resources are concentrated on developing core collections that directly support student requirements, that is, the curriculum. As a result, Oberg maintains, librarians have come to talk in terms of two distinct collections: one that is student-centered, hence practical and necessary, and another that is faculty-centered and relates only to the "esoteric" research interests of individual faculty members. The latter is generally viewed as a luxury best left to university libraries.

However, at the same time as the needs of students and faculty have become dichotomous, faculty have come under increasing pressure to do research and to publish. Oberg's paper explores what faculty research needs are and what portion of those needs are currently being satisfied by the college library. Further, he defines the range of resources required to support faculty research in several fields and suggests which are best satisfied by local collections, by resource sharing, and by development grants that subsidize travel to research collections.

Who should do collection development to support an undergraduate education? Larry Hardesty points out that, historically, members of the classroom faculty have played a major role in book selection for the college library, and there is considerable justification for this arrangement. Faculty are generally well qualified to judge books within their subject areas and can greatly influence the use of those books through assignments.

Hardesty reviews the literature on the development of faculty attitudes and values and relates these to the role of faculty in collection development. He points out that college librarians have become increasingly involved in the selection of library materials. Hardesty further contends that increased knowledge about faculty attitudes and values may allow librarians to decrease the portions of the collections that go unused, thereby increasing the overall value of the collections for users.

Mary and John Scudder come down more on the side of the faculty for college library collection development, and argue that there should be a high level of organization and structure that incorporate a closer working relationship with faculty than is often found in most university libraries. The authors identify some current college library practices designed to foster faculty participation in collection development and to promote library use. In addition, the Scudders present background material to support the formulation of the following practices: a four-point book allocation formula using factors for availability, cost, enrollment, and potential library use; a faculty-librarian liaison program to enhance communication and cooperation; departmental book selection policies listing areas of emphasis; and a faculty library committee to support the purpose and mission of the library and to identify and communicate the needs of users.

The "Survey of Scholars": Collection Development and Library Service Implications

by Ronald H. Epp

Several significant publications appeared in the mid-1980s that raised challenging and novel questions about higher education and the nature of scholarly communication. Two special reports from the Carnegie Foundation for the Advancement of Teaching (*The Academic Life* and *College: The Undergraduate Experience in America*) charted the character of academic life for scholars and students, and although these empirical studies lacked the far-reaching public impact of the more polemical works of that day (e.g., Allan Bloom's *The Closing of the American Mind*), they have provided an agenda of important concerns for the 1990s.

So too the American Council of Learned Societies (ACLS) sponsored in 1985 a Survey of Scholars in order to determine whether scholars and librarians are sufficiently prepared to deal with the challenges of the so-called new technology. Most academics became aware of the Survey through a volatile headline in the *Chronicle of Higher Education*: "Scholars Fault Journals and College Libraries in Survey by Council of Learned Societies." The scholars surveyed seemed to find fault with two important components of scholarly communication: journals and the college libraries that house them. Indeed, a main thrust of Robert L. Jacobson's summary was that "nearly half [the faculty surveyed] rate the book collections in their institutions' libraries only fair or poor in meeting their research needs."[1]

Taking issue with some aspects of the Survey and the interpretation given by the authors of the preliminary report,[2] JoAn Segal, then executive director of the Association for College and Research Libraries, and I responded by emphasizing that the rapidly changing methods of scholarly communication had deeply affected the character of user service in academic libraries. Moreover, we also identified aspects of scholarly communication that should have been addressed by the Survey.[3] We concluded that the Survey was an excellent guide to the ways in which a sample of scholars responded to changes in the means and ends of scholarly communication, raising important implications for academic libraries at every level.

The 3,835 Survey participants were selected from seven ACLS disciplines—classics, history, linguistics, English and American literature, philosophy, political science, and sociology—that are representative of both humanistic and social science approaches to scholarship. They were polled on their attitudes toward research and publication, professional reading, computer resources and their use, forms of scholarly communication, and library resources (the latter accounting for 17% of the questions). Approximately 16 percent of the scholars were faculty at liberal arts colleges, while another 22 percent were at comprehensive institutions (a Carnegie Council classification that includes colleges and universities). Consequently, college faculty represented approximately one-third of the Survey participants.

Although the original report provided limited statistics on college faculty, an article by Survey co-author Anne Price provided expanded commentary and tabular statistics on "how well the transition to the new system is going at this early stage."[4] This paper will concentrate on the documentation in the Price report, noting where appropriate the variances with both the total sample and the scholars at research libraries. In many instances, responses from college and university faculty are statistically similar. Attention will be given to issues where there is significant variance: the availability of library technologies, faculty assessments of the quality of library service, and the adequacy of college library collections to meet teaching and research needs. The paper will conclude with suggestions for modified roles and skills for college librarians that are implied by the Survey.

Before we begin we must bear in mind the Carnegie Report's characterization of academic institutions. In the United States today there are community colleges and research universities, and, in between, doctorate-granting institutions, comprehensive colleges, liberal arts campuses, and specialized institutions. Each has its own culture with different goals, a different mix of students, and separate definitions of academic work.[5] It may be true that liberal arts colleges have a culture of their own, but in considering the Survey statistics we should also bear in mind the diversity of college libraries within this particular cohort and the exceptions to any practice that may be considered commonplace.

RESPONSES TO THE NEW LIBRARY TECHNOLOGIES

The Survey showed an impressive increase over the past five years in the scholarly use of personal computers, with 70 percent of the computer users owning their own PCs. Yet, when we move from the scholar's home and office into the academic library, we see a striking change in involve-ment with the new technology. The Survey concentrated on three library technologies: database searches, online catalogs, and microfiche.

College faculty report a slightly greater satisfaction with computer searches than their colleagues, perhaps because a higher percentage of the college scholars (as opposed to university/research scholars) are present when a librarian does the search. It is curious that, by a two-to-one margin, college faculty (as opposed to faculty at research universities) were able to secure library or institutional funding for the search.

The Survey showed that six out of ten college faculty rate their access to bibliographic utilities as good or better. Four scholars in ten were using available online searching and, regardless of institutional type, roughly seven in ten were satisfied with search results.

At present, most college libraries have only entered the first phase of technological change in their automation of card catalog production, acquisition, circulation, and serials control. At this early stage scholars at every type of institution remain unconvinced that access to the institu-tion's online catalog is important (more than three in five regarded such access as unimportant). Perhaps this is due in part to the slow transition to online catalogs at colleges (where only 17% report the conversion, as opposed to 59% at research universities).

Only one-third of the academic respondents answered questions about the effect of an online catalog on scholarly habits, and we lack a break-down by institutional type. Nonetheless, it is revealing that three in five reported a decrease in the use of the catalog. And slightly more than half reported increased enjoyment in the use of the library coupled with their belief that online catalogs have improved their access to scholarly materi-als. It was not believed by most that the online catalog increased their productivity as teachers or researchers.

The Survey shows considerable familiarity with microfiche as a research tool, with 66 percent of the participants reporting use of fiche in the past three years. There are reservations about the suitability of this medium, especially in the quality of the paper copies. One wishes that the Survey had explored scholarly opinions about the suitability of increasing the percentage of library materials that are in fiche format in response to increased pressure to preserve brittle books.

Dilys Morris argues that in developing the electronic library there will be improvements in storage and communicative technologies that will result in an integrated national network.[6] He envisions a communications network akin to BITNET, which is used by scholars at 1,500 member institutions to exchange manuscripts among themselves and with publish-ers. Moving beyond this, preprint exchange would be only one capacity of a scholar's workstation. Accessing online catalogs, users could browse backward and forward, do call number searching, access tables of contents and indexes of scanned new titles, and order facsimile transmission of journal articles.

The Survey clearly demonstrates that in many disciplines the benefits of technology have been welcomed, even greeted with enthusiasm. In fields that are wedded to the use of historical materials that span centuries, however, bibliographic databases do not begin to reach the sources needed. Most database vendors offer online bibliographic sources for the past twenty or thirty years of scholarship, and this only skims the surface of strongly historical literatures. Humanists are concerned not only with the breadth and depth of online literature searches but with the virtues of the mind. Yet Patricia Battin warns that there is a concept of scholarly autonomy that acts as a barrier to integration of the new technologies. Her electronic scholar in 1984 faced "incompatible hardware, software, and communications networks that . . . developed out of the normal scholarly characteristic of autonomous entrepreneurship in the pursuit of knowledge."[7]

Although very little is known about the way in which humanities research is carried out, we do know that it is solitary, heavily dependent on browsing, and frequently interdisciplinary, and because such research is serendipitous, the involvement of librarians is often presumed to be nonproductive. Humanistic research is also predominantly text-centered and involves a mosaic-like configuration of texts for each scholar who examines a particular problem. Most scholars in the humanities would argue that the essential ambiguities and paradoxes inherent in human knowledge defy resolution.[8]

As Karl Weintraub puts it, "Humanistic knowledge is embedded in the intricacies of language or imagery or sound. . . . [Such] work can rarely be done without those elusive [scholarly] qualities known as sensitivity, . . . wisdom, refined judgment, taste, [and] a sense of proportion."[9] When we combine these characteristics with the conceptual ambiguity that is inherent to any linguistic apparatus, we can better understand why online searching may continue to be a less productive activity for humanists than for the diverse scientific enterprises.

Although most librarians believe that expansion of online databases will be a boon to researchers who want to make sure that every avenue has been explored on a given topic, the Survey data do not show scholarly support for such exhaustiveness. Many faculty show little interest in this presumed scholarly standard; many will argue that it is sufficient to have the best scholarship at hand, the most current, or the resources that support one's own thesis. Moreover, there is contempt for resources presumed to be inadequate because of their lack of polish, sophistication, or clear and hard reasoning.[10]

CD-ROM databases, ever more sophisticated search strategy packages, and the promise of hypertext will continue to be mysteries that college

faculty will want to probe for both their research and teaching applications. Although the conversion of most faculty to the new technologies
seems inevitable to some, librarians need to forge an even larger role for
themselves in this process.[11] Hannalore Rader is quite right when she
predicts that "more [library] staff will be playing a role in the teaching
process" as faculty involvement with the emerging technologies increases.[12]

Nowhere addressed in the Survey is the issue of whether teaching
faculty are put off by the growing range of library information services.
Librarians need to be cautious about adding every new gadget, for even
now many faculty are bewildered by the diversity of media forms available.
The technical complexity of the information transfer process, the range
of formats available, and the volume of references on even the most
specialized topic have frustrated both students and scholars. It is hoped
that with time there will be degrees of integration and standardization
that will make the search process more friendly. Until then, librarians
must be watchful for signs of user weariness.

The Survey does not so much imply that scholars are unreceptive to
the new technologies as it shows their lack of familiarity with present and
future applications. This is especially true in the humanities where search
strategies are so individualized.[13] Moreover, we lack empirical studies of
how these scholars navigate their way back and forth through citations
and source materials. Are there distinguishable strategies? If so, are any
methods distinctive to specific disciplines? Rowland Brown recently detailed the new effort of OCLC to address such questions in order to
produce Electronic Information Delivery Online Systems (EIDOS) that
will enhance information accessibility.[14] Such excursions into unfamiliar
territory need to be coupled with programs to aid faculty in their understanding of the potential of the emerging technologies. The alternative
is "the growing danger of losing at least the older generation of faculties
in the social sciences and humanities."[15]

THE QUALITY OF LIBRARY SERVICE AND COLLECTIONS

When Price compared the responses of college faculty to those of research
university faculty, there was little variance regarding their satisfaction
with the quality of interlibrary loan (ILL) service and their accessibility
to computerized databases. It was, however, in facilitating scholarly research that college libraries were—not unexpectedly—found inadequate.
Whereas 54 percent of those surveyed rated their institutional libraries as
good to excellent in meeting their research needs *through books,* 73 percent
of the university faculty endorsed their institutions while only 43 percent
of the college faculty evaluated their libraries as above average. Journal

collections fared better: 67 percent of all participants rated their serial collections as good to excellent, although nearly twice as many university faculty (81%) as college faculty (49%) were more than satisfied.

It is commonplace for academic librarians to broadcast the sheer size of information resources available to users. Yet the Survey shows that scholars believe that the measure of library adequacy is not the expansive collections in university and research libraries, but their own personal collections. Regardless of the type of scholarly material, whether for teaching or research, 73 percent of all college scholars viewed materials in their personal libraries as of "great importance," whereas only 41 percent (compared with 59% in a research university) so rated their institutional library; perhaps this provides yet another reason for abandoning the goal of comprehensive collections in specific disciplines. Four out of ten college faculty, however, ranked their college libraries as being "of great importance." Moreover, regarding the ability of libraries to meet faculty research needs, journal holdings were rated very good to excellent by only 25 percent of the college faculty compared to 62 percent of the research university scholars.

Traditionally, a library's collection attempts to profile the interests and needs of its users. But college libraries cannot be small versions of university libraries. As Evan Farber argued nearly fifteen years ago, college libraries differ from university libraries "not only in quantitative terms but in their educational roles."[16] Administratively, the primary college library user is the undergraduate student whose needs have an urgency that cannot be rivaled by faculty demands for more specialized sources.

Regarding the convenience of library services, there was little institutional variance on such issues as the promptness of service, the frequency of equipment malfunction, the availability of librarian assistance, or the adequacy of facilities for reading journals.

In meeting teaching needs for both books and journals, college collections were rated fair or poor by nearly three in ten of the scholars, a proportion that was similar for satisfying student needs. Clearly, these assessments should prompt college librarians to carry out needs assessments in partnership with faculty in order to improve local collections. As William Miller and D. S. Rockwood pointed out more than a decade ago, "college collection development officers will continue to use *Choice*, use standard lists, involve faculty in collection decisions, give special attention to the existing strengths of their library, consider the holdings of other area institutions, . . . make interlibrary loan arrangements, and try to anticipate the changing nature of the college curriculum."[17]

It is extremely important that college librarians be even more demonstrative in explaining collection development issues to their users and key campus figures. Alliances must be formed in order to demonstrate anew that there is not only an information explosion but a radical restructuring of the process of scholarly communication that is affecting both the character of education between teacher and student and the nature of communication from scholar to scholar.

BRIDGING THE CLASSROOM-LIBRARY GAP

Characterizing the libraries at most of the institutions is surveyed as "a neglected resource," the Carnegie Report stressed the gap between the classroom and libraries, which are too often viewed by students as quiet study sites. To bridge this gap we should consider the survey as one technique underutilized by college librarians. (Such research should not be confused with the spate of recent articles that focus on faculty perceptions of librarians; neither am I suggesting a complex and expensive study involving many institutions.) Charles B. Osburn puts is well: Library researchers have "not focused so much on the consumer's goals, methods, habits, and motivations as we have on the efficiency of techniques to control and retrieve to our own professional satisfaction."[18] The special collegial relationships between college librarians and their faculties affords them a chance to redirect their library skills so that they might better understand the changing behaviors of teaching faculty.

Since many academics not only enjoy participating in surveys attuned to their interests and use them in teaching and research, library-generated surveys might address large issues (e.g., what mix of books, serials, and computer services are best conducive to undergraduate education, or to scholarly activity?), or concerns peculiar to that institution (e.g., since there is a reduction over the past decade in the number of students enrolled in humanities courses, should the library proportionately reduce acquisition funding to those disciplines?).

Surveys provide empirical documentation that receives attention from faculty and administrators—especially when the survey reveals the unanticipated. Although this technique is hardly untried in academic libraries, it is surprising that it is not used more often at a local level. Not only does it provide much-needed input from users but the very nature of the questions serves to alert faculty to changing practices and policies. Furthermore, such questions could address issues of particular interest to academic librarians that the Survey of Scholars left unanswered.

Have faculty grasped the teaching and research implications of the decreasing importance that many librarians are assigning to collection size? Since growth in the use of online information is anticipated, should hard copy acquisitions be reduced? A majority of ARL librarians surveyed believed that book collections would be reduced in size as the impact of information technology made information available in computerized and multimedia formats.[19]

Teaching faculty on campus might be surveyed to determine whether they believe that it is still important to be able to track the process of scholarship. With the speed of publication and the expanded use of electronic media, caution will be needed to preserve what Warren J. Haas of the Council of Library Resources has called our "intellectual audit trail." He is concerned about electronic changes made to manuscripts and laboratory records, especially when earlier versions are erased. Both librarians and scholars ought to discuss the common concern—that we may have no record of revisions, no track of the progress of experiments, no history of the generation of results.[20]

It is not my intent to delve into the complexities of what constitutes scholarly research. The Survey of Scholars provides considerable insight for revision of some traditional views about the character of scholarly research. Yet, in interpreting Survey documentation, it is important to recognize that scholarship involves not only information but the sharing of different kinds of knowledge: "conclusions, guesses, insights, scenarios, creative interpretations, models, analogies, summaries, speculations, and the whole array of unconventional experimental thought processes."[21] These aspects of knowledge are not sufficiently conveyed by the jargon of those who provide information services. Moreover, these cognitive processes are not the exclusive domain of teaching faculty.

Part of the faculty problem, as Constance McCarthy puts it, is that "the organization of knowledge does not worry them; they are not concerned with its complexities, its problems, or its promise."[22] Although this may overstate the case, it does reflect the dominance in the mind of most scholars of the library as a *place*. Efforts must be made to revise this traditional view so that the library is seen as a part of the process of scholarship, not solely a repository for it.

We are left with a sobering recognition that user perceptions of scholarly needs are at considerable variance with the views of the providers. The ACLS Survey of Scholars supports the report of the 1979 National Enquiry into Scholarly Communication.[23] Murray Martin's blunt characterization of the findings of the earlier ACLS report is reaffirmed: "Users were both ignorant of and did not care to know about the complex processes that produced the information for their use."[24] New efforts to open channels of communication are urgently needed.

In summary, implications of the ACLS Survey of Scholars for college librarians include the following:

1. Because of the nature of humanistic research, librarians should market not every new database available but rather the most efficient new search strategies for accessing online catalogs of books, periodicals, and nonprint media.

2. College librarians need continuing education in new studies of how scholars (and their students) navigate through resources, with special attention to discipline-specific search strategies.

3. Efforts should be made to routinely survey faculty regarding gaps in the collection that undercut the effectiveness of the curriculum.
4. Librarians must experiment with new strategies for educating faculty to the growing importance of how the organization of knowledge—and access to its ever-increasing formats—is vital to the development of their own scholarship.
5. Since many humanistic scholars do not use the library for much of their own research, librarians should imaginatively rethink how they might assist faculty in more efficiently accessing their own personal collections.

College library directors need to encourage their staff to participate more fully in the process of scholarly communication through greater interaction with publishers, learned societies, granting agencies, and journal editors. Through collaborative efforts we may learn to appreciate the reasons for perspectives that might not be entertained within the shelter of the familiar routines of the library. Yet no college librarian ought to find comfort in this notion of library routine, for the Survey conveys at least one telling truism—despite the entrenchment of habit, profound changes are in the wind.

NOTES

1. Robert L. Jacobson, "Scholars Fault Journals and College Libraries in Survey by Council of Learned Societies," *Chronicle of Higher Education* 32 (August 6, 1986): 1.

2. Herbert C. Morton and Anne Jamieson Price, "The ACLS Survey of Scholars," *Scholarly Communication* 5 (Summer 1986): 1–16. Note: The present essay was submitted before the 1989 publication of the ACLS final report by Herbert C. Morton and Anne J. Price, *The ACLS Survey of Scholars: Final Report of Views on Publications, Computers, and Libraries* (Washington, D.C.: Office of Scholarly Communication and Technology, American Council of Learned Societies, 1989).

3. "The ACLS Survey and Academic Library Service," *College and Research Library News* 48 (February 1987): 63–69. See also "Setting the Record Straight on the Survey of Scholars," the Morton/Price response in *College and Research Library News* 48 (May 1987): 273–75.

4. "Librarians and Scholars: The Need for Channels of Communication," in *Library-Scholar Communication in ARL Libraries* (Washington, D.C.: Association of Research Libraries, 1987), 1–16.

5. Burton R. Clark, *The Academic Life: Small Worlds, Different Worlds* (Princeton, N.J.: Carnegie Foundation for the Advancement of Teaching, 1987), chaps. 2, 5.

6. Dilys Morris, "Electronic Information Technology," *College and Research Libraries* 50 (January 1989): 58.

7. Patricia Battin, "The Electronic Library," *Collection Management* 9 (Summer/Fall 1987): 137.

8. See Elaine Broadbent, "A Study of Humanities Faculty Library Information Seeking Behavior," *Cataloguing and Classification Quarterly* 6 (Spring 1986): 23–37.

9. Karl Weintraub, "The Humanistic Scholar and the Library," *Library Quarterly* 50 (1980): 22.

10. See G. R. Jaramillo, "Computer Technology and Its Impact on Collection Development," *Collection Management* 10 (1988): 1–13.

11. See L. W. Helgerson, "CD-ROM and Scholarly Research in the Humanities," *Computers and the Humanities* 22 (1988): 111–16.

12. Hannalore Rader, "Academic Colleagues in Concert," *College and Research Libraries News* 49 (1988): 71. See also the contrasting view of Pauline Wilson, "Librarians as Teachers: The Study of an Organization Fiction," *Library Quarterly* 48 (1979): 146–62.

13. See Peter Stern, "Online in the Humanities," *Journal of Academic Librarianship* 14 (1988): 161–64; and Sue Stone, "Humanities Scholars: Information Needs and Uses," *Journal of Documentation* 38 (1982): 292–313.

14. Rowland Brown, "EIDOS," *OCLC Newsletter* (November/December 1988): 19–23.

15. R. M. O'Neil, "Inter-institutional Cooperation and the Information Needs of Faculty," *Research Libraries in OCLC* 21 (Winter 1987): 5.

16. Evan Farber, "College Librarians and the University-Library Syndrome," in *The Academic Library: Essays in Honor of Guy R. Lyle*, ed. E. Farber and R. Walling (Metuchen, N.J.: Scarecrow Press, 1974): 22. See also Rose Mary Magrill's insightful essay "Evaluation by Type of Library," *Library Trends* 33 (Winter 1985): 267–95.

17. William Miller and D. S. Rockwood, "Collection Development from a College Perspective," *College and Research Libraries* 40 (1979): 320.

18. Charles B. Osburn, "Issues of Structure and Control in the Scholarly Communication System," *Library Quarterly* 54 (1984): 90.

19. See Betty W. Taylor, Elizabeth B. Mann, and Robert J. Munro, *The 21st Century: Technologies Impact on Academic Research and Law Libraries* (Boston: G. K. Hall, 1988), chap. 2.

20. See T. C. Bearman, "Uses of Scientific, Technical, and Societal Information by Policy Makers," *Knowledge in Society* 1 (1988): 27–53.

21. Frederick Praeger, "Librarians, Publishers, and Scholars: Common Interests, Different Views," *Library Quarterly* 54 (1984): 22.

22. Constance McCarthy, "The Faculty Problem," *Journal of Academic Librarianship* 11 (1985): 143.

23. *Scholarly Communication: The Report of the National Enquiry* (Baltimore: Johns Hopkins Univ. Pr., 1979).

24. Murray Martin, "A Future for Collection Management," *Collection Management* 6 (Fall/Winter 1984): 4.

College Library Support for Faculty Research: The Forgotten Obligation

by Larry R. Oberg

Over the past twenty years, the attention of college librarians charged with collection development has shifted sharply away from faculty research needs toward a concentration on student requirements. As librarians entered a period characterized by financial constraints, a proliferation of published information, the advent of electronic access to remote databases, and intensified resource sharing, they began to scale down their expectations of the client activities that a college library collection ought to support.

Today it is necessary to speak of two distinct collections: one that is student-centered and considered essential, and another that is research-oriented and considered inappropriate to the college library. Limited materials resources, insofar as they are controlled by librarians, are concentrated on developing core collections that directly support student requirements. College librarians and administrators often assert that they are neither able to afford nor obligated to purchase materials that satisfy the research interests of individual faculty members. Collections that support original research are viewed as luxuries best left to university libraries.

This change in emphasis has come about for several reasons. In addition to the dramatic increase in the amount of published materials available, declining student competencies and intense faculty specialization have resulted in a dichotomization of need that is reflected in the literature of academe. For example, it is likely that a higher percentage of the academic books and journals produced in previous decades satisfied both faculty and undergraduate requirements. Today, a wide gap exists between those publications that support original research by faculty and those required by students doing survey coursework. At the same time, the splintering of the journals reflects that of the disciplines and reminds us of the increased specialization and diversity in the areas of research pursued by college as well as university faculty. Patricia Battin points out

118

that these factors have led to "a higher cost for the literature of each narrow specialty."[1]

As early as 1974, Evan Farber warned that college librarians ought to cease emulating the practice of their university and research library counterparts. He pointed out that college faculty book selection often emphasizes specialized research materials "purchased at the expense of materials that are less highly regarded by specialists but are more appropriate for undergraduates."[2] By 1981, William Miller and D. Stephen Rockwood cautioned college librarians not "to ignore the obvious disparities between what faculty too often request and what students actually find useful." They admonished us "to build a collection that directly fulfills student needs."[3]

As we heeded their advice, we distanced ourselves from a past in which, as late as 1954, Newton F. McKeon questioned the necessity "to state the obvious, that the college library has a particular obligation to supply teachers with the working materials for scholarship in their fields," and advised librarians that "the journal, the proceedings, the transactions . . . must be secured by the library in full measure."[4]

Farber and others set the stage for college librarians to gain control over book selection, materials budgets, and their professional destinies.[5] In the process, unfortunately, we have managed to become less mindful of the research requirements of the faculty. Although advances in technology offer us a range of new options, we still blur the distinction between our limited ability to purchase specialized materials for the exclusive use of individual researchers and our obligation to provide collection, service, access, and delivery alternatives that support faculty research in general.

These disturbing tendencies are exacerbated by our legitimate concerns over inadequate materials budgets and the quality of faculty book selection. Ironically, this situation has arisen at a time when more original research than ever before is being required of college faculty.

THE CHANGING NATURE OF COLLEGE FACULTY

The changing nature of faculty employment argues strongly for a review of what it is that college librarians should be doing to support faculty research. At many colleges, faculty feel increasingly pressured to conduct research and to publish. Louis F. Brakeman notes "a growing concern among faculty" with "what they see as the increasing emphasis on research." He points out that faculty "feel pressure from presidents, chief academic officers, and in some cases, from their peers. They feel it coming from societal sources as well."[6]

Of course, all colleges, not only the prestigious liberal arts institutions and the "research" colleges, have traditionally had some scholarly expectations of their faculties.[7] As early as 1981, however, Stanley J. Michalak, Jr., and Robert J. Friedrich pointed out that small colleges had begun to rely "more and more on research productivity in coming to decisions about which faculty to hire and which to fire, about which to promote, and about how much faculty should be paid."[8] Among the factors that contribute to this situation are:

1. A desire for increased institutional prestige as administrators attempt to shore up their school's niche in the academic marketplace in anticipation of a decline in student enrollment;
2. Intensified research requirements at the university level that have trickled down to the colleges;
3. The strong, albeit unproven, relationship that is presumed to exist between research productivity and teaching effectiveness;[9]
4. An increase in the number of short-term contractual faculty who must build their vitae if they are to secure tenure-track employment;
5. A competitive academic job market (at least until recently) in which new Ph.D.s who, in earlier times, would have begun and ended their career in research institutions now find their first jobs at teaching colleges where they arrive fired with the desire to do research.[10]

On many college campuses, however, particularly those that are small and isolated, a number of additional factors limit the conditions that encourage or make research possible:

1. Few college library collections today are designed or funded to support original research, even in a very limited number of fields.
2. Teaching, counseling, and committee loads are often heavier at colleges than they are are universities.
3. Funding and other forms of support for research may be limited or difficult to obtain.
4. Mechanisms beyond sabbaticals that provide released time for additional scholarly activity often do not exist.
5. Technical support for research, particularly in the sciences, may not be available.
6. Researchers on college campuses, isolated from colleagues who are working in the same or a closely related field, may not find a supportive local peer group.
7. Research networks may be difficult to establish and professional isolation may occur.
8. Survey courses, unlike graduate seminars, do not serve as incubators of research topics.
9. Local computer facilities may be inadequate for the storage and manipulation of large data sets.
10. The nearest research library may be some distance away.
11. Interlibrary loan and database search fees may be passed along to scholars by local librarians.

In 1986, the Office of Scholarly Communication and Technology of the American Council of Learned Societies (ACLS) conducted a national survey of faculty perceptions of a wide range of scholarly communication issues. The authors found a "mixed" response by scholars to library collections and services. Although research needs were found to be those that are the "least well served at all types of institutions," there is "much less dissatisfaction with [library] collections at research universities" than there is at smaller institutions. Not surprising, college faculty are the least well satisfied. More than half of these respondents state that both their libraries' book and journal holdings are inadequate for their research needs.[11]

Thus, depending on local conditions, college faculty can expect to find it more or less difficult to meet the increasing peer and administrative expectations for promotion and tenure.

THE ALBION COLLEGE PROJECT

The College

Albion College is a small, selective liberal arts college in south-central Michigan that serves approximately 1,600 students, some 85 percent of whom are from within the state. Founded in 1835, Albion is typical of many church-related Midwestern schools that were established in the wake of the westward migration and the prevailing climate of social uplift. Although located within a one-hour drive of several universities, including the University of Michigan at Ann Arbor with its extensive library holdings, the college remains relatively isolated geographically, a factor exacerbated by a residency requirement that obligates college faculty to live within the community of Albion.

Albion College's criteria for promotion and tenure require faculty to demonstrate scholarly development in order to qualify for promotion to the ranks of assistant and associate professor, and scholarly achievement for promotion to the rank of professor. The faculty handbook defines scholarly development as "best demonstrated through publication." Both large and small faculty development grants are available. There is no absolute research requirement, although in recent years scholarly productivity has played an increasingly important role in tenure, promotion, and salary decisions.

In a survey of Albion College faculty perceptions of librarians—conducted in 1988 by Mary Kay Schleiter, Michael Van Houten, and me—respondents were asked to characterize their research. Twenty-four percent responded that their research contributes primarily to updating and revising the courses they teach, 29 percent responded that it contributes primarily to research and publishing, and 47 percent responded that it contributes equally to both.[12] Thus, more than three-quarters of the respondents reported that they are conducting research that may lead to publication.

Justification

Albion College librarians are not charged with an explicit administrative mandate to support the non-curriculum-related research of individual faculty members. Over the past few years, however, we have become increasingly concerned that we may not be doing enough in this area and worry that our inattention could handicap faculty research efforts. In order to clarify scholars' needs and librarians' obligations, a survey of faculty members actively engaged in original research was undertaken. The project was designed to help librarians understand faculty research patterns and determine the nature and extent of the use made of libraries.

The following questions guided the development of the study design and methodology:

1. What research process was followed in the respondent's last published project?
2. What libraries were used and what were the relative percentages of materials and services that the respondent used in each?
3. What frustrations, delays, and problems were encountered in the library portion of the project?
4. What did the respondent think that Albion College librarians could do to provide better support for faculty research?
5. What services provided by librarians proved most useful in the respondent's last research project?

The results were intended to provide the following:

1. Concrete data to inform discussions of faculty and administrative expectations and librarians' obligations toward research support for faculty
2. A baseline for evaluating the level of support for research that library collections and services currently offer
3. A guide for setting collection and service goals for the increased support of faculty research
4. A rationale for discussing funding for research support with faculty and administrators
5. A mechanism for building collegial relationships between librarians and faculty.

Study Design

After considering the strengths and weaknesses of a variety of research techniques, I decided to conduct interviews with faculty who are active researchers. A list was drawn up of those individuals who, within the prior three academic years, had announced the publication of books or articles in the campus academic newsletter, *The Deanery*. Inclusion on the list required that articles had been published in a refereed national or international journal or in a collection. Of approximately 120 full-time faculty members, 30 met these criteria; 25 were available and agreed to participate in the project. The interviews were conducted over the late spring and early summer of 1989.

The previously formulated research questions provided the general framework for interviews that lasted approximately one hour, but respondents were allowed the freedom of shifting topics and moving to related issues. A few questions required that the interviewees quantify their responses: for example, how much of the literature relevant to your research project was in our collection? Interviewees were also prompted for their reactions to a list of both immediately practical and visionary services that might be introduced. A data collection form was designed that included the interview questions and provided space for responses. Extensive notes were taken during the interviews. In a few cases, clarifications and expansions were later sought by telephone.

The interview format had the advantage of allowing maximum freedom to the interviewees in their responses to open-ended questions while requiring a degree of precision when responding to those questions that are quantifiable. The weakness of the technique lies in the fact that the criteria used by the interviewees in formulating their perceptions and assessments may not be comparable.

Summary of Findings

The survey revealed that 92 percent of the interviewees used the Albion College library in their last published research project, 65 percent used the library system at the University of Michigan at Ann Arbor, and 65 percent used other libraries. Collectively, interviewees obtained 47 percent of the books and 49 percent of the journal articles they required for their projects from the Albion College library. Twenty-seven percent of those books and 29 percent of those articles were available in the library's collections; the remaining 20 percent of this latter group of books and articles were obtained through the library's interlibrary loan services.

Thus, slightly more than 50 percent of the materials that the interviewees required in their projects were obtained directly (not through interlibrary loan) from libraries other than Albion's, or from the researchers' personal collections. Two interviewees bypassed the Albion College library altogether. Three stated that they depend heavily on contacts with colleagues nationally and use a relatively limited number of published sources in their projects.

Overall, librarians appear to play a small direct role in faculty research. Only sixteen of the twenty-five interviewees report having sought out the assistance of a reference librarian in the course of their project, and ten of the sixteen qualify this contact as minimal. Twelve of the twenty-five report having requested one or more online database searches. In contrast, twenty-three of the twenty-five interviewees report having used interlibrary loan services.

A high proportion of the interviewees, particularly those in history, the humanities, and the social sciences, depend heavily on libraries in their research, although their contacts at Albion and elsewhere are more likely to be with support staff than with librarians. Interlibrary loan, periodicals, and circulation department staff are their most frequent contacts. Database searching and reference services are most likely to be used when researchers require contextual or background information rather than information in their areas of expertise. Database searches are requested as need and inclination dictate, not necessarily at the outset of the research process.

The survey revealed significant and generalized dissatisfaction with the Albion College library journal collection. Much like the national sample of their college-level colleagues reported in the ACLS survey, interviewees characterize local journal holdings as inadequate for their research.[13] Several pointed out that librarians are not alone in feeling victimized by escalating journal prices, and note that faculty, too, have been forced to cancel subscriptions, many of primary importance to their research. One respondent stated that she has been compelled to cancel personal subscriptions to "the very journals that I know the library cannot be expected to provide." Several others complained that the situation is compounded by copyright restrictions that prohibit librarians from obtaining through interlibrary loan more than five articles a year from the same journal.

Interviewees were less critical of the library book collection. Several suggested that it supports their research as well as they could expect from a college library. Some would prefer to borrow books that are important to their research for longer than the current one-year loan period. A number were concerned that important secondary texts they are sometimes required to obtain through interlibrary loan are circulated for too brief a period by the lending libraries. Three interviewees would like Albion College librarians to provide them with direct access to MIRLYN, the University of Michigan library's new online catalog, or to some other larger database.

The library policy that interferes most with research is that of requiring faculty as well as students to pay the interlibrary loan fees that are increasingly imposed by lending institutions. This policy was spontaneously criticized by ten of the twenty-five faculty members interviewed. Several interviewees felt that these fees should be underwritten by library or faculty development funds. Others protested that Albion College librarians develop collections that force reliance on interlibrary loan, yet punish faculty and students for using the very service that is designed to compensate for limited local collections and geographical isolation.

Several interviewees complained that shortened summer service hours handicap their efforts to accomplish their research agendas and reminded the interviewer that summer is the very time when most college faculty conduct their research. Interviewees also suggested that librarians teach seminars on library research for the faculty, that the name of the selector be written on the verso of the title page of new books to encourage contact by scholars with similar interests, and that faculty development funds be made available to hire reference librarians as research assistants on a contractual basis.

Interviewees were prompted by the author with a number of ideas for improved services. The following suggestions were well received:

1. An automated library catalog distributed to faculty offices through the campus computer network and available from off-campus locations through dial-in ports
2. Direct network access to broader databases of books and journal citations, for example, OCLC's EPIC; UnCover, the CARL (Colorado Alliance of Research Libraries) online journal index; and the catalogs, indexes, and other services available through MERIT, Michigan's higher education computer network
3. The ability to download and merge statistics, text, and bibliographical records from a variety of networked sources in order to create personalized bibliographies or new databases for further manipulation on one's own microcomputer
4. The ability to request articles and books from interlibrary loan through the campus network
5. The ability to place orders for books to be added to the local collection through the campus E-Mail network
6. A library delivery service for books and journal articles
7. Workshops for faculty on library services and collections, conducted by librarians
8. Enhanced online and printed resources to aid in seeking grant sources and writing proposals, for example, the Sponsored Programs Information Network (SPIN) grants index
9. Start-up funds (seed money) for new tenure-track faculty to immediately purchase important texts in their fields
10. *Current Contents* circulated to departments in printed form or made available online through the campus computer network
11. More faculty development funds made available to support the bibliographic needs of researchers
12. Establishment of a computer-based faculty research interest file
13. Initiation by librarians of early contact with new faculty to determine their research as well as their teaching needs and continued close contact through this difficult transition period.

CONCLUSIONS

The results of the survey demonstrate that faculty rely heavily on the Albion College library in the conduct of their research, although the library supplies them with less than 50 percent of the books and journals they require. Although faculty value many of the traditional services that libraries offer, such as interlibrary loan, they do not expect Albion College librarians to provide a particularly high level of support for their research. Faculty depend to a significant degree on the collections of neighboring research universities and, in some cases, bypass the college library entirely.

When prompted during the interview process, few faculty expressed interest in an expanded role for librarians in their research and several appeared genuinely unclear as to what that role might be. One pointed out that she did not expect generalist librarians to be able to make substantive contributions in her area of expertise. Many interviewees seemed satisfied with the passive and reactive stance that librarians have traditionally assumed, and appeared to underestimate the value to their research of librarians' unique knowledge and skills.

Suggestions for the development of local collections and services that support faculty research follow. Although prompted by the Albion survey, they do not necessarily flow directly from the data collected.

1. Promote a shared vision of the library as a primary locus of information access and control, not simply as a repository for books and journals.
2. Commit the library to the support of faculty research in its role-and-mission statement.
3. Create conditions that facilitate research and develop innovative services that satisfy research needs.
4. Collaborate with faculty in the development of programs and services designed to meet their research needs.
5. Demonstrate that innovative access techniques can effectively meet many research needs and compensate for the lack of comprehensive on-site collections.
6. Distinguish clearly between the research materials that must be available in the local collections and those that can be obtained through interlibrary loan and from other sources.
7. Establish expedited, no-fee interlibrary loan service.
8. Develop consortia and coordinated cooperative collection development programs between Albion College and other private and public libraries in state, regional, and national configurations.
9. Evaluate the quality of the collections to determine the supplementary resources needed to support research.
10. Promote an awareness on the part of the faculty of the role in the

research process that generalist librarians can play and the services they can and do offer.

11. Shift the work of librarians away from production toward management and service.

12. Develop in librarians an understanding that even without subject expertise they are able to make significant contributions to the research activities of scholars.

13. Develop a model for deeper librarian involvement in faculty research that emphasizes analytical problem-solving skills, a transition from serving novices to serving experts, and an intellectual commitment to research librarianship.

14. Develop an increasingly proactive stance toward service and teaching on the part of librarians.

15. Promote and reward research by librarians and encourage collaborative research projects between librarians and faculty.

16. Encourage librarians, administrators, and faculty to stop viewing the book budget as the sole wellspring of funding for library research needs and stimulate a search for alternative sources at the institutional and other levels through faculty development funds, endowments, grants, and other non-materials budget sources.

17. Clarify, systematize, and codify the many things that librarians already do that support faculty research.

College librarians, no less than their university-level counterparts, have an obligation to review continuously the level and quality of the research support they provide their teaching faculty colleagues. Further, if we are to develop collections and services that assure the conduct of research at the college level, we must move beyond passivity and our traditional preoccupation with internal procedures and housekeeping tasks.

As professionals who aspire to a status that recognizes and rewards appropriately their contributions to their communities, academic librarians have a particular obligation to support the research efforts of their teaching faculty colleagues. In certain arenas (e.g., automation), college librarians have been successful in seizing the initiative, and some have become sources of innovation on their campuses. No less an assertive effort is required if we are to create conditions that assure the research agendas of the teaching faculty.

As we fulfill our obligation to support faculty research, we enrich the quality of the contacts between teaching faculty and librarians; influence positively faculty perceptions of librarians; and encourage mutual respect, support, and cooperation. Of course, commitment to research further involves librarians in processes that are central to the exchange of scholarly information.

Anne Woodsworth points out that "no matter how a given research library defines its future, collaboration, flexibility, and fluidity will be the key attributes that characterize its operations and services."[14] This is no less true at the college level, as librarians strive to meet not only the research needs of the faculty but also those of students and other clientele. Indeed, Woodsworth's characteristics, as well as creativity, imagination, a tolerance for ambiguity, and a willingness to take risks, are increasingly important survival skills in a rapidly changing technological and academic environment.[15]

NOTES

1. Patricia Battin, "Crossing the Border: Librarianship in the Information Age," *The Harvard Librarian* 19 (September 1985): 8.

2. Evan Ira Farber, "College Librarians and the University-Library Syndrome," in *The Academic Library: Essays in Honor of Guy R. Lyle,* ed. Evan Ira Farber and Ruth Walling (Metuchen, N.J.: Scarecrow Press, 1974), 17.

3. William Miller and D. Stephen Rockwood, "Collection Development from a College Perspective," in *College Librarianship,* ed. William Miller and D. Stephen Rockwood (Metuchen, N.J.: Scarecrow Press, 1981), 137.

4. Newton F. McKeon, "The Nature of the College-Library Book Collection," in *The Function of the Library in the Modern College,* ed. Herman H. Fussler (Chicago: Univ. of Chicago Pr., 1954), 52.

5. The irony of the fact that book selection is dominated by faculty while the college librarian is held responsible for the quality of the collection is noted in Charles A. Gardner, "Book Selection Policies in the College Library: A Reappraisal," *College and Research Libraries* 46 (March 1985): 140–46.

6. Louis F. Brakeman, "We Asked Them: A Report of the Sources of Faculty and Professional Vitality in the Great Lakes Colleges Association; Submitted to the Exxon Education Foundation and the Lilly Endowment, April, 1987." Unpublished manuscript, 1987, p. 20.

7. In a review of scholarship at the selective liberal arts colleges, Ruscio notes that "their strong reputation for quality teaching notwithstanding," these institutions have traditionally had research expectations of their faculty, and "the level and quality of research suggest a professional affinity between faculty in the research universities and in the selective liberal arts colleges." See Kenneth P. Ruscio, "The Distinctive Scholarship of the Selective Liberal Arts College," *Journal of Higher Education* 58 (March–April 1987): 205–22.

8. Stanley J. Michalak, Jr., and Robert J. Friedrich, "Research Productivity and Teaching Effectiveness at a Small Liberal Arts College," *Journal of Higher Education* 52 (1981): 578–97.

9. In a review of the research on the relationship between research productivity and teaching effectiveness, Feldman concludes that "on the whole, scholarly accomplishment or research productivity of college and university faculty members is only slightly associated with teaching proficiency." See Kenneth A. Feldman, "Research Productivity and Scholarly Accomplishment of College Teachers as Related to Their Instructional Effectiveness: A Review and Exploration," *Research in Higher Education* 26 (1987): 227–98.

10. Michalak and Friedrich suggest that there are "many reasons why a small college might want to encourage its faculty to pursue scholarly research and publication," including the publicity it generates among "academic and intellectual elites," the enhanced morale that arises from a sense of working at "an institution of high academic quality," and simply the fact that it helps "to keep faculty members intellectually alive." See Michalak and Friedrich, "Research Productivity and Teaching Effectiveness at a Small Liberal Arts College," 596.

11. Fifty-seven percent of the college respondents rated the adequacy of the book collection at their school as fair or poor; the corresponding figure for the journal collection was 52 percent. At the research university level, the corresponding percentages were 26 and 18. See Herbert C. Morton and Anne J. Price, *The ACLS Survey of Scholars: Final Report of Views on Publications, Computers, and Libraries* (Washington, D.C.: Office of Scholarly Communication and Technology, American Council of Learned Societies, 1989).

12. The entire population of 109 full-time Albion faculty was included in the survey. Eighty-five questionnaires were received for a return rate of 80 percent. See Larry R. Oberg, Mary Kay Schleiter, and Michael Van Houten, "Faculty Perceptions of Librarians at Albion College: Status, Role, Contribution and Contacts," *College and Research Libraries* 50 (1989): 215–30.

13. The library has approximately 1,100 active journal subscriptions.

14. Anne Woodsworth and others, "The Model Research Library: Planning for the Future," *Journal of Academic Librarianship* 15 (July 1989): 132–38.

15. I would like to thank Jeanne L. Narum of the Independent Colleges Office, Washington, D.C.; and Professor Patricia Frick, Provost Daniel Poteet II, Michael Van Houten, and Professors Bruce Weaver and John Williams, all of Albion College, for their thoughtful readings of this report. Thanks are also due Professor Mary Kay Schleiter, University of Wisconsin–Parkside, for her help with the research design of this project.

Faculty Attitudes and Values and Collection Development in the College Library

by Larry Hardesty

Librarians in recent years have taken a more active role in the development and use of the college library's collection. New responsibilities and new job titles reflect this shift. In the 1970s, bibliographic instruction librarians became common on college library staffs. In the 1980s, acquisitions librarians have given way to collection development librarians.

Typically, acquisitions librarians responded to book selections from the classroom faculty. These librarians sought to get faculty-selected books in the quickest and cheapest way possible while keeping the ledgers in order. In contrast, collection development librarians do not just respond to the faculty. They provide overall guidance to faculty and to other librarians in the improvement of the college library's collection. They seek to anticipate needs of students and faculty and to make selections based on their own judgments. These librarians, in fact, may change or reject some recommendations of faculty members.

CHANGE IN ATTITUDES AND VALUES

Why has this change come about? Part of the explanation lies within the library. A higher percentage of college librarians now have graduate degrees in other areas. As a result, they can make a strong argument that they understand the library needs of various disciplines. In addition, societal values have changed. Society not only tolerates but encourages activism. Librarians coming of age in the 1960s and the years since are often less willing than earlier librarians to defer to the faculty.

Equally important, college faculties have changed in recent years. More and more, the attitudes and values of college faculty members have become indistinguishable from those of university and research faculty members. Farber's "university-library syndrome" clearly describes the changes

Table 1

Five-Year Book Circulation at DePauw University
and the University of Pittsburgh

	Circulation				
	None (0)	Light (1–5)	Moderate (6–10)	Heavy (11 +)	Totals
DePauw University	702 (36.9%)	951 (49.9%)	166 (8.7%)	85 (4.5%)	1,904
University of Pittsburgh	17,151 (44.7%)	13,330 (34.7%)	3,934 (10.2%)	3,985 (10.4%)	38,400

that have occurred as research-trained faculty members began taking positions at colleges.[1] More noticeable since the mid-1960s, these changes have been occurring for some time. In the early 1950s, the eminent librarian Louis Round Wilson described the same phenomena.[2] He determined that few college faculty members received training in selecting library materials for teaching purposes or in stimulating their use by undergraduates.

As a result, we find patterns of book use, or nonuse, among college libraries very similar to those of research universities.[3] For example, circulation patterns of library books at the University of Pittsburgh,[4] DePauw University,[5] and Eckerd College[6] are very similar (see tables 1 and 2). At both the research university and the liberal arts colleges a large portion of the books went uncirculated.

How can this occur? Increasingly, colleges recruit faculty members with Ph.D. degrees. As a result, the educational backgrounds and attitudes of

Table 2

Three-Year Book Circulation at DePauw University and Eckerd College

	Circulation				
	None (0)	Light (1–5)	Moderate (6–10)	Heavy (11 +)	Totals
DePauw University	843 (44.3%)	911 (47.8%)	118 (6.2%)	32 (1.7%)	1,904
Eckerd College	464 (33.2%)	844 (60.4%)	68 (4.9%)	22 (1.6%)	1,398

college faculties have become similar to those of the faculties at research institutions. They share, as already noted, a graduate education in which they received little training on how to select books for the undergraduate library and how to encourage the use of those books by undergraduates.[7] The distinct library collection needs for undergraduates may be unfamiliar to most college and university faculty members.

Support for this conclusion comes from a study involving in-depth interviews of undergraduate faculty members.[8] We found that the faculty members interviewed could not describe in a way meaningful to each other how undergraduate library materials might differ from graduate library materials. Some listed specific library items from their disciplines. Others provided general or vague statements. Many of their statements proved unclear, confusing, and baffling to other faculty members. Moreover, the phrase "undergraduate book" meant little to most undergraduate faculty members that we interviewed. As college faculties have become less interested and involved in library collection development, librarians have been forced to become more active.

HISTORICAL BACKGROUND

How have the attitudes and values of college faculties changed? For the answer, we must look back more than a century to the beginnings of modern higher education. The founders of the early colleges in this country had a strong vocational bent—the training of ministers. Toward that purpose, they followed a traditional course of study set up by the middle of the thirteenth century in European universities. The liberal arts, as put forth by the ancient Greeks, included a strong measure of rhetoric, logic, grammar, arithmetic, geometry, astronomy, and music. The first three subjects (the *trivium*) consisted basically of a study of Latin.[9] Early colleges offered only a few courses—all compulsory. The founders *knew* what it took to be an educated man (as was almost always the case).

Frequently, the president taught all the courses. Tutors, usually recent graduates awaiting a ministry, often aided the president. These predecessors to modern faculty had a relatively homogeneous education. They shared considerable common knowledge and a mastery of both Greek and Latin.[10] The tutors had responsibilities for both the intellectual and spiritual development of the students.[11] Enforcement of chapel attendance, disciplinary regulations, and daily recitations (the dominant form of instruction) prevented close relations between the tutors and the students.[12]

Seldom did the tutors have any specialty. In fact, some early presidents interpreted efforts to specialize as disloyalty to the institution. Few regarded college teaching as requiring advanced knowledge or specialized study.[13] The college stressed personality development, community experience, and consideration for the moral ends and social purposes of knowledge.[14] In many ways the faculty members functioned as temporary, inter-changeable parts serving at the pleasure of the president.

Developments in higher education after the Civil War sharply contrast with the old-style colleges. Following the Civil War, newly formed land-grant colleges broadened the curriculum. Among the older colleges, Harvard led the way in expanding the curriculum when it introduced its elective system in 1869. Institutional loyalty deteriorated as faculty gained mobility. As the research Ph.D. became more common during the latter half of the nineteenth century, faculty members began to replace institutional loyalty with disciplinary loyalty.

Presidents, trustees, and faculties competed for more Ph.D.s as a matter of personal reputation.[15] In 1903, William James foretold the results when he called the Ph.D. an octopus.[16] He questioned whether it assured effective teaching and feared the excessive organization that might result.

As the faculties became increasingly specialized, they also became increasingly departmentalized. The department provided a society of equals in which each faculty member could specialize. It provided a balance of power against presidents and trustees. With specialization, faculty members would no longer serve as interchangeable parts.

Specialization also encouraged professionalism. By the early twentieth century, faculty asserted unquestioned authority within the classroom. Concepts of tenure and academic freedom arose. Faculty claimed the right to explore and expound ideas *contrary* to the desires of their institutions or even of society.[17] With such ideas and the weakening of the old classical curriculum came faculty control of the curriculum.

World War II accelerated two trends that had begun after World War I. First, external careers for the faculty through government and private enterprise became more commonplace. While governor of New York in the late 1920s, Franklin Roosevelt consulted faculty members and even appointed them to various state administrative posts. He further involved faculty when he became President. During World War II the federal government considerably expanded its employment of faculty members, which further weakened faculty institutional loyalties.

Second, during World War II, the federal government became deeply involved in higher education. As the armed forces depleted the supply of college-age males, higher education turned to the government for rescue. Many a member of the armed forces spent part of the duration on a college campus in a military training program. After the war, they flooded back to the campuses under the G.I. Bill. Increasingly, colleges and universities looked to the federal government for financial support. In turn, the federal government looked to colleges and universities to support the government's research agenda.

By the early 1960s, researchers began to notice the effect of various forms of federal aid on higher education. A Brookings Institution study in 1962 found:

> The Government (and vaster historical forces) has divided the liberal arts faculty into a contingent of relatively young scientists and social scientists with lighter teaching loads, higher incomes, substantial research support, and other perquisites, and another contingent of older humanists, with heavier teaching loads, lower incomes, and little research support.[18]

One can understand why research and consulting have become more attractive than teaching for many young faculty members.

Circumstances of the 1950s and 1960s further shaped the faculty culture of the 1980s. Those faculty members who entered the profession between 1958 and 1968 experienced a decade of continual growth of higher education in both enrollments and federal funding. Demand for faculty remained high. This demand, which increased mobility, allowed faculty members to achieve satisfying careers. They gained more voice both in their own selection and evaluation and in administration of the college. Prestige, important social goals, and job mobility became major attributes of the faculty culture.[19] Those faculty who entered academia during these years often became highly socialized by their early experiences. They passed on their values and expectations to faculty who came later. As a result, the 1960s have taken on perhaps an undeserved mythology as a "golden age" of higher education—a time many faculty members want to recapture.[20]

CONTEMPORARY FACULTY CULTURE

What is the contemporary faculty culture? The dominant faculty mode emphasizes specialization, expertise, departmentalism, academic freedom, disciplinary loyalty, and the production of knowledge. It de-emphasizes undergraduate teaching, pedagogy, and institutional loyalty. Only a hundred or so institutions realize the ideal of faculty culture. Nevertheless, it serves as a strong force among all institutions of higher education. Few faculty want to return to the insecurities of the old pre–Civil War colleges, however wistfully they may long for their supposed collegiality. Nevertheless, faculty members today often feel their prestige, recognition, and mobility threatened. They feel jeopardized by increased bureaucracy and the general atmosphere of retrenchment in higher education. Faculty members sense an erosion of their rights and privileges. They often feel undervalued and unappreciated. As a result, many faculty are insecure and defensive.

EFFECT ON BOOK SELECTION

How do faculty attitudes and values influence development of the college library collection? Certainly, we owe much of the development of academic libraries today to classroom faculty. The adoption of the graduate seminar and its emulation at the undergraduate level has led to the development of large adacemic libraries. In the 1870s only a handful of colleges had more than 100,000 volumes, none more than 227,650.[21] Largely because of the faculty, many college librarians today can count their collections in the hundreds of thousands of volumes.

Unfortunately, the faculty's emphasis on size has not always been to the benefit of the college library. Farber saw that faculty members first extensively experienced libraries at large research institutions.[22] The libraries of these institutions often have millions of volumes. The newly minted Ph.D. frequently sees the college library as a poor cousin with fewer resources and a less capable staff than the research library. Bigger frequently means better to the neophyte scholar, who gives little thought to the differences in the purposes of the two types of institutions.

Typically, in completing their dissertation, faculty become more knowledgeable about a particular subject than anyone else—period. Their status and even their job security are often highly dependent on the maintenance of their specialization. This specialization predisposes many classroom faculty to think that only they can select books effectively within their areas of mastery. They occasionally succumb to the temptation to transfer the authority provided by this unique knowledge to other areas, such as book selection for the college library. Outside their narrow area of expertise, faculty members' claims of authority are less justified. Certainly, as Wilson pointed out, they have no special training in the selection and use of college library books.[23] In fact, as we found through our interviews, they show limited understanding of books appropriate for undergraduate education.[24] Undergraduates often ignore the books that faculty specifically recommend for student use.[25]

This, however, does not daunt many faculty members. The lack of training in pedagogy does not halt declarations of predominance in teaching and curricular decisions. Academic freedom has come to mean not only the discussion of unpopular ideas in the classroom but also the ability to participate in decision making in other areas. When questioned about the selection of books for the college library, classroom faculty frequently refer both to their particular subject mastery and to academic freedom.

Some faculty members perceive librarians' further involvement in book selection as more erosion of traditional faculty prerogatives. Book selection is one of the few areas in which classroom faculty can manage a budget and make numerous discretionary purchases. Although they may not have time to make careful selections, they often jealously guard the right to do so.

Classroom faculty exhibit this feeling in other ways. They often feel strongly that others should consult them about a wide range of institutional decisions. Nevertheless, they often do not want to spend the time to make informed recommendations. For example, while faculty want involvement, they frequently complain about excessive committee assignments.

Colleges have sought in the post–World War II period to upgrade their faculties by hiring more people with Ph.D.s. Paradoxically, they have created a faculty with less collegiality and less loyalty to the institution. As the institutional loyalties of faculties have been weakened by disciplinary interests, faculty members have committed less time to developing their local library. They think that development of local resources offers fewer rewards than do research and publication. Given the existing reward system in higher education, they may not be wrong.

Time is another concern of faculty. As knowledge has proliferated, the research-centered faculty members often feel they are chasing infinity. That is, each year they can teach proportionally less and less of the content of their discipline. Classroom faculty believe they do not have time to select books for the library. This may explain why college faculty, particularly at less research-oriented institutions, usually are more involved in book selection than are university faculty, who just expect the books to be there.[26] It also may explain why college librarians have felt more need to become increasingly active in developing the college library collection as college faculties have become more research-oriented.

RECOMMENDATIONS

How should college librarians respond to these changes in college faculties? Given classroom faculty influence and sensitivities, a simple answer is not forthcoming. Advising librarians to exercise "maximum control over their materials budget" and to develop "scientific allocation formulas" are not altogether viable solutions.[27] Faculty do have considerable knowledge in their subject areas—they should know how to evaluate the books and journals in those areas. Classroom faculty also highly influence student use of the library since they give assignments and weigh the results. By and large, classroom faculty determine the curriculum.

In addition, it is not completely clear that librarians make better selections for the library. In a DePauw University study, 31.2 percent of the librarian-selected books remained unused after five years. This circulation rate is only 3 percent better than that for faculty-selected books.[28] In an Eckerd College study, more than half (fifteen of twenty-six) of the departments had less than 30 percent of faculty-selected books uncirculated after only three years.[29]

Librarians need to tread very carefully in working with faculty. As Jasper Schad pointed out, perceptions of the fairness of allocation formulas differ.[30] The underlying rationales of most allocation formulas may be questionable if followed too rigidly.[31] Even use of literature-size information has some disadvantages when applied in the college setting.[32] A college administration may decide to provide additional support to a particular department or discipline beyond what a formula might support—for several good reasons. For example, a college may have a geographical location that favors a particular discipline. The members of a certain discipline may provide the extra effort to attract good students and enhance the prestige of the college. They may want to involve extensively their students in use of the college library. Might there not be a reason to allow them to select more books than the literature size would indicate?

For some problems there are no definite solutions, only accommodations. The attitudes and values of faculty and their strengths within an institution are such that seldom do administrative decrees accomplish their intent. It matters little whether the edicts come from the president, the academic dean, or the library director. We agree with Scudder that collection development should be a shared responsibility of librarians and classroom faculty.[33]

College librarians should appreciate the concerns and sensibilities of classroom faculty. Librarians must take advantage of faculty members' strengths. Both librarians and faculty have credible areas of specialization and valid perspectives. Nevertheless, both groups also have shortcomings. Faculty may want the college library to acquire highly esoteric, specialized materials to support narrow research. They may not give the needed time to select library materials. Librarians may not fully understand the nuances of specialized areas and may uncritically select books from standard lists. Both groups more effectively serve the educational needs of college students when they share their knowledge in the development of the college library.

In the college setting, informal persuasion, accommodation, and respect accomplish much more than rigid formulas and unyielding collection development policies. The faculty consists of highly diverse and specialized individuals who function within the broad parameters of the predominant values of contemporary faculty culture. Despite the difficulties involved, librarians do have considerable opportunity in the limited confines of the college to understand and to work with the faculty. The single most important commandment for the college librarian is to "know thy faculty."

NOTES

1. Evan Ira Farber, "College Librarians and the University-Library Syndrome," in *The Academic Library: Essays in Honor of Guy R. Lyle*, ed. Evan Ira Farber and Ruth Walling (Metuchen, N.J.: Scarecrow Press, 1974), 14.

2. Louis Round Wilson, Mildred Hawksworth Lowell, and Sarah Rebecca Reed, *The Library in College Instruction* (New York: H. W. Wilson, 1951), 13.

3. F. W. Lancaster, *If You Want to Evaluate Your Library . . .* (Urbana: Univ. of Illinois Graduate School of Library and Information Science, 1988), 37.

4. Allen Kent and others, *Use of Library Marterials: The University of Pittsburgh Study* (New York: Dekker, 1979).

5. Larry Hardesty, "Use of Library Materials at a Small Liberal Arts College," *Library Research* 3 (Fall 1981): 261–82.

6. Larry Hardesty, "Use of Library Materials at a Small Liberal Arts College: A Replication," *Collection Management* 10 (1988): 61–80.

7. Wilson, *The Library in College Instruction*, 13.

8. Larry Hardesty, "Book Selection for Undergraduate Libraries: A Study of Faculty Attitudes," *Journal of Academic Librarianship* 12 (March 1986): 19–25.

9. Frederick Rudolph, *Curriculum: A History of the American Undergraduate Course of Study Since 1636* (San Francisco: Jossey-Bass, 1977), 29–30.

10. Burton R. Clark, *The Academic Life* (Princeton, N.J.: Carnegie Foundation for the Advancement of Teaching, 1987), 27.

11. Martin J. Finkelstein, *The American Academic Profession* (Columbus: Ohio State Univ., 1984), 9.

12. John S. Brubacher and Willis Rudy, *Higher Education in Transition: A History of American Colleges and Universities, 1636–1968.* Rev. and enl. (New York: Harper & Row, 1968), 48.

13. Howard R. Bowen and Jack H. Schuster, *American Professors: A National Resource Imperiled* (New York: Oxford Univ. Pr., 1986), 30.

14. Douglas Sloan, "Harmony, Chaos, and Consensus: The American College Curriculum," *Teacher's College Record* 73 (December 1971): 222–23.

15. Edward Shils, "The Order of Learning in the United States: The Ascendancy of the University," in *The Organization of Knowledge in Modern America, 1860–1920,* ed. Alexandra Oleson and John Voss (Baltimore: Johns Hopkins Univ. Pr., 1979), 43.

16. William James, "The Ph.D. Octopus," *Harvard Monthly* 36 (March 1903): 1–9.

17. Rudolph, *Curriculum*, 157.

18. Robert Orlans, *The Effects of Federal Programs on Higher Education* (Washington, D.C.: Brookings Institution, 1962), 62–64, quoted in Brubacher and Rudy, *Higher Education in Transition*, 237.

19. Carol Herrnstadt Shulman, *Old Expectations, New Realities: The Academic Profession Revisited* (Washington, D.C.: American Association for Higher Education, 1979), 17.

20. David D. Henry, *Challenges Past, Challenges Present: An Analysis of American Higher Education Since 1930* (San Francisco: Jossey-Bass, 1975), 150.

21. Edward G. Holley, "Academic Libraries in 1876," *College and Research Libraries* 37 (January 1976): 23.

22. Farber, "College Librarians and the University-Library Syndrome," 52.

23. Wilson, *The Library in College Instruction*, 13.

24. Hardesty, "Book Selection for Undergraduate Libraries," 19–25.

25. Stewart Saunders, "Student Reliance on Faculty Guidance in the Selection of Reading Materials: The Use of Core Collections," *Collection Management* 4 (Winter 1982): 21–22.

26. Joan H. Worley, "Collection Development in a Small College Library: Can Less Be More?" *Choice* 25 (June 1988): 1513.

27. William Miller and D. Stephen Rockwood, "Collection Development from a College Perspective," in *College Librarianship*, ed. William Miller and

D. Stephen Rockwood (Metuchen, N.J.: Scarecrow Press, 1981), 145; Gary M. Shirk, "Allocating Formulas for Budgeting Library Materials: Science or Procedure?" *Collection Management* 6 (Fall/Winter 1984): 46.

28. Hardesty, "Use of Library Materials at a Small Liberal Arts College," 274.

29. Larry Hardesty, "Recent Developments in Bibliographic Instruction," paper presented at the Southern Education Foundation, "Networking for the Future: Developing Collections and Implementing New Technologies," Atlanta, Ga., September 8, 1988.

30. Jasper G. Schad, "Fairness in Book Allocation," *College and Research Libraries* 48 (November 1987): 479–86.

31. Richard Hume Werking, "Allocating the Academic Library's Book Budget: Historical Perspectives and Current Reflections," *Journal of Academic Librarianship* 14 (July 1988): 140–44.

32. Richard Hume Werking and Charles M. Getchell, Jr., "Using *Choice* as a Mechanism for Allocating Book Funds in an Academic Library," *College and Research Libraries* 42 (March 1981): 134–38.

33. Mary C. Scudder, "Using *Choice* in an Allocation Formula in a Small Academic Library," *Choice* 24 (June 1987): 1506.

Faculty Involvement in College Library Collection Development

by Mary C. Scudder and John R. Scudder, Jr.

Should faculty be involved in collection development? If so, how should they be involved and why? José Ortega y Gasset's well-known interpretation of the essence of librarianship suggests why faculty involvement is necessary in building a library collection. According to Ortega, librarians were at first primarily collectors of documents, then later organizers of materials in preparation for their actual use. Finally, in contemporary times, the role of the librarian is that of "a filter interposed between man and the torrent of books."[1] The filter concept has become one of the primary views of the essence of contemporary librarianship, according to Lester Asheim.[2] But for the filter analogy to function as the essence of librarianship, it needs to be stated positively rather than negatively. Stated positively it means that a librarian's primary responsibility is to build a strong collection of materials by making judicious selections based on the library's purpose within the mission of the college.

We will argue that fulfilling the filter function of building a strong collection of well-chosen materials for a college library requires extensive faculty involvement in the selection process. We will show that the charges that faculty involvement leads to elitism and to favoring research over instruction are unfounded. After showing why faculty involvement is necessary, we will discuss how Lynchburg College has dealt with three major problems concerning faculty involvement: (1) ensuring an equitable distribution of book funds, (2) fostering adequate involvement by all departments, and (3) assisting and supporting faculty research while maintaining a library primarily devoted to instruction.

NEED FOR FACULTY INVOLVEMENT

One way to bring the need for faculty involvement in selection into clear relief is by responding to its opponents. Lester Asheim, interpreting Ortega negatively, argues that the use of expertise as a filter in collection building is elitist and prescriptive.

> Any librarian who turns to subject experts for assistance in selecting materials in a special field discovers how much narrower a limit the experts apply to their definition of what would be useful in the library. Their view is frequently colored by their personal prejudices, by their adherence to a particular "school of thought" in their field, by the personal animosity they feel for the writer or the approach, by the arrogant assumption—shared by Ortega—that they can define and eliminate, for everyone else, the "useless" and the "stupid." Librarians, almost alone among professionals, do not, in that sense, "prescribe."[3]

Asheim obviously interprets a filter as a means of eliminating impurities. Following this negative interpretation, he contends that subject experts act as elitist, prescriptive filters. But does his contention that librarians do not prescribe mean that librarians should not use expert appraisal in book selection? When stated positively the filter interpretation entails not elitist censorship but judicious assessment in selecting library materials. When librarians use *Choice* in book selection they are, in fact, using expertise as a filter. Written by experts in their fields, *Choice* reviews assist both faculty and librarians to make judicious selections of books for the library collections.

Informed appraisal of books for potential acquisitions in the college library is elitist only in the sense that a college is elitist. A college is elitist in the sense that it restricts its membership by academic criteria. Furthermore, it is prescriptive in the sense of expecting certain levels of academic achievement. Whatever may be the criteria by which other libraries build their collections, a college library collection must reflect the purpose of the institution and the requirements of its users. To state the matter in less emotional language than "elitist" and "prescriptive," a college library should select books that support the instructional purpose of the college and are appropriate for students and faculty.

Since the primary purpose of a college library is to support instruction and since the faculty are the experts in instruction, it would seem that they would need to be very involved in the selection process. However, William Miller and D. Stephen Rockwood argue against faculty involvement by contending that faculty are experts in research while librarians are experts in what materials students find useful. Since Miller and Rockwood believe that libraries should be student-centered and that librarians know what materials students use, those librarians should be the primary selectors. In short, they argue that client use should be the primary determinant of the collection rather than instructional use, and that librarians rather than faculty should be the primary selectors of materials for that collection.[4]

Miller and Rockwood draw on a study made by Massman and Olson to support their position:

> Faculty members are too often either "overburdened with other duties," lacking in their knowledge of books, disinterested in books, unconvinced that library materials are really of value in instruction, prone to selecting only narrow research works on the one hand or textbooks on the other, or simply too lazy to care what happens to their book budget, even though believing that "only they are capable of selection."[5]

Evan I. Farber counters Miller and Rockwood's contention by asserting "that the few faculty members who fit that description will not even bother to order, and then the librarian can fill that gap."[6]

Our experience with the faculty of the two colleges in which we have worked supports Farber's characterization rather than that of Miller and Rockwood. Their statement that "the faculty member's needs are secondary, for the library, to those of the students" implies that the faculty's need for books, periodicals, and other materials are primarily for research and not for instructional purposes.[7] In our experience, most faculty are very concerned about acquiring materials that support instruction.

Our observations are in accord with the findings of a study at Pennsylvania State University–Behrend College. In that study, a questionnaire sent to faculty produced a 45 percent response that revealed several items relevant to the concerns of this paper. For example, 84 percent of the respondents believed that books should be selected by librarians and faculty, with 2 percent favoring librarians only and 4 percent faculty only (the rest were undecided). Sixty-four percent indicated that book selection had "a high priority" for their work, with 11 percent undecided and 25 percent disagreeing. Fifty-nine percent indicated that book selection was important to their research, while 16 percent said that it was not and 23 percent were undecided. Nearly 70 percent, however, indicated that book selection was important to the courses they teach, while only 9 percent indicated that it was not (the rest were undecided). These findings are especially significant when one considers that some introductory courses in such disciplines as mathematics and accounting make little use of the library. The study concluded that "librarians should not underestimate the interest and concerns of faculty in the book-selection process," that "selection plays an important role in the faculty members' responsibilities," and that "selection seemed more important for teaching responsibilities than research."[8]

Faculty who are most engaged in research at Lynchburg College share the conviction that library materials should be selected primarily to support instruction. Our associate dean polled the ten faculty members who have been awarded the annual Distinguished Faculty Scholar Award to determine whether they believed that the primary purpose of the

Lynchburg College library is to support instruction or faculty research. Eight responded that the primary purpose was to support instruction, two indicated both, and none favored research. Their support in building a collection primarily devoted to instruction helps account for the fact that during the time of expansion of both the library collection and research there has not been the tension between the scholars and the librarians that one would expect to find if Miller and Rockwood's assessment of faculty is accurate. On the contrary, the ten Distinguished Faculty Scholars not only advocate a library that supports instruction but are among the strongest supporters of the library.

Not only does Miller and Rockwood's contention that most faculty in colleges select materials to supply their research needs seem questionable, but so do their claims that librarians are in a better position than faculty to determine which library materials are being used by the students. Although automation makes it possible for librarians to determine which materials are being circulated, there is no adequate way of measuring in-house use or circulated materials that are unused. Faculty can estimate the use of such materials by checking citations in papers. Also, because of their expertise, faculty are better judges of the academic quality of materials cited. Obviously, librarians need to work with faculty to determine which materials are and should be used. Both are engaged in a common instructional enterprise that requires the expertise and cooperation of both to select appropriate materials and ensure their use.

PROBLEMS WITH FACULTY INVOLVEMENT

We have argued that elitism and faculty preoccupation with research are not major issues concerned with faculty involvement in collection development. We also contend that college librarians need to utilize faculty in materials selection because these materials should be selected by academic (not elitist) and instructional (not client-use) criteria. When faculty are much involved in collection building, what major problems do librarians face? Here we can speak only from experience in two colleges in which faculty were very involved in the selection process. The first problem is how to equitably distribute funds between departments. The second is how to involve all departments in the selection of materials commensurate with their interest in the library. And the third is how to assist faculty and students with research while building a collection focused primarily on instruction.

Equitable Distribution of Resources

Limited funds for acquisitions often foster competition between academic departments. One advantage small colleges have over universities, however, is the capacity to develop a sense of community, which facilitates cooperation between librarians and the faculty. Before a positive relationship of mutual trust can develop between faculty, librarians, and administrators, a collegial relationship of appreciation needs to be fostered. Such a relationship builds over time and requires continuous cultivation. In years past, a positive relationship and trust in the librarian were not always present at Lynchburg College. Book budgets were meager and there was strong competition for control of book funds. The library received very limited funding for collection development. Gradually, both the quantity and quality of the librarians and technical assistants improved so that they are now highly professional, commanding faculty respect. Continued administrative support of the materials budget, along with endowment funds, provides both increased departmental allocations and larger budgets for librarians.

Currently, collection building at Lynchburg College is a cooperative responsibility of the librarians and the teaching faculty. Book selection follows a written collection development policy developed by the library staff in consultation with the Faculty Library Committee. Each department is encouraged to develop a selection policy specifically geared to its particular curricular emphasis. For example, the history department developed an order of priorities for future library acquisitions that gives the library disciplinary direction (see fig. 1). Another department appoints a Library Materials Selection Committee that evaluates each request before submitting it for purchase. (This procedure fosters judicious selection but sometimes delays acquisition until late in the budget year.)

The faculty are directly involved in the distribution of book funds by participating in an allocation formula developed by the librarian and approved by the Faculty Library Committee in 1976. This formula distributes 60 percent of the total book budget to the departments, and 40 percent to the library. The library is responsible for the purchase of all reference, interdisciplinary, replacement, and retrospective volumes. A full explanation of this plan was published in *Choice.*[9]

Briefly, the formula consists of the following four factors:

1. *Availability:* Current titles published on a college level by department, ascertained by tabulating *Choice* reviews for one year.
2. *Cost:* The average cost of books by department as reported in *Choice.*
3. *Enrollment:* The number of students enrolled in individual courses by department.
4. *Library use:* Potential use of library resources by department, determined by faculty assigning a point value to each course on a scale ranging from 4 for heavy use to 0 for no use.

After the data are collected for each departmental factor, funding is calculated based on a percentage of the total factors for that category.

Figure 1. History Department
Order Priorities for Library Acquisitions, November 1989

	HEAVY	CONSIDERABLE	MEDIUM	LIGHT
United States				
Political—All periods				
Social and Cultural				
Labor				
Economic and Business				
Black History				
Urban History				
Southern History				
Diplomacy and Foreign Policy				
Ethnic and Minorities				
Ancient				
Greek				
Roman				
Europe				
General European Political				
Medieval				
Renaissance/ Reformation				
A.D. 500–1500				
A.D. 1500–1800				
1800 to Present				
European Intellectual				
A.D. 500–1500				
A.D. 1500 to Present				
National Histories				
England				
France				
Germany				
Italy				
Russia				
Spain/Portugal				
Other Regions				
Hapsburg Empire				
Balkans (20th century)				
Other East Europe (20th century)				
Benelux				
Scandinavia				
European historiography				

(cont.)

Figure 1. History Department
Order Priorities for Library Acquisitions (cont.)

	HEAVY	CONSIDERABLE	MEDIUM	LIGHT
Canada				
Latin America/Caribbean				
Africa				
Political				
West Africa				
East Africa				
Arab Africa				
Social and cultural				
Asia				
South Asia				
India				
Pakistan				
Bangladesh				
Sri Lanka				
Southeast Asia				
Burma				
Thailand				
Malaysia				
Singapore				
East Asia				
China				
Japan				
Korea				
Taiwan				
Hong Kong				
History of Communism and Communist States				
Women's history				

The four percentages are then totaled, multiplied by the total book funds available, and divided by four. We have developed a computer program that simplifies these calculations. (David Hillman, library director at Virginia Western Community College, uses the Lotus 1-2-3 program on a microcomputer in applying a variation of our formula.[10])

The first three factors apply equally to each department, but the rating of potential library use by the faculty provides a direct way to solicit their participation. After all, a senior seminar in history requires greater library resources than a senior laboratory course in chemistry. Reviewing the course list each year may serve as a reminder of how dependent each course may be on library resources. Judging by the positive response by the faculty and library staff to our allocation formula, the problem of distributing funds has been satisfactorily solved for Lynchburg College, at least for the present.

Equitable Faculty Involvement

Total faculty involvement in materials selection is far from being realized in our college. Some departments are lax in utilizing their book funds, and some faculty fail to utilize the many resources available to them and their students. Considerable progress is being made, however, through our liaison program; a librarian is assigned to work with faculty in each academic department, thereby strengthening the lines of communication. The departments that have responded are enthusiastic about the plan. Faculty members are encouraged to share with the liaison librarian their course assignments and other information (e.g., the particular style manual used). The librarian offers bibliographic instruction, provides helpful selection aids, and points out deficiencies and demands on the collection. The liaison librarian informs faculty of recent acquisitions in reference, serials, and nonprint media that may be of interest to them. The librarian also introduces new faculty to library services, to the facility and equipment, and to materials related to their discipline. Faculty members are called on, and sometimes volunteer, to assist in the removal of outdated and unwanted materials from the collection.

Supporting Faculty Research

One way a college can keep strong, outstanding faculty and encourage scholarship is by providing the basic reference services and access to resources that are available at major universities. Farber believes that a college library must have "a good reference collection that will serve as a key and not just to the immediate library, but for finding resources elsewhere."[11] Funds for supporting research are much better used to strengthen reference resources and offer computer-assisted bibliographic search services to access large research collections than to purchase a limited number of research materials.

At Lynchburg College we strive to provide access to research materials through the expertise of librarians, "key" reference sources, and automated services, including CD-ROM indexes, DIALOG, and OCLC. There is no charge to faculty for online searching. To support both the undergraduate and graduate programs we provide Compact Disclosure for the School of Business as well as DIALOG OnDisc and ERIC for the School of Education. *Academic Index* and the *Readers' Guide* on CD-ROM are also available. Recently, an in-house tabulation of microforms used in the library revealed a striking increase in the use of periodical literature and ERIC documents since the introduction of the CD-ROM indexing services. Correspondingly, requests for interlibrary loans have greatly increased, and, through use of telefacsimile equipment, copies are obtained promptly.

Librarians should not only assist faculty with research but also make the college community and others aware of faculty scholarship. Lynchburg College has a high percentage of faculty actively involved in research and writing. The library maintains a cataloged collection of faculty monographs and journal articles that are exhibited in a prominently located antique breakfront where they are viewed by the campus community, visitors, and prospective students. An exhibit catalog of faculty publications has been produced by the library, offering further recognition for research efforts. This bibliography is updated and reproduced from time to time. Faculty publications also appear in the library's list of recent acquisitions.

CONCLUSION

If Ortega were speaking to librarians today, imagine how perplexed he would be by the increased number of books from which to choose since he first spoke of the need for filters. The sheer number of books to be filtered is not the major problem for college librarians, however. The problem is how to select from the abundance of books and other materials available, those which serve the instructional purposes of the college. To accomplish this, librarians need to take advantage of faculty expertise in order to make judicious selection of materials using academic and instructional criteria. When faculty are involved in collection development, librarians are faced with three problems: equitable distribution of funds, adequate involvement of all academic departments, and energetic support of faculty research. We have suggested an allocation formula to help with the first problem, a liaison program to help with the second, and diversified reference resources and services for the third. But resolution of such issues is more a matter of positive attitude and cooperative spirit than of procedures. When collection building becomes positive rather than negative, so does the "welter of books." Rather than posing a problem requiring a filter, they provide a rich resource from which to make judicious selections. Such selection requires the expertise of the faculty in conjunction with the professional knowledge and experience of the librarians.

NOTES

1. José Ortega y Gasset, "The Mission of the Librarian," trans. James Lewis and Ray Carpenter, *The Antioch Review* 21 (Summer 1961): 154.

2. Lester Asheim, "Ortega Revisited," *The Library Quarterly* 52 (July 1982): 215–26.

3. Ibid., 222.

4. William Miller and D. Stephen Rockwood, "Collection Development from a College Perspective," *College and Research Libraries* 40 (July 1979): 323.

5. Ibid.

6. Evan I. Farber, "Collection Development from a College Perspective: A Comment and a Response," *College and Research Libraries* 40 (July 1979): 326.

7. Miller and Rockwood, "Collection Development from a College Perspective," 320.

8. Mary Sellen, "Book Selection in the College Library: The Faculty Perspective," *Collection Building* 5 (Spring 1985): 9.

9. Mary C. Scudder, "Using *Choice* in an Allocation Formula in a Small Academic Library," *Choice* 24 (June 1987): 1506–11.

10. David Hillman, "Book Budgets, Community College Libraries and Lotus 1-2-3," *Computers in Libraries* 9 (April 1989): 17–21.

11. Evan I. Farber, "Limiting College Library Growth: Bane or Boon?" *Journal of Academic Librarianship* 1 (November 1975): 14.

Part 5

Trends in Collection Development

Assumptions that remain untested never obtain the status of fact, nor are they refuted. Some long-standing assumptions regarding practices that are appropriate for large research libraries but not for college libraries are beginning to be tested, with mixed results. The validity of several of these assumptions is covered in this last section and, regardless of the outcome of the application of these assumptions to a particular collection, it is reasonable to conclude that continued investigation is appropriate for each.

One assumption in the academic library community is that an approval plan is a useful collection development tool for large academic and research libraries with breadth and depth of subject coverage, graduate programs, and large materials budgets. A corollary to this assumption holds that an approval plan is an inappropriate collection development tool for a four-year undergraduate library; even more so, for libraries serving two-year institutions, such as community colleges, junior colleges, and satellite campuses of larger institutions with small to modest budgets and limited breadth and depth of collections. Two papers in this section address the issue of approval plans from different small academic library perspectives, that of varying institutional scope and that of varying materials budget size. While neither author found approval plans to apply to their particular collection development program, their research suggests further avenues of approach for interested college libraries.

Wanda Dole notes that smaller college libraries represent a sizable percentage of all academic libraries, and that they suffer from the same shortage of staff—for title-by-title ordering—that makes approval plans attractive to larger libraries. After reviewing the extant literature on approval plans, Dole challenges the assumption that they are not feasible for small college libraries by presenting a model of what would have been acquired through an approval plan against what actually was acquired for the collection of the library of Pennsylvania State University, Ogontz. Actual book acquisitions of this library for a three-year period are compared to the book titles that would have been sent on approval by two major vendors, using a profile based on the library's collection development policy and modified by level, subject, and publisher.

Ann Niles addresses the issue of the appropriateness of approval plans for college libraries from the vantage point of a traditional four-year liberal arts institution. She presents the results of a three-year trial of an approval plan at Carleton College. Major factors anticipated in the effectiveness of such a plan were a limited budget and reliance on faculty, rather than on library subject bibliographers or selectors, to choose the majority of materials for the library's collections. The decisive factor was found to be who selects, rather than the size of the budget available to pay for what is selected.

The lack of coverage in the professional literature suggests another implicit assumption; that is, that preservation, a concern within the last decade for most university library collections, applies only to research materials usually excluded from college library collections. Two papers argue that significant research materials, frequently of local interest, are often found in the rarified atmosphere of college special collections.

Charlotte Brown and Kathleen Moretto Spencer investigate whether there is a role in the national preservation effort for the liberal arts college library. Further, they ask, what is the preservation responsibility of this type of library and, assuming there is one, how can college librarians meet it? They identify the preservation decision-making process as one component of a traditional preservation program that may be isolated and applied to a college library's collection development program, providing both rationale and methodology for identifying and treating materials that require preservation. This paper describes how the preservation decision-making process was applied to a collection of Classics materials having substantive research value that was identified in the library collection at Franklin and Marshall College. This experience enabled Brown and Spencer to speculate that there is a significant amount of material of value to the scholarly community located in college libraries. The authors conclude that college librarians have a definite responsibility to preserve and conserve collections beyond the traditional "Does it support our curriculum?" rationale.

While Spencer and Brown speculate that college libraries may have research materials requiring preservation treatment, Joanne Hill focuses on less specialized materials in college library collections. In researching the extent to which preservation is an issue for college library general collections, she addresses a middle ground of materials where the dominant factor is use combined with age and quality of paper and construction. Fifty-five college libraries responded to a survey whose threefold purpose was to assess, for a liberal arts undergraduate collection, the degree to which preservation is an issue; to evaluate the status of current and planned preservation activity; and to determine an appropriate level of response. Hill found that a majority of respondents judged that preservation is, indeed, a problem for their general collections and that a subset of options utilized by university libraries to address the issue of preservation are being used by college libraries and adapted to address their own unique needs.

Peter Deekle's paper, "The College Library Collection Revisited: A Bibliographic Essay," performs two functions at once. The first is to determine whether the attention given college library collection development in this book is currently reflected in the professional journal literature. The second, and perhaps more important, function is to provide a fifty-year perspective on collection development in college libraries in order to give clarity to the editors' finding that, in the past, literature in the field has been concerned less with college libraries than with larger institutions. Deekle reviews the professional literature on collection development since the mid-1940s and finds that, despite the attention given to academic library collection development, few published works of note directly address the college library. Although this paper demonstrates a growing breadth of coverage, it reinforces evidence of a prevailing focus on larger academic library needs and issues. It therefore provides significant support for the editors' attempt to further the dialogue by focusing on issues specific to college library collection development.

The Feasibility of Approval Plans for Small College Libraries

by Wanda V. Dole

In her study of publisher-based and subject-based approval plans, Karen Schmidt suggested that it is more interesting and useful to review what approval plans are and what they can do than to ask why academic libraries should employ such plans.[1] One interesting but not frequently asked question is what approval plans can do for the small undergraduate library.

Approval plans have become accepted collection development tools for large academic and research libraries. They have also been adopted by libraries at well-endowed colleges with graduate programs and/or strong commitments to research and quality education. Librarians and book vendors, however, have maintained that approval plans are inappropriate, if not impossible, collection development tools for libraries serving small to medium-sized undergraduate institutions with small budgets and few research pretensions. Approval plans are considered especially inappropriate for libraries serving two-year institutions, such as community colleges, junior colleges, and satellite campuses of large universities.

Small college libraries, however, represent a sizable percentage of all academic libraries. Sixty-one percent of all academic libraries contain fewer than 100,000 volumes and the majority of academic libraries serve institutions with enrollments of fewer than 5,000.[2] These libraries suffer from the same shortage of staff to devote to title-by-title ordering that make approval plans attractive to larger libraries.

Hunter Kevil refuted most of the standard arguments against the use of approval plans in college libraries and convincingly argued that approval plans are not only feasible but also desirable methods of acquisition for such libraries.[3] The present paper tests Kevil's theory about the use of approval plans in smaller libraries by showing its impact on the Ogontz Campus Library at Pennsylvania State University; other general assumptions about approval plans are also considered.

ASSUMPTIONS

Although there is a sizable body of literature on approval plans,[4] Kevil's "The Approval Plan of Smaller Scope" is a theoretical study on the feasibility of approval plans for college libraries. To my knowledge, the literature contains no serious studies on the implementation of approval plans at small college libraries.

The literature does contain a number of general assumptions that have bearing on the question of approval plans and small college libraries. These assumptions include:

1. *Budget size:* Approval plans are feasible only for libraries with large acquisitions budgets.
2. *Approval versus librarian/faculty selection:* Approval plans will not bring in the same materials as title-by-title selection by librarians and/or faculty.
3. *Approvals bring in "core" materials:* Approval plans bring in those current publications from mainstream publishers that every academic library would automatically acquire on a title-by-title basis.
4. *Publisher-based versus subject-based plans:* For domestic publications, publisher-based approval plans work better than subject-based plans.

BUDGET SIZE

In 1969, Hendrik Edelman argued that

> no library should start comprehensive blanket order programs unless its retrospective holdings are already significant and its book budget is at least $500,000. In the case of a library with weak retrospective holdings while supposedly supporting rapidly growing graduate programs, the book budget should be $700,000.[5]

Without specifying a dollar amount, Dudley, and McCullough et al. have supported Edelman's assumption that approval plans do not work well when there is a "relatively small book budget to cover a wide range of subject areas."[6] Only Holleman and Kevil have suggested that approval plans are possible for libraries with book budgets as small as $40,000 or $50,000.[7]

APPROVAL PLAN SELECTION VERSUS LIBRARIAN OR FACULTY SELECTION

Critics have maintained that approval plans do not furnish libraries with the same materials as would have been selected on a title-by-title basis by librarians and/or teaching faculty. Connected with this assumption is the implication that some materials are better than others and hence one method of acquisition (approval or title-by-title) is better.

A study at California Polytechnic University (Pomona) comparing an approval plan collection to a collection built by faculty or library selectors showed that

> there are significant differences between the collection which will result from approval buying and the collection which will result from the traditional selection and order procedures, given current vendor service.[8]

These results contradict an earlier study of an approval-built collection at an unidentified medium-sized academic library where Leon Raney found that the approval system took the same action (selection or rejection of a title) on 82 percent of the 4,559 titles treated.[9]

APPROVAL PLANS AND CORE COLLECTIONS

Approval plans have frequently been heralded as an economic means of supplying "core" materials—those titles of mainstream publishers that every academic library would automatically purchase.[10]

As early as 1970, Marion Wilden-Hart argued for the value of approval plans in supplying this basic core.[11] A decade later, in Noreen Alldredge's survey of collection development officers or acquisitions librarians in forty-four academic libraries, 90 percent of those responding said that the purpose of their approval plans was to build a broadbased collection, not a core collection.[12] DeVilbiss's California Polytechnic study is also at variance with Wilden-Hart's contention that approvals furnish core materials.[13] More recently, Ross Atkinson supported the use of approval plans to build a basic, instructional collection. He maintained that such a collection can be built "more or less automatically" by developing a vendor profile and designating relevant subjects and standard publishers.[14]

PUBLISHER-BASED VERSUS SUBJECT-BASED PLANS

Schmidt compared publisher-based and subject-based approval plans at the University of Illinois (Urbana-Champaign) and concluded that publisher-based plans work better for domestic publications.[15] Kevil, however, pointed out that "a publisher approach simplifies acquisitions routines (by permitting easy disposition of firm-order requests simply on the basis of the publisher)."[16]

After a one-year review of publisher-based and subject-based plans at the University of Nebraska–Lincoln, Womack et al. concluded that "the current publishing phenomena of mergers, buyouts, and increased small press publishing seemed to be detrimental to a publisher-based profile."[17]

APPROVAL PLANS AND COLLEGE LIBRARIES

The Carnegie Foundation for the Advancement of Teaching groups institutions of higher education into categories on the basis of the level of degree offered and the comprehensiveness of their missions. These categories comprise 75 percent of all institutions of higher learning and enroll 68 percent of all students.[18]

The present study on the feasibility of approval plans and small college libraries was carried out at the Ogontz campus of Penn State University, an institution which combines aspects of several Carnegie categories. Like two-year colleges, the Ogontz campus offers certificate and associate degree programs. The campus also offers the baccalaureate degree to a growing number of "location-bound" students. The first two years of coursework in more than 120 Penn State baccalaureate majors are available at the campus, which enrolls approximately 3,500 students (2,100 full-time and 1,400 part-time) and employs 162 faculty members (75 full-time, tenure-track and 87 fixed-term).

As part of Penn State University, the campus shares the mission "to provide programs of instruction, research, and public service, and thus act as an instrument of self-renewal for the Commonwealth."[19] According to the campus mission statement, Ogontz

> combines the breadth and excellence of a Penn State education with the individual attention to students fostered by a small-college setting. . . . The campus attracts students seeking four-year baccalaureate and two-year associate degrees.[20]

Campus administrators maintain that at Ogontz "students can experience the ambiance of a private liberal arts college like Swarthmore—but at K-mart prices."[21]

The primary mission of the Penn State University libraries is "to support, by the acquisition of books and other materials, the research and teaching programs of the University."[22] The Ogontz campus library, "guided by the mission of the University Libraries, has the primary duty to develop and maintain collections appropriate to the Ogontz Campus."[23] To this end, the library contains approximately 50,000 volumes and adds on average 922 titles a year. The monographic budget is $21,000—well below the lower limit recommended by Kevil for approvals. The monographic budget, however, is devoted entirely to materials that support undergraduate instruction. Advanced undergraduate, graduate, and research materials are not acquired by the library.

Titles are recommended by faculty and selected by librarians who use a variety of selection tools ranging from publisher announcements to the review media (e.g., *Choice*, *New York Times*).

An examination of orders placed over a three-year period (1985–88) showed a tendency to order a small number of titles from each publisher. The most frequent (21% orders) ordering pattern was that of placing one order per publisher. Next frequent were two titles per publisher (14%), three titles (9%), four titles (7%), five titles (7%), and six titles (6%).

APPROVAL PLAN STUDY

Kevil maintained that approval plans could be effective collection development tools for libraries with monographic budgets as small as $50,000. His statements, however, apply to tightly defined plans limited to certain publishers (such as university press plans) or subjects (such as art or history of the Southwest). We know of no author who suggests that an approval plan profile could be written to supply books from a larger universe of publishers or in all the subject areas taught at a comprehensive undergraduate institution for a library with a monographic budget under $50,000. Moreover, no one suggests that the approval plan is a vehicle to acquire only "initial study level" materials (materials adequate to support undergraduate instruction). Edelman and others propose that there are budgetary and intensity levels below which approval plans are not effective. The following studies at the Ogontz campus were conducted to determine the lower ranges of those levels. The goal was to test the feasibility of approval plans for a small undergraduate library supporting basic instruction in general arts and sciences with a small monographic acquisitions budget.

The methodology of the study was as follows:

1. Evaluation of the scope of the approval profile limited by collection level ("instructional" or "undergraduate").
2. Comparison of titles that would have been supplied on a publisher-based approval plan to actual acquisitions.
3. Comparison of titles that would have been supplied on a subject-based profile to actual acquisitions.

Approval plan statistics and lists of titles supplied on the hypothetical approval plans were obtained from two vendors: Blackwell North America (BNA) and Baker & Taylor. It should be noted that the project was not a vendor evaluation. The object was to learn if approval plans could work for a broad spectrum of subjects at the instructional level within the budget constraints.

METHODOLOGY

In June 1988, an initial profile based on the Ogontz library collection development policy and using the Blackwell North America thesaurus was drafted. The profile was very broad in regard to both subjects and non-subject parameters. It was hoped that the modifier or non-subject parameter "undergraduate library" would be the key factor in defining a plan for an initial-study-level collection. Unfortunately, the term is broadly applied by BNA: In 1987–88, 54 percent (15,955 titles) of the total (29,300) titles treated on approval by BNA were coded "undergraduate library."[24] A match against the BNA database for a three-year period (July 1985 through June 1988) showed that the BNA profile would produce 30,000 titles, yet during the same period the Ogontz library had purchased only 3,000 titles.

A more restrictive publisher-based profile was then adopted. Titles that Blackwell North America would have supplied on this profile from July 1987 through June 1988 were checked against the Ogontz library catalog and the on-order file. The examination revealed that the library had actually acquired or had on order only 3 percent of the titles that would have been supplied by this profile.

Finally, the effectiveness of a subject-based approach was studied. Titles that would have been supplied on a Baker & Taylor subject-based plan for a nine-month period (July 1988 through March 1989) were checked against the Ogontz catalog and the on-order file. The library had acquired or had on order only 3 percent of this total approval list.

CONCLUSIONS

Although there were limitations to the Ogontz library study, it did provide an answer to the specific question of whether a broad-based, all-subject approval plan is an effective collection development tool for a small, low-budget undergraduate library collecting at the initial study level. It also tested some general assumptions concerning approval plans.

The study was limited by the nature of the institution (a hybrid somewhere between college and community college) and the budget of the library. Results of such a study at a prestigious college with a large budget and a commitment to faculty research would be different.

The study was entirely quantitative. It does not and cannot determine quality. The question of which would be the "better" book—that selected by Ogontz or that selected by the approval plan—cannot be answered. There is no agreement about what constitutes a better book or better collection. Recently, David Vidor and Elizabeth Futas attempted to address the better book question in their comparison of the effectiveness of faculty and librarians as selectors of business materials at Emory University. In their assessment of who selected better books, they defined as "better" those books included in standard lists and reviews.[25] This definition supports the selection tools used by Ogontz selectors.

The study provided information on the feasibility of approval plans for small undergraduate libraries and the validity of some of the general assumptions contained in the literature.

1. *Budget:* The study confirmed the assumption that approval plans do not work well below a certain budget level unless there is some other distinct factor, such as limiting the plan to certain publishers or subjects.

2. *Approval versus traditional selection:* The study confirmed the assumption that approval selections were significantly different from the titles actually ordered by library and faculty selectors. Only 3 percent of the approval titles were ordered by the library.

3. *Publisher-based versus subject-based plans:* The study did not confirm the assumption that publisher-based plans were more successful than subject-based plans for the acquisition of domestic publications. The success rate of both types of plans was the same: 3 percent.

The study also reaffirmed the need for self-study and careful planning in the initial stages of an approval plan. Any small college library contemplating an approval plan should:

1. Ascertain its annual acquisitions rate in each subject.
2. Identify purchasing patterns by publisher.
3. Draw up an initial profile and obtain an estimate of the number of titles in each subject that would be supplied against that profile. If the estimate is radically different from the library's actual acquisition rate and purchasing pattern, obtain a list of titles that would have been supplied in a previous period and check the list against the library's holdings and order file.

Finally, we must all remember Kathleen McCullough's admonition that each approval plan should be evaluated individually, since "one library's experience cannot be transferred directly to another without allowances for the specific library."[26]

NOTES

1. Karen Schmidt, "Capturing the Mainstream: An Examination of Publisher-Based and Subject-Based Approval Plans in Academic Libraries," *College and Research Libraries* 47 (July 1986): 369.

2. Mary Jo Lynch, *Libraries in an Information Age: A Statistical Summary* (Chicago: American Library Association, 1970), figs. 1, 4.

3. L. Hunter Kevil, "The Approval Plan of Smaller Scope," *Library Acquisitions: Practice and Theory* 9 (1985): 13–20.

4. For an overview of the literature on approval plans, see Gary J. Rossi, "Library Approval Plans: A Selected Annotated Bibliography," *Library Acquisitions: Practice & Theory* 11 (1987): 3–34. See also Robert D. Stueart, "Mass Buying Programs in the Development Process," in *Collection Development in Libraries*, ed. Robert D. Stueart and George B. Miller, Jr. (Greenwich, Conn.: JAI Press, 1980), 203–17; and Helen Lloyd Snoke and Jean L. Loup, "Comparison of Approval Plan Profiles and Supplementary Collection Development Activities in Selected ARL Libraries," a Report to the Council on Library Resources (November 1986), 1–3.

5. Hendrik Edelman, "The Joint University Libraries and Blanket Orders," in *Approval and Gathering Plans in Academic Libraries*, ed. Peter Spyers-Duran (Littleton, Colo.: Libraries Unlimited, 1969), 14.

6. Norman Dudley, "Organizational Model for Collection Development," in *Collection Development in Libraries*, 27; Kathleen McCullough, Edwin D. Posey, and Doyle C. Pickett, *Approval Plans and Academic Libraries* (Phoenix, Ariz.: Oryx, 1977), 2.

7. Curt Holleman, "A Distinguished Press Approval Plan for Academic Libraries of Medium-Size," in *Shaping Library Collections for the 1980s*, ed. Peter Spyers-Duran and Thomas Mann, Jr. (Phoenix, Ariz.: Oryx, 1980), 93–99; Kevil, "The Approval Plan of Smaller Scope," 15.

8. Mary Lee DeVilbiss, "Approval Built Collection in the Medium-Sized Academic Library," *College and Research Libraries News* 36 (November 1975): 487–92.

9. Leon Raney, "An Investigation into the Adaptability of a Domestic Approval Plan to the Existing Pattern of Book Selection in a Medium-size Academic Library" (Ph.D. diss., Indiana University, 1972).

10. McCullough et al., *Approval Plans and Academic Libraries*, 131.

11. Marion Wilden-Hart, "The Long-Term Effects of Approval Plans," *Library Resources and Technical Services* 4 (Summer 1970), 400–6.

12. Noreen S. Alldredge, "Symbiotic Relationship of Approval Plans and Collection Development," in *Shaping Library Collections for the 1980s*, ibid., 174–77.

13. DeVilbiss, "Approval Built Collection in the Medium-Sized Academic Library," 489, 492.

14. Ross Atkinson, "The Language of the Levels: Reflections on the Communication of Collection Development Policy," *College and Research Libraries* 47 (March 1986): 147.

15. Schmidt, "Capturing the Mainstream," 365–69.

16. Kevil, "The Approval Plan of Smaller Scope," 19.

17. Kay Womack et al., "An Approval Plan Vendor Review: The Organization and Process," *Library Acquisitions: Practice and Theory* 12 (1988): 373.

18. Carnegie Foundation for the Advancement of Teaching, *A Classification of Institutions of Higher Education* (Princeton, N.J.: The Foundation, 1987), 7 and tables 4, 5.

19. *Pennsylvania State University Bulletin* 72, no. 4 (March 1988), 11.

20. Pennsylvania State University, Ogontz Campus, *Strategic Plan, 1985–90* (Abington, Pa.: Ogontz Campus, 1986), 8.

21. Huntly Collins, "At Penn State, Learning Is Spread Around," *The Philadelphia Inquirer* (August 30, 1987): 12-B.

22. Pennsylvania State University. Commonwealth Campuses Libraries Division, *Procedures and Reference Manual* (University Park: Pennsylvania State Univ. Libraries, 1988), 1.1.

23. Pennsylvania State University, Ogontz Campus Library, "Collection Development Policy" (1988), Appendix 1.

24. Blackwell North America, *Approval Program Coverage and Cost Study, 1987/88* (Lake Oswego, Ore.: Blackwell North America, 1988), 1-1.

25. David L. Vidor and Elizabeth Futas, "Effective Collection Developers: Librarians or Faculty?" *Library Resources and Technical Services* 32 (April 1988): 127–36.

26. McCullough et al., *Approval Plans and Academic Libraries*, 123.

An Approval Plan Combined with Faculty Selection

by Ann Niles

Approval plans have been used to build library collections for the past twenty-five years, especially in university libraries. As the volume of publishing increased and library budgets grew in the 1960s, university libraries hired subject bibliographers to develop their collections, a responsibility formerly assumed by faculty. The practice of using subject bibliographers was accompanied by the adoption of approval plans.[1] College libraries, in contrast, have not used approval plans.[2] Only 12 percent of Blackwell North America's current approval plans are for college libraries.[3] L. Hunter Kevil, in his paper on the approval plan of smaller scope, suggests that the liberal arts college library "can overcome some of the many disadvantages of its small scale" by using an approval plan.[4] College libraries are often reluctant to use approval plans because their budgets are too small. But Kevil argues that "generally a library with a budget for current imprints of this magnitude [$50,000] or greater can make an approval arrangement work."[5] Since we spend about $200,000 annually on current imprints at Carleton, we decided in 1986 to use an approval plan to assist in developing the collection. This paper will describe how our plan worked.

Carleton is a midwestern college with a national student body of 1,800 and a faculty of 150. The curriculum emphasizes the liberal arts and about 75 percent of the graduates go on to graduate or professional schools. The academic environment is serious with faculty committed to teaching and students to learning. Traditionally, faculty have taken a great interest in the library, selecting books and assigning papers requiring students to use the collection. The collection consists of 365,000 books, 70,000 periodical volumes, 53,000 microforms, and 260,000 government documents. The primary purpose of the collection, like that of most college libraries, is to support what is taught. Faculty are responsible for selecting those books that support the curriculum. We allocate about 60 percent of the book budget to faculty departments; librarians are responsible for selecting reference, general, interdisciplinary materials, and for filling gaps in the collection. The library both encourages and depends on faculty to select for the collection because we have a small professional staff (seven librarians) with neither the time nor expertise to assume full responsibility for book selection. Faculty are familiar with the collection they help develop, and they know what resources they need to support their courses and the work of their students. Most faculty recommend books because the collection is such a central part of their teaching.

We adopted an approval plan at Carleton to assist us in getting systematic coverage of what was being published. The library staff wanted to make sure that titles useful in supporting our curriculum were not being overlooked. We intended the approval plan to be used primarily by the faculty. Since they could examine the actual books, we believed that the plan would help faculty decide which books to select for the collection. Faculty would define the profile to supply those books needed to support their teaching and they would be responsible for selecting from weekly shipments. As Acquisitions Librarian, I would review approval titles due to be returned and select any I thought should be kept. We expected that defining a profile of those subjects we collect to support the curriculum would provide useful information for managing the collection. The staff also hoped to save time since an approval plan would provide automatically most of the books we would have ordered anyway.

The first step in implementing the approval plan was to define the profile of those subject areas faculty wanted to collect. A representative from our vendor, Blackwell North America, conducted extensive interviews with faculty members from each of our twenty-three departments. Faculty designated subjects in which they wanted to receive books on approval and subjects in which they wanted to receive forms with bibliographic information only. The library would receive shipments of approval books for the nine-month academic year and forms only for the three summer months. During the three years of the approval plan, faculty twice completely reworked the subject profile and library staff periodically made other adjustments. We defined the profile to supply about 6,000 books on approval annually, or for somewhat more than half of our annual acquisitions budget of $400,000.

We encouraged faculty participation in reviewing approval books by creating an approval room where we displayed each shipment for four weeks, Monday through Friday from 8:00 A.M. until 5:00 P.M. We arranged the books by department on book trucks and once a week displayed shipments during the faculty coffee hour held in the library's meeting room. Faculty were sent a weekly list of newly received approval titles for their department as a reminder to visit the library and select books.

Our approval plan worked well in attracting a loyal group of faculty who regularly visited the library and signed for approval books. We know that at least one member from every department generally reviewed approval shipments. For example, in January and February 1989 during a four-week period, faculty from each of the twenty departments profiled to receive books also signed for approval books. Many faculty members were enthusiastic about examining a book before deciding on its appropriateness for our collection. They also liked seeing books for other departments. Some faculty were pleased that new books were quickly available, and others remarked on the usefulness of the approval plan in making them aware of what was being published.

But a loyal group of faculty was not enough for our approval plan to succeed. Over one-third of the books we received on approval were returned over the three years of our plan. For most vendors and libraries "a rejection rate of less than 10% seems to be considered characteristic of a satisfactory approval plan arrangement."[6] Blackwell North America has a return rate of 7.5 percent for all approval plans and a 9 percent return rate for approval plans in college libraries.[7] At Carleton we returned 28 percent of our approval books during the first year of our plan, 40 percent the second year, and 36 percent the third year, a total of 5,474 titles. Our return rate would have been even higher if I had not selected from approval books due to be returned. During a three-week period in December 1988, for example, we received 589 approval titles. Faculty selected 254 books, or 43 percent of those sent. From the remaining 335 titles, I chose another 189, or 32 percent, and we finally returned 146 (25%). We have tried to analyze why our return rate was so high. The books we returned were not duplicates of books that had already been on firm order because we did not place firm orders until we determined how Blackwell North America had treated a title. The reason why our approval plan was not successful seems to be simply that faculty—rather than subject bibliographers—are selecting books for the collection.

Unlike subject bibliographers, faculty are not present in the library to review approval shipments as they arrive. They must remember to make a special trip to the library in order to select from approval shipments— only one or two members of each department visited the approval room regularly. Faculty told us that coming to the library to review approval books was just an added responsibility. Rather than visit the library, some simply returned their weekly approval notification lists through campus mail after indicating those books they wanted. Others remarked that they preferred to read reviews, publishers' flyers, or *Choice* cards. An examination of book orders for one week in January 1989 confirms these faculty preferences. During that week, nineteen faculty members (12.6%) signed for approval books while we placed firm and form orders requested by fifty-one faculty members (34%). Of the books selected for the library that week, faculty chose almost 75 percent of the titles from their offices or homes—not from the library.

We found that faculty choose books differently from subject bibliographers who select for an entire subject. At Carleton, faculty view their collection responsibility exclusively as selecting books for their own area of teaching, not for those subjects taught by colleagues in their department. Faculty observe that a certain book would probably interest a member of their department, but they expect that person to come to the library to decide. Most faculty participated in drawing up the departmental subject profile, although only one or two members of a department actually selected approval books, and then only from their own area of the profile. Consequently, even if a profile brings in the books faculty want, unless most members regularly review shipments, only a fraction of the books received may actually be kept.

Faculty choose books differently from subject bibliographers in yet another way. Unlike subject bibliographers who select to cover a field, faculty generally choose books for the library individually. In the ten college libraries he studied, Hannaford found that "selection is done on a title-by-title basis with many, if not most, of the selections coming from the faculty."[8] One aspect of title-by-title selection is that faculty are selective in what they choose for the collection. In the college library "when few materials can be ordered, faculty want to make sure that the right materials are selected."[9] Carleton faculty told us that they were very discriminating in choosing approval books for the library. They expected to look at several titles before deciding which one was best for our collection. The difficulty with this method is that faculty, in contrast to subject bibliographers, did not expect to choose all or even most of the books sent on approval.

Faculty select title-by-title for the college library because they respond to changes in the curriculum. When using an approval plan to build a collection that is influenced by the curriculum, it is important to change the profile as new courses are offered. One reason faculty did not select more titles from approval shipments is the extent of curriculum changes—many of the titles supplied did not match current needs. For example, from 1985 to 1988, the Curriculum Committee at Carleton approved 162 new courses, or an average of 54 new courses each year for our 23 teaching departments. In addition to materials for new courses, we need to purchase materials for our "integrative exercise" requirement. Every senior student participates in this exercise "intended to help students relate the subjects they have studied in their major field." Many students fulfill this requirement through "extensive research projects, papers, or public lectures."[10] Since each student does an individual project, books needed to support this kind of research will vary widely. It would be difficult for any profile to respond to this magnitude of changing requirements. Profile changes take time to describe, implement, and take effect. The difficulty of supplying books following profile changes is evident in the number of approval books we received late. During a five-week period in November and December 1988, we received 904 books, 130 of which had earlier invoice dates and should have been returned during the previous six months.

Only about half of the current imprints selected for the collection were supplied by the approval plan. In 1987/88, for example, we selected 7,261 titles with current imprint dates, excluding foreign and standing orders, but only 3,817 (53%) of these titles were provided from approval books. We know that the firm orders we placed were not for titles treated for book shipment on our approval plan since all incoming book requests with a current publication date were held until we determined from Blackwell North America's fiche that the company was not supplying the book. Further, few of our firm orders were for approval books we had returned. In 1988/89, for example, we reordered only 23 of the 6,194 titles Blackwell North America sent us. Other titles faculty selected simply could not be supplied on the approval plan because they were outside the scope of Blackwell North America's program. We sent Blackwell North America a small sample of book requests that had not appeared on its fiche six months after we had received the faculty request. After researching the status of these 67 titles, Blackwell North America reported that it could not supply 41 (61%) of them—the publisher was "outside of approval scope," the items were reprints, the titles were too popular, the items were not "offered on approval," or the items were "not usually available on approval because of publisher terms."[11]

Using an approval plan for books to supply only half of our current domestic imprints was expensive, not only because our return rate was so high but also because we had to maintain our regular firm order acquisition procedures. Throughout the three years of our approval plan, faculty members continued to submit requests because they wanted a particular book for the collection—regardless of how we acquired it. Consequently, we had to maintain files of those requests until we either received the book on approval or placed a firm order for it. We devoted twenty hours of regular staff time and twenty hours of student time each week to activities related solely to the approval plan. We checked all incoming book requests with a current publication date against Blackwell North America's fiche to determine treatment for our approval plan in order to avoid ordering duplicates. The staff also maintained a forthcoming file for all requests listed on order or not listed in Blackwell North America's fiche and checked each approval shipment against this file. Each month the six hundred requests in this forthcoming file were reviewed with Blackwell North America's updated fiche, and those titles not in their program were ordered. We periodically searched OCLC records for holdings for faculty requests not yet treated by or still on order at Blackwell North America in order to decide if we should place a form order for those titles already held by several libraries. A database was created for approval shipments in order to produce weekly notification lists for the faculty. In addition, we had to unpack, display, pack up, pay postage, and process invoices and credit memos for titles we did not select for our collection.

Our experience suggests why approval plans tend to be found in the university library. Approval plans work well with subject bibliographers because it is convenient for them to review weekly shipments. In a college setting, however, faculty must make a special trip to the library to choose approval books and, as a result, shipments are often not reviewed. Approval plans are easier to administer with subject bibliographers because they are responsible for defining the subject profile and for selecting from it. In a college library, on the other hand, we found that faculty who had participated in defining the profile did not necessarily review shipments, and since faculty tended to select only in their own area of teaching, many books in a department's profile were not kept simply because no one reviewed them.

Approval plans complement collection development in a university library where bibliographers are responsible for collecting comprehensively in most subject areas. As Bonk and Magrill observed, "breadth, depth, and variety are key characteristics of university collections."[12] Approval plans provide systematic coverage in depth for all publishing output. Subject bibliographers "monitor the intake. . . . Book selection [is] a selection of fields, a selection of emphases . . . not . . . a selection of individual books."[13] The bibliographer's responsibility is to ensure that important titles are not missed, rather than to select the best titles from an approval shipment. In a college library, in contrast, the collection is selective and is governed by what faculty are teaching. Only a few of the books published annually in a subject may be added to the collection. We found that faculty are discriminating in which books they select, and approval plans are simply not designed for this type of selection. Kevil agrees that "an approval plan . . . is used by libraries conceiving their collection development responsibilities, not in title-by-title terms, but in terms of covering publishing output."[14] We returned one-third of our approval shipments because many of the books were either not needed by the faculty or not selected for the collection. For example, I chose 328 titles from the April 1988 issue of *Choice;* of these, Blackwell North America offered only 191 (or 58%) on our plan.

Our experience suggests that size of budget is not the critical factor in determining the success of an approval plan in a college library. Rather, the effectiveness of an approval plan seems to depend on who is selecting. In the university setting, selection is centered in the library with subject bibliographers. Kevil assumes this model of librarians responsible for selection when he suggests that an approval plan supplies "automatic books in the right quantity for each subject so the college librarian can make the final decision to keep or reject the book in hand."[15] In most of the college libraries that have approval plans provided by Blackwell North America and Yankee Book Peddler, the library assumes responsibility for selecting books, similar to the subject bibliographer model for the university library. Though these approval plans differ in some respects, they are similar in that someone within the library is responsible, rather than an external faculty selector. One type of plan is the limited university press plan in which librarians define the profile and select from shipments. Another approach is the limited subject plan in which a librarian is responsible for selecting in a specific subject area, for example, the music librarian for the music library. Yet another type is the comprehensive plan in which selection is shared by faculty and a librarian. Still another is the comprehensive plan in which the library director defines the profile and is responsible for choosing approval books.[16] Our comprehensive approval plan with faculty responsible for selecting seems to be the exception and, based on our experience, the college library should not adopt it. Rather, an approval plan for the college library probably should be limited by subject or publisher, with the library staff maintaining a major role in defining the profile and selecting books. Carleton College library staff will continue to encourage faculty to select books for the collection since our professional staff is small, but instead of a comprehensive plan for approval books, we will use a forms-only plan to assist us in covering publishing output.

NOTES

1. "Robert G. Vosper," in *The Librarian Speaking: Interviews with University Librarians,* by Guy R. Lyle (Athens: Univ. of Georgia Pr., 1970), 175.

2. Wallace John Bonk and Rose Mary Magrill, *Building Library Collections* (New York: Scarecrow Press, 1979), 38.

3. Scott A. Smith, Blackwell North America, telephone conversation, January 16, 1989.

4. L. Hunter Kevil, "The Approval Plan of Smaller Scope," *Library Acquisitions: Practice & Theory* 9 (1985): 13.

5. Ibid., 15.

6. Rose Mary Magrill and Doralyn J. Hickey, *Acquisitions Management and Collection Development in Libraries* (Chicago: American Library Association, 1984), 101–2.

7. Scott A. Smith, telephone conversation, January 16, 1989.

8. W. E. Hannaford, Jr., *Collection Development in Ten Small Academic Libraries: A Report to the Council on Library Resources* (Washington, D.C.: Council on Library Resources, 1979), 10.

9. Joan H. Worley, "Collection Development in a Small College Library: Can Less Be More?" *Choice* 25 (June 1988): 1513.

10. Carleton College, *Academic Catalog 1988–1989,* 14.

11. Douglas Duchin, Blackwell North America, letter, September 2, 1988.

12. Bonk and Magrill, *Building Library Collections,* 27.

13. Vosper, 175.

14. Kevil, "The Approval Plan of Smaller Scope," 14.

15. Ibid., 17.

16. Scott A. Smith, telephone conversation, October 12, 1989; Bob Nardini, Yankee Book Peddler, telephone conversation, October 12, 1989.

Preservation, a Critical Element of Collection Development in College Libraries

by Charlotte B. Brown and Kathleen Moretto Spencer

An estimated one-fourth of the books housed in our nation's major research libraries are in a state of serious embrittlement. This is primarily due to the acid paper on which nearly all books have been printed since the mid-nineteenth century.[1] Concerned librarians have been sounding the alarm for decades, but it is only recently that the devastating reality of the deterioration of library collections has become a national priority.

Authors and publishers are taking the alkaline paper pledge. The budget of the National Endowment for the Humanities Office of Preservation has been increased from $4.5 million to $12.5 million in FY 1989, with continuing increases planned up to a level of $20.3 million in the next four years. In the United States Congress, resolutions have been introduced in both houses that seek to establish a national policy to promote the printing of books and other publications of enduring value on alkaline, permanent papers.[2] Many U.S. research libraries have long-standing preservation programs; many more are organizing programs and hiring staff to manage enormous quantities of disintegrating books and other materials.[3]

Based on the recommendation of a committee of nineteen organizations supporting a brittle books program, the Council on Library Resources established the Commission on Preservation and Access in 1986. The commission works closely with libraries and other involved organizations that have the primary responsibility to do the work of preservation. It is engaged in an intensive effort to broaden the base of support for preservation initiatives and to coordinate preservation activities. The commission is currently working with librarians from all sizes of academic libraries, including college librarians, and with scholars, archivists, book publishers, paper manufacturers, and physical plant administrators.

There is no denying that major research libraries face a problem of such magnitude that they rightly command first place in priority as the national preservation effort is launched. There is, however, something of an anomaly in the exclusive use of the adjective *research* in describing those libraries whose collections contain large quantities of books, many brittle, published in the nineteenth and twentieth centuries. College library collections are just as vulnerable as their research counterparts, particularly those collections located in colleges founded in the nineteenth century. The age of a collection, however, is not the only consideration.

The 1987 Bowdoin College Library compilation of "Selected Library Statistics" indicates that the forty liberal arts college libraries that responded to the survey have holdings in excess of 18 million volumes.[4] Assuming that the results of the brittle book studies of research collections are applicable to college collections, the libraries represented by the "Bowdoin Statistics" house 4.5 million brittle books—an enormous problem in the aggregate.

What is the place of college libraries in the national preservation effort? What are the responsibilities of college libraries? How can and should college librarians participate?

First, it is imperative for college librarians to acknowledge that substantial portions of their collections may be endangered and then to commit themselves to salvaging those endangered collections. It is also imperative for college librarians to realize that it may no longer be acceptable to withdraw books from collections simply because they do not circulate locally. Before librarians deaccession materials, they have a responsibility to ascertain the scholarly value of those materials, to check the availability and (if possible) the physical condition in other collections, and thereby to make decisions based on criteria beyond local use. Such a process is a tall order, to be sure, but one that can be met with a reasonable local preservation program in place.

In this paper, we will report on the results of a study that not only heightened our awareness of the unique research value of one underutilized collection housed in the Shadek-Fackenthal Library at Franklin and Marshall College, but also reinforced our belief in the value of sound preservation decision-making techniques as an integral part of collection development.

THE FRANKLIN AND MARSHALL COLLEGE LIBRARY PRESERVATION PROGRAM

The preservation program at Franklin and Marshall College Library was initiated in May 1985. Its purpose was to extend the useful life of library materials from the point when an item was ordered to the point when the decision was made regarding its permanent retention or deselection.

Franklin and Marshall's preservation program was intentionally designed along the Yale University Library model because the Yale model actively promoted the coordination of preservation activities with collection development functions. We were of the opinion that these two activities had to work in tandem if the goals of either were to be competently achieved.[5] And as it turned out, there was a specific subject collection and a rather serendipitous set of events that not only tested our assumptions but also confirmed the benefits of this dual approach.

An item's physical condition as well as its intellectual content figure prominently in the decision-making process of a preservation program with a strong collection development component. Too often collection development decision making, particularly as it is practiced in the acquisitions phase, ignores the physical state of an item. It is questionable whether an item acquired in poor physical condition can fulfill its intended intellectual function, be it newly published or used. To address this problem, Franklin and Marshall's coordinated program includes a binding contract reflecting sound preservation principles, and a preservation searching technique that fosters informed decisions. As a result, every book acquired by the library undergoes a physical and intellectual assessment that, in turn, increases our knowledge of the physical condition and intellectual content of the collections as a whole. As our knowledge of the collections increases, decisions involving out-of-scope collections and/or collections in poor physical condition can be undertaken with greater confidence.

"Who will save the books?" This is the preservation question of the 1980s, and also the title of an article written by historian Roger Bagnall.[6] In the article, Bagnall not only examines the process known as selection for preservation from the perspective of the scholar, but he also searches for assurances that time and money are not being squandered on efforts to preserve what he and his fellow classical historians consider to be low-priority brittle books.[7] To this end, Bagnall was involved with a project sponsored by the American Philological Association (APA). The goals of the project were (1) to undertake the "preservation of a substantial body of the most important materials from classical studies—mature but now endangered scholarship," the publication dates of most titles falling between 1860 and 1920; (2) to improve access to this body of scholarship; and (3) to assess the APA project by focusing on one specific aspect of the methodology: having scholars make the preservation selection and access choices.[8] The targets for the APA project were major U.S. research libraries known to have collection strengths in the classics, primarily members of the Association of Research Libraries and the Research Libraries Group. What Bagnall could not have anticipated was the existence of the Gonzalez Lodge Classics Collection at Franklin and Marshall College.

THE GONZALEZ LODGE CLASSICS COLLECTION

Gonzalez Lodge (1863–1942) was a professor of classics who taught at Bryn Mawr College and at Teacher's College, Columbia University. In 1901, he received an honorary degree from Franklin and Marshall College, and in 1944, Franklin and Marshall received from Lodge's estate what was understood to be Lodge's personal library, a collection of approximately 2,500 volumes of mostly nineteenth-century European imprints of classical Greek and Latin texts and secondary scholarship. The collection included numerous sets of bound pamphlets consisting of dissertations, *Gymnasium* studies, and *Programschriften*. The collection was, for the most part, cataloged for the general stacks collection and entered into the OCLC database; however, item cataloging for the hundreds of bound pamphlets did not exist.

It was during the first few months of the newly established preservation program that the Lodge materials came under review. After a cursory physical sampling of the collection, two characteristics were evident: (1) the materials received low or no use and (2) a majority of the titles were brittle. In addition, the intellectual content was out of scope with the stated mission of the college library, that is, to support the current or anticipated curriculum of the college and to support, as feasible, faculty research.

The following collection options were then considered: Should the collection be allowed to remain on the shelf, unused? Should the collection be transferred to a noncirculating, brittle books section within the library? Should the materials be discarded or transferred to a library known to have a strength in the classics? Should the collection be maintained at Franklin and Marshall and preserved through reformatting? All are valid and typical preservation–collection development options. Until this point in the assessment of the Lodge Collection, we were unaware of Bagnall's American Philological Association classics project.

When we learned of the APA project, we contacted Bagnall and arranged for him to assess the Lodge collection. Immediately the question of the collection's provenance emerged. By coincidence, Bagnall held a position at Columbia University, one of the institutions where Gonzalez Lodge had taught, and he knew that the Columbia University Libraries held Lodge materials in their collections. What was the source of Franklin and Marshall's Lodge items and how did Lodge-owned materials come to be held by two institutions? It is conjectured that his personal library came to Franklin and Marshall and that the collection from his faculty office was transferred from Bryn Mawr to Columbia. In any case, Bagnall was surprised to learn of the Lodge materials at Franklin and Marshall. After some analysis, Bagnall concluded that no bibliographic records existed for an estimated 40 percent of the dissertation pamphlet material in the Franklin and Marshall collection, nor were these titles duplicated in the APA project. He asked if Franklin and Marshall would consider transferring the materials to Columbia for microfilming. The decision was made to defer transferring the collection pending further investigation.

CLASSICS AND LINGUISTICS: A CASE STUDY

In an effort to gain an understanding of the preservation–collection development implications of the Lodge Collection, we decided to survey the collection by using an assessment typology described by Ross Atkinson and Margaret Child in 1986.[9] Charlotte Brown, Franklin and Marshall's archivist and special collection librarian, was eager to test Atkinson's methodology because it combined a systematic approach to collection development with the goals and objectives of a preservation program. Atkinson describes the partnership between collection development and preservation in these words: "Decisions to preserve library materials affect the quality and composition of library collections; [therefore] such decisions clearly must be made in consultation with collection development staff."[10] This typology supplied Brown and her colleague Janet E. Gertz, preservation librarian at Columbia University, with an appropriate methodology to continue the assessment of the Lodge Collection.

Atkinson sets forth a decision-making process that begins by determining an item's intrinsic value, intellectual value, and pattern of use. This information is then used to categorize the item into one of three classes: (1) "special"—those items having high economic value, particularly special collections materials, and items belonging to level five collections as defined in the RLG Conspectus; (2) "on-going research and teaching support"—those items having relevance of subject to the institution's current or anticipated curriculum and research; and (3) "low-use, long-term research"—those items having long-term research value and that fail to fit into class 1 or 2. The class assigned to the item then determines the type of preservation treatment.

Although Atkinson devised his typology for application at major research libraries, Brown and Gertz decided to test it on the classics collection (Library of Congress Classification PA) at Franklin and Marshall. This collection contained many of the Lodge items, and Brown and Gertz anticipated that much of the Lodge Collection would be documented as class 3 material when the study was completed. For comparison, the results of the classics survey were matched with the results of a survey of the linguistics collection (Library of Congress Classification P). The linguistics collection was selected as the control because it was younger and contained titles purchased, for the most part, to support the current curriculum.

The study applied an "at-the-shelf" preservation decision-making methodology that enabled Brown and Gertz to analyze every title held in the linguistics collection and an equivalent number of randomly selected classics titles (986 volumes in the PAs). A form was completed for every title analyzed. First, the bibliographic information was entered (the shelf-list card was photocopied onto the form) and then the physical condition was documented according to the following criteria: Is the cover functional? Is the paper brittle? Is the text block intact? Has the text been mutilated? Is there environmental damage (water, insects, etc.)? It was noted if the item was part of the Gonzalez Lodge Collection, if the item had circulated within the past ten years, and if the item had circulated on interlibrary loan and/or reserve. Then the intellectual content was analyzed. Finally, after all the information was gathered, the item was assigned to one of Atkinson's three classes.

The results of the Brown-Gertz study verified what was suspected all along: (1) the majority of titles in the linguistics collection (88%) were either class 1 or class 2 and that over one-third of the classics titles (35%) were designated as class 3; (2) almost 25 percent of Franklin and Marshall's class 3 titles were reported as being held by five or fewer libraries in the United States; (3) 41.7 percent of the class 3 titles analyzed were part of the Lodge Collection; and (4) 67 percent of class 3 titles were brittle.

Of the 986 classics titles surveyed, 468 (47%) were categorized as class 3. According to Atkinson's theory, these titles have research value to the scholarly community beyond Franklin and Marshall. These titles, on the other hand, generate preservation and housing expenses disproportionate to their usefulness at an undergraduate liberal arts college, especially if the stated collection mission of the college is taken seriously.[11]

We retell the story of the Gonzalez Lodge Collection and describe the Brown-Gertz study because we believe that collections like Lodge's are certainly not unique to Franklin and Marshall, but exist in the stacks of many college libraries. In order to test this belief, Franklin and Marshall has been awarded a grant from the Council on Library Resources to replicate the Brown-Gertz study at Franklin and Marshall, and also at the libraries of Amherst College and Grinnell College.

If the results of the replication of the Brown-Gertz study reflect more than a singular event at one college library, and we suspect they do, then college libraries hold significant amounts of materials with substantial research value to the scholarly community. These materials, if identified by means of an integrated preservation and collection development program, may indeed be candidates for designation as preservation copies as part of the national brittle books microfilming program. Coordinating the identification and preservation of other class 3 collections at college libraries, perhaps through the use of a modified conspectus, surely is feasible, and certainly would help lessen the burden of the major U.S. research libraries in their preservation efforts.[12]

College libraries have a responsibility to preserve and conserve collections beyond the traditional "does it support our curriculum" rationale. By the adoption of policies and procedures that report, assess, and preserve their collections, college libraries will contribute substantially to the enhancement of the national bibliographic resource, and therefore increase the availability of library resources to the scholarly community.

At the June 21, 1989, meeting of the Committee on College Libraries of the Commission on Preservation and Access, George Farr, director of the National Endowment for the Humanities Office of Preservation, urged college libraries to enter the competition for NEH preservation funds. There is every indication that financial support for the preservation of college library collections will be available, and that college libraries have the potential for becoming full partners in the national preservation effort.

NOTES

1. Patricia Battin, "President's Column; Commission on Preservation and Access," *C.L.R. Reports* 2, no. 2 (July 1988), unpaginated insert.

2. S.J. Resolution 57 and H.J. Resolution 226; 101st Congress, 1st session.

3. For the purposes of this paper, the use of the term *preservation* and of its distinction from the term *conservation* follow the definition employed by Pamela Darling: "Libraries are responsible for the care of materials which are physically endangered, and library preservation encompasses everything which serves to prolong the life of those materials and/or their informational content. I use the term 'preservation' in this broadest sense, reserving the term 'conservation' for those activities which involve physical treatment of individual items by a 'conservation technician' or professional 'conservator' . . . [and the term] *conservation* to refer to that subset of activities dealing with physical treatment, within a comprehensive *preservation* program which also includes preventative care and replacement or reformatting of information." Pamela W. Darling, "Preservation vs. Conservation," *The Abbey Newsletter* 9 (November 1985): 96–97.

4. Arthur Monke, comp., "Selected Library Statistics for 1987–88" (Brunswick, Maine: Bowdoin College, 1988), unpublished survey.

5. For a fuller description of the preservation program at Franklin and Marshall, see Charlotte B. Brown, "The Preservation Program at Franklin and Marshall College," *Conservation Administration News* 30 (July 1987): 6–7.

6. Roger Bagnall, "Who Will Save the Books? The Case of the Classics," *New Library Scene* (April 1987): 16–18.

7. For a discussion of similar concerns by scholars affiliated with the Modern Language Association, see Danielle Mihram, "Online Databases and Book Preservation," *College and Research Libraries News* 49 (March 1988): 152–55.

8. Bagnall, "Who Will Save the Books?" 16.

9. Ross W. Atkinson, "Selection for Preservation: A Materialistic Approach," *Library Resources and Technical Services* 30 (October/December 1986): 341–53;

Margaret Child, "Further Thoughts on 'Selection for Preservation: A Materialistic Approach' " *Library Resources and Technical Services* 30 (October/December 1986): 354–62.

10. Atkinson, "Selection for Preservation," 341.

11. Charlotte B. Brown and Janet E. Gertz, " 'Selection for Preservation': Applications for College Libraries," in *Building on the First Century: Proceedings of the Fifth National Conference of the Association of College and Research Libraries* (Chicago: American Library Association, 1989), 288–94.

12. See Larry R. Oberg, "Evaluating the Conspectus Approach for Smaller Library Collections," *College and Research Libraries* 49 (May 1988): 187–96.

An Ounce of Prevention: Preservation Organization and Practice in College Libraries

by Joanne Schneider Hill

> *Through and through the inspired leaves,*
> *Ye maggots make your windings;*
> *But, oh! respect his lordship's taste;*
> *And spare his golden bindings.*

Robert Burns's little verse composed toward the end of the eighteenth century upon visiting a nobleman's impressive library may go far to describe the very real damage done to books by little creatures. Taken to its larger context today, "Ye maggots" images the effects on books from three major sources of deterioration: the methods and materials used in their manufacture; the unsuitable environments housing them, especially in libraries; and repeated use.

Relatively little has been written on the need for preservation organization and practice in college libraries. As with other issues in the library world, preservation concern has been primarily focused on university collections housing massive amounts of aging materials, while small, private academic libraries housing far smaller but also aging collections have yet to be adequately addressed. All academic libraries may not have the extensive variety and depth of research materials found in university libraries. One may assume, however, that all share concern for the intellectual and historical integrity of materials in their collections that are disintegrating, for quality cannot be determined by quantity. Frazer Poole, former head of preservation at the Library of Congress, has often been quoted as predicting in 1973 that most nonfiction published between 1900 and 1939 will be unusable by the year 2000. Actually, his prediction applies to all books published in the "age of poor paper," initiated in 1850 by industrial processes applied to the mass production of paper. It is obvious to those of us in constant contact with library collections that both the use of acidic materials in book construction and repeated handling have resulted in books that are becoming unusable. Although many trends in the library world, particularly in Western culture, are youth-oriented (read technologically fixated), librarians still yearn to pay homage to age, to the antiquarian as well as the intellectual value of books.

BACKGROUND

Preservation librarianship has evolved as an area of specialization in the profession simply because research collections are deteriorating. Predictably, the largest libraries were the first to address the problem. Even as long ago as the 1930s, the New York Public Library and Columbia University began microfilming fragile materials. In 1973, the Library of Congress completed a collection review, estimating it had six million brittle books. Major research libraries, such as the New York Public, Columbia, and the Newberry, followed suit by conducting preservation reviews of their collections, with one of the most touted initiated at Yale. Gay Walker, head of the university's Preservation Department, reported on the results of a study conducted from 1979 to 1983 that reviewed a random sample of 36,500 volumes published between 1860 and 1940. In 37 percent of the books sampled, paper had become embrittled, breaking after two double folds, and 82.6 percent had acidic paper with a pH of below 5.4.[1] In the research library community, the results of this study generated much discussion centered on the concern that, while it is not too late to address the problem of disintegrating materials, it may be later than we think.

In response to widespread concern in the profession, the Association of Research Libraries (ARL) Office of Management Studies completed an assisted self-study program known as the ARL/OMS Preservation Planning Program.[2] The program provides a structure and methodology for conducting self-studies that result in documents covering all major aspects of preservation for libraries studied. This tool has permitted yet another echelon of research libraries to review their needs and set up similar programs at such institutions as Ohio State University, Northwestern University, and the University of Tennessee–Knoxville.[3] The cumulation of these reports has provided sufficient data to cite 30 percent as an average proportion of American library books that are embrittled. Typically, areas covered in the self-study are:

1. Survey on the condition of the collection
2. Review of environmental conditions
3. Storage and handling
4. Education of staff and public
5. Replacement and reformatting

6. Treatment (binding, repair, conservation)
7. Organization (acid-free materials, cooperation, funding, personnel, policy)

One caveat is that self-studies require considerable time and expense. Background information must be absorbed and gathered, a committee formed, and assignments made. One may assume that the average study consumes eleven months or 2,000 staff hours, pervades all library operations, typically involves the time of twenty-five to thirty-eight people, and costs $4,000 to $9,000 in fees to ARL (depending on the size of the study). Other library expenses typically run between $750 and $1,500 for environmental monitoring equipment. An additional hidden expense occurs when most self-studies result in a recommendation to establish a professional position devoted to preservation.

The focus of such studies has not been solely on rare materials. Atkinson has suggested a typology of preservation that catagorizes library materials for the purposes of preservation.[4] His class 1 category includes special or unique items, rare books, and manuscripts, which represent considerable capital investment for any library. Although of research value, their use is subsidiary to their economic value. These "jewel-in-the-crown" artifactual materials reside in special collections and obviously are much more a presence in research collections.[5] Their primary mode of preservation tends to be restorative and expensive. Atkinson's class 2 category consists of higher-use items currently in demand for curriculum and research purposes. High use determines that the primary mode of preservation will be replacement. Class 3 includes lower-use research materials that, nevertheless, should be retained for posterity. This is the most problematic category due to low use and the format utilized for preservation (i.e., microfilming). These three classes comprise the body of materials reviewed and treated for preservation in research collections.

PRESERVATION, AN ISSUE FOR COLLEGE LIBRARIES?

With a full range of preservation review and treatment procedures developed to address university collections, what faces college librarians is the extent to which preservation is an issue for items in their collections falling outside the rarified atmosphere of special collections. The large-scale concerns of research libraries about rare artifactual materials (Atkinson's class 1) or an item that is one of a dwindling number of copies contributing to the national record (Atkinson's class 3) have traditionally affected college libraries with regard only to small special collections. Those opposed to considering preservation important for college libraries might argue that the appropriate focus for undergraduate collections is to collect and maintain general study–level materials supporting the teaching function of the institution, and that, by definition, precludes the need to consider preservation an issue. This middle ground of materials, however, is contained in Atkinson's class 2 typology where the dominant factors are use combined with age and quality of paper and construction. Therefore, the traditional lack of emphasis on research materials in college libraries is not reason enough to preclude all materials from preservation consideration.

While college collections always lacked the archival function maintained by research libraries, older materials infiltrated these collections through gifts of faculty and donations of personal libraries that sometimes span several generations. Many libraries established in the nineteenth and early twentieth centuries contain significant numbers of disintegrating materials having intellectual value for the collections and for the programs they support.

Even though preservation is primarily addressed to embrittled or disintegrating materials, it is also useful for preventative measures such as spine reinforcement or the use of alkaline mending materials to ensure the continued usefulness of materials not yet obviously in decline. Despite the growing importance of information in electronic formats, it is reasonable to assume that paper-based materials will continue to be maintained for some time to come. Therefore, preservation of material not yet embrittled "becomes the process of maximizing its useful life in that appropriate format, or in another acceptable format, until that information is no longer required by the library and its users."[6] A portion of this group of materials has value to the collection in the long term, satisfying Atkinson's class 2 typology. Since these materials may be difficult or expensive to replace, preventative strategies are available to reinforce and otherwise protect materials to some degree against the natural depredations of time. This is especially significant at a time of inadequate or shrinking materials budgets when efforts made to prolong the life of newer useful materials may result in real long-term benefits.

THE OBERLIN GROUP COLLEGE LIBRARY PRESERVATION SURVEY

Middlebury College is one of New England's better-known small, residential liberal arts colleges of long tradition. Founded in 1800, it has been devoted to the liberal arts, offering its students a broad curriculum embracing the humanities, foreign languages, the social sciences, and natural sciences. The central library facility, Egbert Starr Library, and three branches house 800,000 items and 2,000 journal and newspaper subscriptions. The library adds 15,000 or more volumes to its collections each year through purchase and gifts. Since 1884 the library has been a selective depository for U.S. government documents. Starr Library was first built in 1900 and has been enlarged three times, in 1925, 1962, and 1979. Special holdings of the library include the Abernethy Library of American Literature, the Vermont Collection, the College Archives, general rare book and manuscript materials, the Flanders Ballad Collection, and the Vermont Archive of Traditional Music. In the state, Middlebury's collections are surpassed in number and depth only by the University of Vermont, located within an hour's drive to the north.

Justification

For some years, the Curator of Special Collections at Starr Library has reviewed all imprints published before 1900 culled from the general stacks to determine whether any have artifactual value that would require them to be transferred into the protective custodianship of special collections. The collection development librarian also reviews transferred materials to determine whether to acquire a replacement for the general stacks. Since most of these items are in poor condition, those lacking artifactual value and not qualifying for transfer are then reviewed to determine whether they hold intellectual value for the collection and, if so, what kind of treatment may be necessary to prolong and maximize their life.

As the preservation of library materials gathered interest and attention in the professional literature, Middlebury instituted additional measures to prolong the life of materials in its collections. Paperbound items are reviewed for preventative reinforcement; all gift materials are inspected for brittle paper and, if present, rejected; a disaster policy and procedures, along with an active disaster team, was established; and all materials used in mending were analyzed for nonalkaline content. Most of these measures were initiated by the head of collection development or the college librarian.[7] Yet it was difficult to establish a full-fledged preservation and review program without standard parameters for staffing, funding, and procedures. Questions arose regarding realistic expectations for such a program within the context of stable staffing and monetary constraints. Stymied by insufficient preservation standards for college libraries, it seemed reasonable to me to seek information on what is done at peer libraries and to determine whether expectations for Middlebury's collections are in keeping with those of comparable institutions.

The Survey Group

Middlebury's library exchanges statistics with several groups of similar institutions. The largest, called the Oberlin Group, currently includes sixty-two small colleges that have in common a dedication to the liberal arts and maintain professional staffs ranging from four to nineteen librarians. The *raison d'être* of the group was to provide ready access for directors of small college libraries to a body of peers to discuss and formulate practice and policy for this type of academic library. Member directors meet once every one or two years to discuss topics of mutual concern and interest.

Obviously here was the most appropriate group to canvass regarding the need for preservation and the level of activity currently in place. This group largely subsumes colleges included in a smaller group of forty-one institutions known as the Bowdoin Group, which also exchanges statistics on a regular basis. Seven from the Bowdoin Group not included in the Oberlin Group were added to the final survey list for a total of sixty-nine institutions. Although at first glance many of the institutions included may be regarded as privileged—with generous budgets and large collections—they actually vary considerably with regard to these two factors. It also seemed reasonable that data extracted from these libraries would suggest an appropriate level of preservation activity for a wide range of college libraries.

The Survey

The purposes of the survey were to evaluate the status of preservation activity in this group of libraries, to assess the degree to which preservation is an issue for college libraries, and to determine an appropriate level of involvement or activity. For purposes of the survey, the term *preservation* may be defined as action taken to anticipate, prevent, stop, or retard deterioration and that may require substituting an original item with one in a different format. Modeled on the major areas covered by the ARL/OMS Preservation Planning Program, the following principles guided the development of the survey:

1. What is the pattern of organization in college libraries regarding preservation? Is preservation a responsibility designated to an individual and, if so, to whom?
2. Is preservation an issue for primary collections? Have collections been reviewed for brittleness? Have environmental conditions been reviewed and are primary collections housed under appropriate environmentally controlled conditions?
3. What types and levels of materials review methods and preservation procedures are currently in place, both in-house and through contractual services? How many staff are involved? What type of documentation exists regarding commercial binding and disaster planning?
4. How is preservation funded and what are the major obstacles faced in development of preservation assessment, review, and treatment procedures?

5. What level and type of preservation education is in place for staff?
6. Are college libraries willing to expend staff and budgetary resources to contribute to the national bibliographic record?

One major question we attempted to resolve is whether a trickle-down effect exists. Can colleges simply downscale what has been established practice in a research environment to one that suppresses the long-term research aspect of the collection in favor of direct support for the undergraduate curriculum? Or is there something unique to college library collections that requires a very different perspective and methodology?

The cover letter accompanying the survey specified that I was interested in preservation practices regarding collections not currently housed under the protective custody of a special collection or an archive. The focus was the intellectual value of materials that may be at risk due to the combination of several factors (i.e., age, level of acidity in materials used to construct books, fluctuating temperature and levels of humidity, and high or careless use) resulting in brittle and damaged materials. Therefore, the target collections in the survey were general stacks materials, including periodicals, reference collections, and any other collections readily available to users. As is customary, institutional anonymity was guaranteed.

SUMMARY OF FINDINGS

The survey was conducted in 1988. Fifty-five out of sixty-nine college libraries responded for a response rate of 80 percent. One was unusable since it was applied to a special collection within a college library and not, as specified, to the library's primary collections. Two additional responses were received well after the completion date and results from these could not be included.

Need for Preservation

Eighty-six percent of the respondents report preservation as an issue for their library's primary collections. Of the 14 percent reporting that it is not an issue, several commented that their collections were too new for preservation to be an issue or remonstrated that theirs was an undergraduate, not a research, library, clearly implying that preservation should not be an issue for college libraries. Using random sampling or personal examination, 9 percent had reviewed their primary collections to determine the extent to which materials are brittle, with 26 percent planning to do so over the following two years. Seventy-three percent had reviewed environmental conditions for their primary collections, with another 13 percent planning on doing so in two years. Significantly, over half (53%)

house their primary collections under environmentally controlled conditions, with another 23 percent planning on doing so within the next five years.

Pattern of Organization

Sixty percent have assigned the responsibility of preservation to an existing professional position, in one case to a support staff position. Nine percent of the assignments in this group do not suit the preservation needs in their libraries. The primary holders of this responsibility are directors and special collections librarians (both at 13%), followed by collection development librarians (9%), and head of technical services and archivists (each 7%). None of the libraries had established a separate position of preservation librarian. Of the 40 percent not having assigned preservation as a responsibility to any position, 16 percent report that this does not suit the needs of their libraries, leaving 24 percent reporting no need for assigning preservation responsibility to any position.

Since many university libraries affiliate the function of preservation with offices of collection development, the survey contained questions regarding establishment of the position of collection development librarian. Frankly, it seemed that if many of the sample libraries had established a collection development position, it would be the ideal locus of preservation responsibility as programs developed. While 33 percent include the position of collection development or collection management librarian, only 9 percent assign preservation as a responsibility to this position. Collection development policies are maintained by 51 percent, with 29 percent containing stated policies regarding preferred materials formats for preservation.

Existing Activities

Thirty-one percent of the respondents developed a procedure to identify and recommend treatment for brittle and disintegrating materials in their collections. Eleven percent have formalized a written preservation policy, and 31 percent plan to produce one within the next two years. A related question focused on the methods either currently utilized or thought reasonable to support a brittle books program, delineating respondent preferences for a variety of in-house and contractual treatments (see table 1). The responses clearly distinguish those treatments that are or seem to be appropriate for preservation, those that are not appropriate, and those for which no consensus can be reached.

As to who should be responsible for deciding which treatment is utilized, 40 percent chose the library director, 31 percent chose the collection development librarian, and most of the remainder split between the head of technical services, the special collections librarian, and the archivist. Sixty-nine percent reported using alkaline mending supplies and pam

Table 1
Treatments for Brittle Books Developed, Judged Reasonable to Develop,
and Unreasonable to Develop

	Been developed	Reasonable to develop	Unreasonable to develop
In-house			
Transfer to special collections	35%	31%	22%
Transfer to storage	13	22	44
Transfer to brittle stacks section	4	22	42
Withdraw	55	40	2
Purchase paper replacement	69	26	4
Photoduplication	36	35	16
Microfilming brittle materials	20	26	38
Encapsulation in polyester film	27	26	24
Phase box/custom enclosure	46	33	7
Deacidification	18	18	36
Contractual services			
Photoduplication	13	44	15
Microfilming brittle materials	15	44	16
Encapsulation in polyester film	13	13	22
Phase box/custom enclosure	16	36	18
Deacidification	7	38	18

binders. With regard to the number of full-time equivalent support staff available to carry out both standard mending activities as well as the more specialized treatment required for brittle books, 36 percent reported fewer than one, 26 percent reported one, 22 percent reported between one and two, and 4 percent reported a maximum of three.

Significantly, 67 percent reported that their library does not knowingly add brittle materials to its primary collections, and 31 percent have developed a procedure to identify new materials that may be particularly susceptible to damage for treatment before processing them for the collections. If it is known that a library's commercial binder adheres to standards established by the Library Binding Institute, it is unnecessary to have a written contract. On the other hand, 33 percent maintain written contracts with their binders. As a further indication of the degree to which libraries are organized to protect their collections, 36 percent have written disaster plans and 29 percent have established preservation education programs for staff.

Funding for Preservation

With regard to major obstacles facing college librarians in developing preservation assessment, review, and treatment procedures, 53 percent reported a lack of budgetary support for adequate staffing, with one-third of the respondents indicating lack of budgetary support for materials or services. While 20 percent of the libraries have a separate budget allocation earmarked for preservation, 78 percent report that current funding for preservation is maintained through binding and/or microform allocations. Since several funds may be drawn upon to fund preservation, however, 40 percent acknowledged using operating fund allocations when necessary.

Seventy-two percent provided material funding data with allocations ranging from $39,000 to $1.03 million, a span of almost $1 million. The arithmetic mean was $435,260, with a median of $411,150. Obviously, some of the institutions in the survey group maintain large collections supported by materials budgets large enough to carry them beyond the level usually regarded as fitting for a small college library. Divided into quintiles, almost one-third of the libraries fell in the least-funded group, with the fewest number distributed in the highest-funded group (see table 2). The remaining institutions were fairly equally distributed among the middle three groups. The 40 percent maintaining well-developed preservation programs are distributed among the five groups.

Table 2
Distribution of College Libraries Surveyed and Proportion with Preservation Program by Materials Allocation

Materials Allocation	Distribution of Respondents	% with Preservation Program
$ 39,000–200,000	30%	9%
200,100–400,000	18	7
400,100–600,000	24	5
600,100–800,000	20	15
800,100–1,034,900	8	4

Preservation of the National Bibliographic Record

Because many small, private liberal arts colleges maintain collections begun a century or so ago, it is probable that these collections contain scarce research materials of significant scholarly value that would contribute to the national bibliographic record. Much of this material may have its greatest application to local or regional history, although some collections may have been established or enhanced through rather significant gifts of scholarly collections. It is possible, therefore, that these collections contain materials not readily available elsewhere.

Twenty-nine percent of the respondents reported that their collections included these materials, while another 29 percent acknowledged their ignorance of the existence of these materials in their collections. For the former group, the proportion estimated as brittle ranged from 20 to 35 percent, which matches the figures found in university collections. Significantly, 69 percent indicated a willingness on the part of their libraries to expend staff and budgetary resources to preserve low-use, long-term research materials in their collections.

CONCLUSIONS

The majority of the college librarians surveyed thought that preservation was important to their collections, with a smaller number actually addressing the problem by assigning responsibility for preservation to an existing professional position. But preservation must vie with a number of other functions for attention by a single person. The university model, where a separate position has been established to focus exclusively on preservation, is not easily applied to a college library. For college libraries, fewer professionals are present to address a broad range of library services and one librarian often, quite literally, wears several different hats. Frequently, as well, college library directors assume added responsibility for new administrative tasks with a majority taking responsibility for collection development, and a number also taking on preservation duties.

For university libraries, the trend has been to place preservation under the aegis of collection development or administrative services.[8] As a result, a section of the survey focused on the presence of a collection development librarian and whether preservation responsibility was assigned to this position. Survey findings indicate that the locus of preservation responsibility in college libraries, even when a collection development librarian is on the staff, does not always reside with the individual that has most direct knowledge of the collections. Instead, responsibility is distributed among a number of administrative positions. What seems clear is that preservation shares a similarity with collection development in that both functions are more than the sum of their parts. As Hannaford defines collection development as the intentional and systematic building of a library collection, so may preservation be defined as the intentional and systematic review and treatment of a library collection.[9] The whole is more than merely the sum of the parts—the separate activities of preservation review, treatment, funding, environmental review and controls, and education. But without a designated librarian to give intention and system to the process, all the parts can be in place without actually having an ongoing and effective preservation program. The assignment of this responsibility to a person having in-depth knowledge of the collection is vital. In a college library, this person could well be the director, although incorporating added responsibilities here is problematic—the director may not have sufficient time to carry them out. Preservation should, nonetheless, be assigned to a high-level librarian who has extensive knowledge of the library's collections and the college's curriculum.

Only a small number of libraries had reviewed their collections to assess the extent to which materials had become embrittled; a majority housed their collections under environmentally controlled conditions and had reviewed the efficacy of these conditions. This least costly and time-consuming step, monitoring an existing environmental system, indicates concern for prolonging the life of materials not yet damaged. One-fourth of the libraries responding indicated plans to install environmental control systems within five years. Though this is still expensive, it involves the least amount of staff and time commitment for the library.

Roughly one-third of the libraries routinely review and treat brittle books. From survey responses concerning methods of treatment, it is possible to segregate types of activities regarded as reasonable or unreasonable for college libraries, recognizing that there was no consensus about some methods (see table 3). Transfer to storage or to a stacks section for brittle books is considered an unreasonable option. Unlike university libraries, which have established remote storage facilities as a solution to housing and maintaining little-used but worthwhile materials at low cost, college libraries have not been required to do so since they do not maintain an archival function outside of a special collection.

Table 3
Methods Considered Reasonable and Unreasonable for Treating Brittle Books in College Libraries

In-house	
Transfer to special collections	
Withdraw	
Purchase paper replacement	Been developed or
Photoduplication	reasonable to develop
Phase box/custom enclosure	
Contractual services	
Photoduplication	
Microfilming brittle materials	Reasonable to develop
Encapsulation in polyester film	but not currently utilized
Phase box/custom enclosure	
Deacidification	
In-house	
Microfilming brittle materials	
Encapsulation in polyester film	No real consensus
Deacidification	
Transfer to storage	Unreasonable to develop
Transfer to brittle stacks section	

In research collections, the preferable format for materials preservation has been microfilming, often carried out within the library, for items containing intellectual but not artifactual value; deacidification, encapsulation, and other restorative procedures are used for items with artifactual value. Staff, budget, training, and space inadequacies in college libraries, along with an insufficient number of materials to justify the cost of these expensive treatments, may be reason enough for the lack of consensus about such in-house options. The uncertainty about these specialized procedures may be a sign of what has been termed "the myth of the expensive expert," a factor retarding development of preservation planning.[10] Because some aspects of physical deterioration of materials are technically complex, involving costly physical treatment and highly skilled professional work, the myth holds that a professional conservator is required. Therefore, college libraries, awed by the enormity of the problem and fearful of a lack of in-house technical knowledge, may limit or postpone response to the problem until more funds or expertise are available.

Demonstrated support, however, for a variety of in-house and contractual treatments isolates an effective array of methods with which to address the challenge of brittle books in college library collections. Acceptance of contractual services is especially important when only limited support staff are available to carry out these treatments along with mending and book processing routines. Though a majority of respondents do not add embrittled materials to their collections, only half of those have developed procedures to identify and treat new materials susceptible to damage, written contracts with commercial binders, written disaster plans, and formal ongoing preservation education programs. Preservation education programs, one of the least costly and easiest to implement aspects of a preservation program, have yet to be developed.

Not surprisingly, the major obstacle to addressing preservation is a lack of budgetary resources for adequate staffing. Only a minority have established separate budget lines expressly for preservation, with most providing funding through established budget allocations for binding and microforms, although a significant number also extract funds from their operating budgets. A major question begging to be answered from the budget allocation data collected concerns the relationship between materials allocations and meeting the preservation challenge. With such a wide range of allocations spanning the sum of a million dollars, an obvious assumption is that libraries with the most money maintain the highest level of preservation activity. Significantly enough, this is not the case. To address that issue, I established basic components for analyzing the data that seemed reasonable and necessary in order to determine whether a well-organized preservation program was, indeed, in place in any one library. These components are:

1. Preservation assigned as a responsibility to a librarian

2. Preservation identified as an issue for the library's primary collections
3. Development of a review and treatment procedure for embrittled and disintegrating books
4. A reasonable array of methods developed to treat these materials
5. Evidence of a preservation education program for staff

While only 18 percent of those surveyed maintain this full menu of preservation activities, they represent a wide range of college libraries with materials allocations of $39,000 to $917,000. Even though one or two libraries with small allocations do not necessarily provide a well-established model for the smaller college library, they do demonstrate that a full program is possible if the need for preservation has been recognized as such and established as a priority. A slightly larger group of libraries (25%) met all but one of the preceding criteria. Their budgets ranged from $127,000 to $771,000, a smaller span than exists for the first group. As a whole, libraries falling in either of these two groups are fairly widely distributed among the budget allocation quintiles (see table 2) with the least number placed among the highest allocations. This is encouraging evidence for those librarians in particularly small college libraries since it sets a precedent for preservation being adequately addressed regardless of materials budget size.

Not surprising, an overwhelming proportion of college libraries expressed a willingness to devote staff and budgetary resources to preserve materials that contribute to the national bibliographic record even if these have little application to the program of the college. These materials have yet to be identified in most college collections but may be defined as the most specialized of Atkinson's class 3 materials. Clearly, this category of materials in college libraries requires further research.

SUMMARY

The preservation challenge facing college libraries is largely recognized. Certainly, a trickle-down effect has occurred from the university model, not of the whole but of those aspects that best suit the particular needs of college libraries. They do not face the full range of materials requiring preservation that are present in university libraries. Due to budget constraints, only the least costly steps have been taken to preserve materials with intellectual value. These steps include: assigning part-time responsibility for preservation to an existing professional position; testing the efficacy of existing environmental-control systems; using alkaline mending and reinforcement materials; and preventing brittle gift materials from being added to collections. Most college libraries are willing to implement more costly and involved measures. With the majority lacking the necessary budget support for adequate staffing and materials, however, an approach as extensive as the ARL/OMS Preservation Planning Program is beyond their means. Another method must be developed that better suits their budgetary and staffing parameters. Rather than merely downscaling established preservation practices in university libraries, it seems clear that college libraries will extract only certain aspects of these and tailor them to their own unique needs.

NOTES

1. Gay Walker et al., "The Yale Survey: A Large-Scale Study of Book Deterioration in the Yale University Library," *College and Research Libraries* 46 (March 1985): 111.

2. Pamela W. Darling and Duane E. Webster, *Preservation Planning Program: An Assisted Self-Study Manual for Libraries* (Washington, D.C.: Association of Research Libraries, Office of Management Studies, 1987).

3. Ellen McCrady, "Nine Preservation Self-Studies," *Abbey Newsletter* 12 (February 1988): 33.

4. Ross W. Atkinson, "Selection for Preservation: A Materialistic Approach," *Library Resources and Technical Services* 30 (October–December 1986): 341–53.

5. Margaret S. Child, "Further Thoughts on 'Selection for Preservation: A Materialistic Approach,' " *Library Resources and Technical Services* 30 (October–December 1986): 355.

6. Wesley L. Boomgaarden, "Preservation Planning for the Small Special Library," *Special Libraries* 76 (Summer 1985): 205.

7. For a good overview of procedures utilized to review and treat materials about to be added to collections or items already contained in them, see Charlotte B. Brown, "The Preservation Program at Franklin and Marshall College," CAN: *Conservation Administration News* 30 (July 1987): 6–7; Marsha J. Hamilton, "Poor Condition: Procedures for Identifying and Treating Materials Before Adding to the Collections," *RTSD Newsletter* 13 (1988): 19–22; and Marcia Duncan Lowry, *Preservation and Conservation in the Small Library* (Chicago: Library Administration and Management Association, ALA, 1989).

8. *Organizing for Preservation in ARL Libraries* (Washington, D.C.: Association of Research Libraries, Office of Management Studies, 1985), 2.

9. William E. Hannaford, Jr., "Collection Development in College Libraries," in *Library Resources for College Scholars: Transactions of a Conference Held at Washington and Lee University, Lexington, Virginia, February 14–15, 1980*, ed. Robert E. Danforth (Lexington, Va.: University Library, 1980), 13.

10. *Basic Preservation Procedures* (Washington, D.C.: Association of Research Libraries, Office of Management Studies, 1981), 1.

The College Library Collection Revisited: A Bibliographic Essay

by Peter V. Deekle

Although *Collection Development in College Libraries* focuses primarily on the last quarter century, this chapter reflects a fifty-year perspective in order to give clarity to the editors' finding that recent literature in the field has been concerned less with college libraries than with larger institutions. The professional literature about collection development since the mid-1940s has included very few published works of note that directly concern the college library, as this selected bibliography demonstrates (see the College Libraries section). Rather, during the past half century, attention has been focused on the development of collections in large academic institutions.

Where particular aspects of academic library collection development reported in the literature have been pertinent to college libraries, the corresponding articles have been cited for the reader's understanding in this essay. These citations concern such topics as collection evaluation, cooperative collection development, the organization of collection development, roles of librarian and faculty selectors, and subject specialization. Despite their interest to college librarians, these citations reinforce the evidence of a prevailing focus on larger academic library needs and issues.

Harvie Branscombe expressed concern in 1940 (*Teaching with Books*) about the strong popularity of textbook instruction in higher education. He advocated the use of an academic library's entire collection as the appropriate "text" for undergraduate study. This bibliographic essay includes selected references from 1940 to the present, illustrating the early and important recognition of an academic library's central role as a significant learning resource.

The citations in this essay were selected based on several parameters. No news items or announcements were included; the references selected generally exceed two pages in length. Although both citations to periodical literature and monographs were listed, periodical references were predominant. Among the functions associated with collection development, the following topics, often cited in the literature, were emphasized in this essay: book selection, collection analysis and evaluation, deselection, and collection management (including cooperative collection development). Deliberate attention was focused on literature most relevant to the four-year institution; however, as the editors stated in their introduction, it was appropriate to cite relevant writing concerning the university library because of its predominance in the body of literature.

Few articles and books devoted solely or primarily to academic library collection development at two-year institutions were included in this essay. Although often relevant to the essay's guiding theme, these writings devoted to lower-division programs of study were considered beyond the scope of this publication. Also excluded were citations to foreign language references and those primarily concerned with academic libraries in foreign countries.

Despite these qualifications, exclusions, and distinctions, the essay's bibliographic content (representing the university library perspective) should be beneficial to any academic librarian who desires to selectively review recent collection development literature. Where the literature directly concerns the college library, it tends to be an exception to the prevailing treatment of an issue. The bibliography is organized by topic into eleven sections: book selection in academic libraries, collection development in academic libraries (general; specific, e.g., concerning individual libraries or aspects of the topic; and college libraries, e.g., concerning solely or primarily undergraduate institutions), collection development roles of academic libraries and librarians, cooperative collection development, evaluating academic library collections, policy statements, special topics, structuring collection development, and tools for collection development.

During the fifty years represented in this chapter, the literature reported a succession of trends and conditions in American higher education. For example, a pervasive interest at Harvard College and other liberal arts institutions in a core curriculum was later balanced by a trend toward subject specialization and professional education. The professional library literature during this same period reflected curriculum-driven collection development. Persistent examination of the roles of academic libraries and librarians with regard to the development of collections was also a recurrent theme throughout the fifty-year period. These trends were seen in college as well as university library practices.

There was early recognition in the literature of qualitative differences between college and university libraries (Laing, "Library for the Undergraduate College," see College Libraries). The nature and size of collections to meet the needs of undergraduate curricula were comparatively considered in Blanchard's 1968 article, "Planning the Conversion of a

College to a University Library" (see Special Topics). Information access and collection development for distance learners were discussed by Gorman in 1986 ("Collection Development and Acquisitions in a Distance Learning Environment," see Special Topics).

Collection development literature has included considerable discussion concerning the creation and management of subject specialties in academic libraries. Usually, this discussion has related most directly to university libraries or large undergraduate collections (Anders, "Selection of a Divisional Reading Room Collection," see Book Selection in Academic Libraries). However, Norton wrote in 1941 about the special aspects in developing a small college browsing room collection (see Special Topics). Bixler, in *Administration of the College Library*, has written about the identification and selection of special types of materials for college libraries (see Book Selection in Academic Libraries).

This review of the literature has demonstrated the profession's high degree of interest in standards and philosophical bases for collection development. The importance of a systematic plan was documented by several writers, including Kirkpatrick ("Does Your Library Lack a Plan?" see the General section). Some writers considered the prospect of the complete and direct creation of library collections (Sutton, "Search for the Instant Library," see Special Topics); others were more concerned with collection maintenance (Benjamin, "Feed and Weed: A Philosophy of Book Selection," see Book Selection in Academic Libraries). In the 1970s the application of systems theory to college library development was increasingly reported in the literature (Beilby and Evans, "Information System for Collection Development," see the Specific section; "Toward an Information System for Responsive Collection Development," see Special Topics).

Throughout the fifty-year period of this literature review, the creation and evaluation of standard selection tools has been a topic of discussion. In 1941, Gosnell considered the positive and negative elements of such tools ("Values and Dangers of Standard Book and Periodical Lists for College Libraries," see the General section). The question of actual collection quality has persisted. Futas and Vidor, writing in 1987, addressed the question directly—"What Constitutes a 'Good' Collection?" (see the General section).

Where there has been expressed concern with college library collection quality it has centered on a consideration of collection size. This tendency reflects the dominant influence of the university and large institution over college library practices. Oboler and Stevens, writing in 1960, expressed the "get-em-all" theory of collection development (see Special Topics). Davidson (1951) considered the 150,000-volume standard (see the General section); almost twenty-five years later, Lee questioned, "College Libraries: Are 100,000 Volumes Enough?" (see College Libraries). The appropriate size of collections has continued to be a topic of interest for many collection development theorists and practitioners (McCrum, "Book Selection in Relation to the Optimum Size of a College Library," see Book Selection in Academic Libraries).

Evidence of economic conditions throughout the period of this review has been reflected in the literature. During the mid-1970s, for example, Thomas discussed the impact of library budget cuts on collection development ("Book Selection in an Economic Recession," see Book Selection in Academic Libraries).

As librarians looked increasingly toward approval plans and other "automatic" means to acquire materials, college library collection development specialists questioned the effect of these convenient and standardized techniques and tools. Turner studied the prospects for collection development assisted by new information technology; Simmons documented computer applications of loan records in selection decisions (see College Libraries). The virtues of book approval plans were analyzed comprehensively by Emery (see Book Selection in Academic Libraries).

From the earliest date in this review of the literature there has been discussion of the librarian's role in collection development. Brenni wrote an article in 1969 entitled "Bibliographer in the College Library," which pointedly illuminated the selector's role (see Cooperative Collection Development). Equally prevalent in the literature has been consideration of the role of faculty in collection development (Pickett, "Faculty Participation in Book Selection," see Book Selection in Academic Libraries; Vidor and Futas, "Effective Collection Developers: Librarians or Faculty?" see Collection Development Roles of Academic Libraries and Librarians).

The continuing consideration of a librarian's role in collection development relates to the role of the library itself in the instructional program. This relationship may have a heightened significance for college libraries. In 1957, Kuhlman, referring to Branscombe's earlier proposal, questioned whether library book collections could form the basis of undergraduate instruction (see Cooperative Collection Development). In 1960, Lester defined a "Library's Role in a Liberal Education" (see Collection Development Roles of Academic Libraries and Librarians). The information needs of undergraduate students have been an increasingly evident concern of collection development specialists in recent years. Dole has written an article representative of this concern ("Acquisitions and Collection Development: 2001—The End User," see the General section).

Limited attention has been given in the literature to building college library collections that support bibliographic services. McAllister expressed this interest in 1949 ("Building a Book Collection for Service," see the General section); Rice focused on the same issue in a university context ("Development of Working Collections . . . ," see the General section).

The interest in an undergraduate core curriculum has paralleled an interest in a core collection for academic libraries. Van Jackson wrote in

1967 of a college library's role in relation to the academic core (see Collection Development Roles of Academic Libraries). The literature includes many references to building the core collections of libraries, Horny's 1971 article in *Library Journal* being a notable example (see the Specific section).

Interlibrary cooperation has been a pervasive topic for discussion among large institutions for many years. In 1942, Heathcote wrote briefly about "Cooperative Book Selection" (see Cooperative Collection Development). The discussions of cooperative collection development have increased markedly in number during the past decade. Recently, some authors have discussed the particular issues associated with this topic for small or medium-sized college libraries (for example, Holicky, "Collection Development vs. Resource Sharing: The View from the Small Academic Library," see Cooperative Collection Development).

Perhaps most significantly, this review of the literature has demonstrated the continuing presence of some fundamental themes for all academic libraries. As college librarians further the creation and use of systems for the effective development of collections, they continue to recognize the need to define their place and function in the academic environment. Increasingly, this is a collaborative dialogue with faculty with regard to the growing sophistication of learning needs for the undergraduate students of today and tomorrow.

COLLECTION DEVELOPMENT BIBLIOGRAPHY

Book Selection in Academic Libraries

Alley, B., and Cargill, J. S. "Inventory and Selection Techniques for Large Unorganized Collections." *Library Acquisitions* 21 (1978): 23–28.

Anders, M. E. "Selection of a Divisional Reading Room Collection." *College and Research Libraries* 22 (November 1961): 430–34.

Benjamin, P. M. "Feed and Weed: A Philosophy of Book Selection." *College and Research Libraries* 23 (November 1962): 500–3.

Bixler, P. H. "Book Selection and Acquisition; Selection and Acquisition of Special Types of Materials." In *Administration of the College Library*, 4th ed., edited by G. R. Lyle and others, 330–431. New York: H. W. Wilson, 1974.

"Book Selection and Standing Orders." *The Bookmark* 20 (September 1967): 11–12.

Blackney, A. L. "Principles of Book Selection Based on an Analysis of Book Usage in a Liberal Arts College." Master's thesis, University of Chicago, 1941.

Brenni, V. J. "Book Selection and the University Library." *Catholic Library World* 38 (March 1967): 425–29.

Calhoun, J. C., and Bracken, J. K. "Index of Publisher Quality for the Academic Library." *College and Research Libraries* 44 (May 1983): 257–59.

Carlson, J. F. "Book Selection and the Small College Library." *Learning Today* 4 (Fall 1971): 37–43.

Clarke, J. A., and Cooklock, R. A. "Book Selection: From Teachers College to University." *College and Research Libraries* 27 (May 1966): 222–24.

Copeland, A. T. "Philosophy Journals as Current Book Selection Guides." *College and Research Libraries* 27 (November 1966): 455–60.

Danton, J. P. *Book Selection and Collections: A Comparison of German and American University Libraries.* New York: Columbia Univ. Pr., 1963.

DeVilbiss, M. L. "Approval-Built Collection in the Medium-sized Academic Library." *College and Research Libraries* 36 (November 1975): 487–92.

Dickinson, D. W. "Rationalist's Critique of Book Selection for Academic Libraries." *Journal of Academic Librarianship* 7 (July 1981): 138–51.

Emery, C. D. "Efficiency and Effectiveness: Approval Plans from a Management Perspective." In *Shaping Library Collections for the 1980s,* edited by Peter Spyers-Duran and Thomas Mann, Jr., 183–99. Phoenix: Oryx Press, 1980.

Ettinger, J. R. T. "Through a Glass Darkly: Academic Book Selection in Crisis." *APLA Bulletin* 32 (June 1968): 32–40.

Grace, Sr. M. "Selecting Books in the 900's." *Catholic Library World* 27 (May 1956): 355–58.

Haro, R. P. "Book Selection in Academic Libraries." *College and Research Libraries* 28 (March 1967): 104–6.

Harris, T. C. "Book Purchasing or Book Selection: A Study of Values." In *Advances in Understanding Approval and Gathering Plans in Academic Libraries,* edited by Peter Spyers-Duran and Daniel Gore, 53–62. Kalamazoo: Western Michigan Univ., 1970.

Jenks, G. M. "Book Selection: An Approach for Small and Medium-Sized Libraries." *College and Research Libraries* 33 (January 1972): 28–30.

Josey, E. J. "New Clarification of an Old Problem: Book Selection for College Libraries," *Savannah State College Bulletin* 18 (December 1964): 107–13.

Kosa, G. A. "Book Selection Trends in American Academic Libraries." *Australian Library Journal* 21 (November 1972): 416–24.

Kraft, M. "Argument for Selectivity in the Acquisitions of Materials for Research Libraries." *Library Quarterly* 37 (July 1967): 284–95.

Lane, D. O. "Selection of Academic Library Materials, a Literature Survey." *College and Research Libraries* 29 (September 1968): 364–72.

Lansberg, W. R. "Book Selection at Dartmouth." *Library Journal* 80 (October 1, 1955): 2048–52.

Lehman, J. O. "*Choice* as a Selection Tool." *Wilson Library Bulletin* 44 (May 1970): 957–61.

Logsdon, R. H. "Selecting Books for a College Library." *Madison Quarterly* 2 (May 1942): 114–16.

Lopez, M. D. "Guide for Beginning Bibliographers." *Library Resources and Technical Services* 13 (Fall 1969): 462–70.

Lyle, G. "Book Selection and Acquisition." In *Administration of the College Library,* 4th ed., edited by G. R. Lyle and others, 170–200. New York: H. W. Wilson, 1974.

McCrum, B. P. "Book Selection in Relation to the Optimum Size of a College Library." *College and Research Libraries* 11 (April 1950): 138–42.

Metcalf, K. D., and Williams, E. E. "Book Selection for the Harvard Library." *Harvard Library Bulletin* 6 (Spring 1952): 193–201.

Orr, R. W. "Book Selection: I.S.U. (Iowa State University) Style." *The Bookmark* 18 (September 1965): 15.

Ottemiller, J. H. and others. "Selective Book Retirement Program at Yale." *Yale University Library Gazette* 34 (October 1959): 64–72.

Pate, M. "Selecting and Ordering Books for Waukesha and Rock County Centers, University of Wisconsin." *Illinois Libraries* 49 (November 1967): 851–61.

Pickett, A. S. "Faculty Participation in Book Selection." *Indiana Librarian* 15 (June 1960): 32–35.

Randall, W. M., and Goodrich, F. L. D. "Books: Their Selection, Purchase, and Preparation for the Shelves." In *Principles of College Library Administration*, 75–108. Chicago: American Library Association and University of Chicago Press, 1941.

Reparata, M. "Some Book Selection Practices in Certain College and University Libraries and the Bylaws of Rosary College Library." *Illinois Catholic Librarian* 2 (January–April 1946): 9–13.

Schwartz, C. A. "Book Selection, Collection Development, and Bounded Rationality." *College and Research Libraries* 50 (May 1989): 328–43.

Snyder, M. B. "Examination of Methods Used in a Study of Decision-Making in the Selection of Science Library Materials." *ALA Bulletin* 61 (December 1967): 1319–23.

Stiffler, S. A. "Philosophy of Book Selection for Smaller Academic Libraries." *College and Research Libraries* 24 (May 1963): 204–8.

Thakore, A. V. "Practice of Book Selection in a University Library." *Indiana Librarian* 15 (September 1960): 71–75.

Theall, B. "College Book Selection and the Social Order." In *Conference Proceedings, 1960*, 63–67. New York: Catholic Library Association, 1960.

Thomas, A. F. "Book Selection in an Economic Recession." *Catholic Library World* 47 (February 1976): 299–300.

Thompson, L. S. "Dogma of Book Selection in University Libraries." *College and Research Libraries* 21 (November 1960): 441–45.

Trump, A. G. "Book Selection in a College Library." *South Dakota Library Bulletin* 46 (October 1960): 156–58.

Wilks, J. "Book Selection." In *Manual of University and College Library Practice*, edited by G. Woledge and B. S. Page, 25–46. London: The Library Association, 1940.

Williams, E. E. "Selection of Books for Lamont." *Harvard Library Bulletin* 3 (Autumn 1949): 386–94.

Wisconsin State College. "Library Selection of Materials." *Kentucky Library Association Bulletin* 23 (July 1959): 64–66.

Wyrick, J. "Inquiry into the Need for a New Book Selection Aid for College Libraries." *The Southeastern Librarian* 12 (Fall 1962): 153–58.

Collection Development in Academic Libraries

GENERAL

Axford, H. W. "Collection Management: A New Dimension." *Journal of Academic Librarianship* 6 (January 1981): 324–32.

Baker, J. W. "Acquisitions and Collection Development: 2001 [Collection Management at the University of California, Berkeley]." *Library Acquisitions* 12 (1988): 243–48.

Cline, L. "Collection Management, Academic Libraries, and Service." *Show-Me Libraries* 36 (October–November 1984): 50–53.

Davidson, D. C. "150,000 Volumes Are Enough, They Say." *Library Journal* 76 (August 1951): 1190 + .

Dole, W. V. "Acquisitions and Collection Development: 2001—The End User [Information Needs of Future College Students]." *Library Acquisitions* 12 (1988): 2, 249–53.

Downs, R. B. "Collection Development for Academic Libraries: An Overview." *North Carolina Libraries* 34 (Fall 1976): 31–38.

Frankie, S. O. "Collection Development in Academic Libraries." *Catholic Library World* 54 (October 1982): 103–9.

Futas, E., and Vidor, D. L. "What Constitutes a 'Good' Collection?" *Library Journal* 112 (April 15, 1987): 45–47.

Gosnell, C. F. "Values and Dangers of Standard Book and Periodical Lists for College Libraries." *College and Research Libraries* 2 (June 1941): 216–20.

Hartje, G. N. "Parameter of Developing and Managing a Library Collection." *Collection Management* 3 (Summer–Fall 1979): 247–56.

Hitchcock-Mort, K. A. "Collection Management in the Eighties—Where Are We Now?" *Library Acquisitions* 9 (1985): 3–12.

Kaser, D. E. "Collection Building in American Universities." In *University Library History: An International Review*, edited by James Thompson, 33–55. New York: Saur Verlag, 1980.

Kirkpatrick, L. H. "Does Your Library Lack a Plan?" *Library Journal* 71 (June 1, 1946): 782–88.

McAllister, D. M. "Building a Book Collection for Service." *Wilson Library Bulletin* 24 (November 1949): 227–28.

McKeon, N. F. "Nature of the College-Library Book Collection." *Library Quarterly* 24 (October 1954): 322–35.

Metz, P. "Collection Development in Academic Libraries: New Media, New Choices." *Journal of Academic Librarianship* 13 (November 1987): 298c–98d.

Mosher, P. H. "Collection Development to Collection Management: Toward Stewardship of Library Resources." *Collection Management* 4 (Winter 1982): 41–48.

Orne, J. "Current Trends in Collection Development in University Libraries." *Library Trends* 15 (October 1966): 197–334.

Osborn, C. B. "Collection Development: The Link Between Scholarship and Library Resources." *New Directions for Higher Education* 34 (September 1982): 45–54.

Pargellis, S. "Building a Research Library." *College and Research Libraries* 5 (March 1944): 110–14.

Propas, S. W. "Cincinnati Collection Management and Development Institute, November 6–9, 1983." *Library Acquisitions* 8 (1984): 51–64.

"Report on Conference [To Explore Some Current and Anticipated Problems in the Building of Book Collections in Libraries]." *Library Journal* 84 (June 1, 1959): 1765–67.

Rice, B. A. "Development of Working Collections in University Libraries." *College and Research Libraries* 38 (July 1977): 309–12.

Rotkowicz, R., and Nabors, K. L. "Collection Development in Academic Libraries." *Show-Me Libraries* 36 (October–November 1984): 30–35.

Sankowski, A. "The Challenges in Developing Academic Library Collections." *Catholic Library World* 58 (May–June 1987): 269–72.

Schad, J. G. "Allocating Book Funds: Control or Planning." *College and Research Libraries* 31 (May 1970): 155–59.

Schad, J. G., and Tanis, N. E. *Problems in Developing Academic Library Collections.* New York: Bowker, 1974.

Simpson, M. L. "Experiment in Acquisitions with the Lamont Library List." *College and Research Libraries* 15 (October 1954): 430–33.

Thomas, L. "Tradition and Expertise in Academic Library Collection Development." *College and Research Libraries* 48 (November 1987): 487–93.

"Variations by Type of Library." In *Building Library Collections*, 5th ed., edited by John Bonko and Rose Mary Magrill, 25–60. Metuchen, N.J.: Scarecrow Press, 1979.

Vosper, R. G. "Books to Build Our Colleges." *ALA Bulletin* 51 (April 1957): 247–52.

Werking, R. H. "Allocating the Academic Library's Book Budget: Historical Perspectives and Current Reflections." *Journal of Academic Librarianship* 14 (July 1988): 140–44.

SPECIFIC

Alldredge, N. G. "Symbiotic Relationship of Approval Plans and Collection Development." In *Shaping Library Collections*, edited by Peter Spyers-Duran and Thomas Mann, Jr., 174–77. Phoenix: Oryx Press, 1980.

Bellby, M. H., and Evans, G. T. "Information System for Collection Development in SUNY: A Progress Report." *Collection Management* 2 (Fall 1978): 217–28.

Biggs, M., and Biggs, V. "Reference Collection Development in Academic Libraries: Report of a Survey." *RQ* 27 (Fall 1987): 67–79.

Boyer, J. W. "Selective Duplication and Approval Plans." In *Advances in Understanding Approval and Gathering Plans in Academic Libraries*, edited by Peter Spyers-Duran and Daniel Gore, 85–97. Kalamazoo: Western Michigan Univ., 1970.

Chernofsky, J. L. "Collecting the Twentieth Century [25th RBMS Preconference in Austin, Texas]." *AB Bookman's Weekly* 74 (August 6, 1984): 771 +.

Collection Development and Management at Cornell: A Concluding Report on Activities of the Cornell University Libraries Project for Collection Development and Management, July 1979–June 1980. Ithaca, N.Y.: Cornell Univ. Libraries, 1981.

"College Book Collection." In *Conference Proceedings*, 50–62. New York: Catholic Library Association, 1960.

Horny, K. "Building Northwestern's Core." *Library Journal* 96 (May 1, 1971): 1580–83.

Moffett, H. S. "Examination of the Plan and Method of Book Purchase in the Library of Flora Stone Mather College." Master's thesis, Western Reserve University, 1955.

Nisonger, T. E. "Acquisitions and Collection Development: Cooperation in a Changing Environment [Report on the AMIGOS Workshop of 1987]." *Library Acquisitions* 12 (1988): 73–77.

O'Connor, T. F. "Collection Development in the Yale University Library, 1865– 1931." *Journal of Library History, Philosophy, and Comparative Librarianship* 22 (Spring 1987): 164–89.

Osborn, A. D. "Development of Library Resources at Harvard; Problems and Potentialities." *Harvard Library Bulletin* 9 (Spring 1955): 197–212.

Rouse, R. "Automation Stops Here: A Case for Man-made Book Collections." In *Advances in Understanding Approval and Gathering Plans in Academic Libraries,* edited by Peter Spyers-Duran and Daniel Gore, 35–51. Kalamazoo: Western Michigan Univ., 1970.

Simmons, P. *Collection Development and the Computer: A Case Study in the Analysis of Machine Readable Loan Records and Their Application to Book Selection.* Vancouver: Univ. of British Columbia, 1971.

Turner, E. F. and others. *Study of the Implications of Modern Technology for Small College Libraries.* Washington, D.C.: U.S. Office of Education, Bureau of Research, 1969.

White, R. F. "History of Science and Technology for Liberal Arts Colleges: Building a Useful Collection." *Choice* 24 (April 1987): 1181–82 +.

COLLEGE LIBRARIES

Bixler, P. H. "Development of the Book Collection in the College Library; Book Collection and Its Functions." *College and Research Libraries* 12 (October 1951): 355–59.

Corbett, E. M. "Collection Development in a Liberal Arts College Library." *The Bookmark* 41 (Fall 1982): 27–31.

Hannaford, W. E. "Collection Development in College Libraries." In *Library Resources for College Scholars,* edited by Robert E. Danford, 13–17. Lexington, Va.: Washington and Lee Univ. Library, 1980.

Harloe, B. "Achieving Client-Centered Collection Development in Small and Medium-Sized Academic Libraries." *College and Research Libraries* 50 (May 1989): 344–53.

Johnson, R. D. "The College Library Collection." *Advances in Librarianship* 14 (1986): 143–74.

Kraus, J. W. "Book Collections of Early American College Libraries." *Library Quarterly* 43 (April 1973): 142–59.

Laing, A. "Library for the Undergraduate College." *College and Research Libraries* 1 (September 1940): 314–21.

Lee, J. D. "College Libraries: Are 100,000 Volumes Enough?" *North Carolina Libraries* 33 (Spring 1975): 5–7.

Miller, W. "Collection Development from a College Perspective: A Response." In *College Librarianship,* edited by William Miller and D. Stephen Rockwood, 151–53. Metuchen, N.J.: Scarecrow Press, 1981.

Moskowitz, M. "Collection Development and the College Library: A State-of-the-Art Review." *Collection Building* 6 (Summer 1984): 5–10.

Seely, E. C. "Development of the Book Collection in the College Library; Cost of Books." *College and Research Libraries* 12 (October 1951): 359–61.

Stickle, N. R. "College Library Problems: A Symposium: Weeding the College Library." *ILA Record* 8 (April 1955): 70–71.

Collection Development Roles of Academic Libraries and Librarians

Bailey, L. C. "Role of the College and University Library in the Fields of the Humanities and the Social Sciences." In *Role of the Library in Collecting Information and Giving Service to the Serious Student and Research Worker*, edited by Esther Stallman, 78–87. Austin: University of Texas. Graduate School of Library Science, 1954.

Bonn, G. S. "Role of the College and University in the Fields of Sciences and Technology." In *Role of the Library in Collecting Information and Giving Service to the Serious Student and Research Worker*, edited by Esther Stallman, 88–95. Austin: University of Texas, Graduate School of Library Science, 1954.

Brenni, V. J. "Bibliographer in the College Library." *Catholic Library World* 40 (April 1969): 497–99.

Fussler, H. H. "Bibliographer Working in a Broad Area of Knowledge." *College and Research Libraries* 10 (July 1949): 199–202.

Haro, R. P. "Bibliographer in the Academic Library." *Library Resources and Technical Services* 13 (Spring 1969): 163–69.

Lester, J. A., Jr. "Library's Role in a Liberal Education." *Library Journal* 85 (February 1, 1960): 491–94.

Rana, M. S. "Role of Librarian in Building Book Collection in Academic Libraries." *Herald of Library Science* 12 (January 1973): 35–38.

Reichman, F. "Acquisition Librarian as Bibliographer." *College and Research Libraries* 10 (July 1949): 203–7.

Van Jackson, W. "Role of the College Library: The Academic Core." *Virginia Librarian* 14 (Summer 1967): 6–11.

Vidor, D. L., and Futas, E. "Effective Collection Developers: Librarians or Faculty?" *Library Resources and Technical Services* 32 (April 1988): 127–36.

Cooperative Collection Development

Branin, J. J. "Issues in Cooperative Collection Development: The Promise and Frustration of Resource Sharing." In *Issues in Cooperative Collection Development*, edited by June L. Engle and Sue O. Medina, 1–38. Atlanta: Southeastern Library Network, Inc., 1986.

Dougherty, R. M. "A Conceptual Framework for Organizing Resource Sharing and Shared Collection Development Programs." *Journal of Academic Librarianship* 14 (November 1988): 287–91.

Gribbin, J. H. "Interlibrary Cooperation and Collection Building." In *Academic Library: Essays in Honor of Guy R. Lyle*, edited by Evan Ira Farber and Ruth Walling, 105–17. Metuchen, N.J.: Scarecrow Press, 1974.

Heathcote, L. M. "Cooperative Book Selection." *Library Journal* 67 (January 1, 1942): 3.

Holicky, B. H. "Collection Development vs. Resource Sharing: The View from the Small Academic Library." *Journal of Academic Librarianship* 10 (July 1984): 146–47.

Kuhlman, A. F. "Teaching with Books—A Symposium: Can We Teach with Books?" *Southeastern Librarian* 7 (Spring 1957): 5–9.

Lockwood, D. P. "Cooperative Acquisitions in the United States versus a World Library." *College and Research Libraries* 8 (April 1947): 110–12.

Maltese, S. M., and Weech, T. I. "Cooperative Collection Development in Illinois Academic Libraries—A Report on IACRL/IBHE Activities." *Illinois Libraries* 69 (January 1987): 69–74.

Meachen, E., and Scharfenorth, G. R. "Cooperative Collection Management in Higher Education: The IACRL/IBHE Initiative." *Illinois Libraries* 71 (January 1989): 46–52.

Moore, J. A. "Case for Cooperation Based on Two Talks Given at the Fall Workshop of the Oregon Chapter of ACRL." *PNLA Quarterly* 45 (Spring 1981): 9–39.

Munn, R. F. "Collection Development vs. Resource Sharing: The Dilemma of the Middle-Level Institutions." *Journal of Academic Librarianship* 8 (January 1983): 352–53.

Neumann, J. "Impact of New York's Collection Development Funds on Resource Sharing." *The Bookmark* 45 (Fall 1986): 26–29.

Evaluating Academic Library Collections

Alexander, N. D. "Suggested Model Designed to Serve as a Guide for Evaluating the Adequacy of Academic Library Collections in American Colleges and Universities." Ph.D. diss., University of Southern California, 1975.

Basart, A. "Criteria for Weeding Books in a University Music Library." *Music Library Association Notes* 36 (June 1980): 819–36.

Burns, R. W., Jr., "Evaluation of the Holdings in Science and Technology in the University of Idaho Library." *The Library.* Moscow, Idaho: Univ. of Idaho, 1968.

Carnovsky, L. "Self-evaluation; or, How Good Is My Library?" *College and Research Libraries* 3 (Spring 1942): 304–10.

Cassata, M. B., and Dewey, G. L. "Evaluation of a University Library Collection: Some Guidelines." *Library Resources and Technical Services* 13 (Fall 1969): 450–57.

Cooper, M. "Criteria for Weeding of Collections." *Library Resources and Technical Services* 12 (Summer 1968): 339–51.

Ferguson, A. W. "Assessing the Collection Development Need for CR-ROM Products [at Columbia University]." *Library Acquisitions* 12 (1988): 3–4, 325–32.

Grover, M. L. "Collection Assessment in the 1980s." *Collection Building* 8 (1987): 23–26.

Hall, B. H. *Collection Assessment Manual for College and University Libraries.* Phoenix: Oryx Press, 1985.

Ifidon, S. E. "Qualitative/Quantitative Evaluation of Academic Library Collections: A Literature Survey." *International Library Review* 8 (June 1976): 299–308.

King, E. "Evaluation of the Biology Collection of the Trevor Arnett Library of Atlanta University." Master's thesis, Atlanta University, 1963.

Mitchell, R. K. "Methodology for Assessing Academic Library Collection Development." Ph.D. diss., University of Pittsburgh, 1976.

Nisonger, T. E. "Annotated Bibliography of Items Relating to Collection Evaluation in Academic Libraries, 1969–1981." *College and Research Libraries* 43 (July 1982): 300–11.

Porta, M. A., and Lancaster, F. W. "Evaluation of a Scholarly Collection in a Specific Subject Area by Bibliographic Checking: A Comparison of Sources [at University of Illinois at Urbana-Champaign Library]." *Libri* 38 (June 1988): 131–37.

Sanders, N. P. and others. "Automated Collection Analysis Using the OCLC and RLG Bibliographic Databases." *College and Research Libraries* 49 (July 1988): 305–14.

Schofield, J. L. and others. "Evaluation of an Academic Library's Stock Effectiveness." *Journal of Academic Librarianship* 7 (July 1975): 207–27.

Stieg, L. F. "Technique for Evaluating the College Library Book Collection." *Library Quarterly* 13 (January 1943): 34–44.

Stielow, F. J., and Tibbo, H. R. "Collection Analysis and the Humanities: A Practicum with the RLG Conspectus." *Journal of Education for Library and Information Science* 27 (Winter 1987): 148–57.

Stone, E. O. "Measuring the College Book Collection." *Library Journal* 66 (November 1, 1941): 941–43.

———. "University Library Reappraises Its Holdings." *Wilson Library Bulletin* 29 (May 1955): 712–14+.

Tjarks, L. "Evaluating Literature Collections." *RQ* 12 (Winter 1972): 183–85.

Webbert, C. A. "Evaluation of the Holdings in Social Science in the University of Idaho Library." *The Bookmark* 14 (1962): 3, supp.

Whaley, J. H. "Approach to Collection Analysis." *Library Resources and Technical Services* 25 (July 1981): 330–38.

Wiemers, E. "Collection Evaluation: A Practical Guide to the Literature." *Library Acquisitions* 8 (1984): 65–76.

Policy Statements

Book Selection Policies of the Libraries of Stanford University. Stanford, Calif.: The University, 1970.

Cargill, J. S. "Collection Development Policies: An Alternative Viewpoint." *Library Acquisitions* 8 (1984): 47–49.

Cline, H. F., and Sinnott, L. T. *Building Library Collections: Policies and Practices in Academic Libraries*. Lexington, Mass.: D. C. Heath, 1981.

Coleman, K. L., and Dickinson, P. "Drafting a Reference Collection Policy." *College and Research Libraries* 38 (May 1977): 227–33.

Gardner, C. A. "Book Selection Policies in the College Library: A Reappraisal." *College and Research Libraries* 46 (March 1985): 140–46.

Koenig, D. A. "Rushmore at Berkeley: The Dynamics of Developing a Written Collection Development Policy Statement." *Journal of Academic Librarianship* 7 (January 1982): 344–50.

Kozumplik, W. A. "Oregon State College Has Replacement Policy." *Library Journal* 75 (October 1, 1950): 1604–6.

Krause, P. "Collection Development Policy and the Future for Academic Libraries." In *Festschrift in Honor of Dr. Arnulfo D. Trejo*, edited by Christopher F. Grippo, 25–32. Tucson: University of Arizona, Graduate Library School, 1984.

Morrow, A. L. "Study of the Book Selection Policies and Practices of Southern Baptist College, University, and Seminary Libraries, 1952–1963." Master's thesis, University of North Carolina, 1965.

Osborn, C. B. "Planning for a University Library Policy on Collection Development." *International Library Review* 9 (April 1977): 209–24.

Reeder, D. "Value of Written Book Selection Policies for College Libraries." *Maryland Libraries* 26 (Winter 1959): 24–25.

Say, P. C. "Plan for the Development of the Book and Periodical Collection of San Beda College Library." Master's thesis, Catholic University, 1965.

Ward, K. L. "Collection Policy in College and University Libraries." *Music Library Association Notes* 29 (March 1973): 432–40.

Special Topics

Beilby, M. H., and Evans, G. T. "Toward an Information System for Responsive Collection Development." In *New Horizons for Academic Libraries,* edited by Robert D. Stueart and Richard D. Johnson, 424–31. New York: Saur Verlag, 1979.

Bingham, R. B. "Collection Development in University Libraries: An Investigation of the Relationship Between Categories of Selectors and Usage of Selected Items." Ph.D. diss., Rutgers University, 1979.

Blanchard, J. R. "Planning the Conversion of a College to a University Library." *College and Research Libraries* 29 (July 1968): 297–302.

Clarke, J. A. "Textbooks in College Libraries?" *Choice* 4 (July 1967): 509–11.

Fainsod, M., and Bryant, D. W. "Science Collections at Harvard." *Harvard Library Bulletin* 17 (April 1969): 238–39.

Ferguson, A. W. "University Library Collection Development and Management Using a Structural-Functional Systems Model." *Collection Management* 8 (Spring 1986): 1–14.

Garland, K. "Application of Information Theory for Materials Selection and Collection Evaluation." Ph.D. diss., Case Western Reserve University, 1980.

Gorman, G. E. "Collection Development and Acquisitions in a Distance Learning Environment." *Library Acquisitions* 10 (1986): 9–66.

Harmon, C. L. "Impact of Serials on Collection Development: A Report of the Conference Proceedings [May 1981, University of Oklahoma]." *Library Acquisitions* 5 (1981): 95–99.

Haywood, C. R. "Old, Bold Librarians: An Acquisitions Program to Fit the Library-College." *Library-College Journal* 1 (Summer 1968): 11–14.

Heinzkill, R. "Retrospective Collection Development in English Literature: An Overview [Improving an Academic Library's Holdings]." *Collection Management* 9 (Spring 1987): 55–65.

Helen, Sr. "Book Purchasing for the Small College Library." *Catholic Library World* 29 (December 1957): 147–52 +.

Hewitt, J. A., and Shipman, J. S. "Cooperative Collection Development Among Research Libraries in the Age of Networking: Report of a Survey of ARL Libraries." In *Advances in Library Automation and Networking* 1 (1987): 189–232.

Kohut, J. J. "Allocating the Book Budget: A Model." *College and Research Libraries* 35 (May 1974): 192–99.

Ludington, F. B. "Promotional Considerations in the Selection of Scholarly Books." *Publishers Weekly* 169 (June 25, 1956): 2739–40.

Metz, P. "Duplication in Library Collections: What We Know and What We Need to Know." *Collection Building* 2 (1980): 27–33.

Norton, T. E. "Browsing Room for a Small College." *Library Journal* 66 (February 15, 1941): 151–54.

Oboler, E. M. "Get-Em-All Theory of Book Buying." *Library Journal* 85 (October 1, 1960): 3391–92.

Schmidt, C. J. "Administering the Book Budget: A Survey of State-Supported Academic Libraries in Texas." *Texas Library Journal* 42 (Summer 1966): 51–53.

Schreiner-Robles, R. "Collection Development in Foreign Literatures at Medium-Sized Academic Libraries." *Library Resources and Technical Services* 32 (April 1988): 139–47.

Stevens, R. E. "Get-Em-All Theory of Book Buying." *Library Journal* 85 (October 1, 1960): 3392–93.

Sutton, L. "Search for the Instant Library." *Saturday Review* 49 (April 16, 1966): 24–25.

Vosper, R. G. "Collection Building and Rare Books." In *Research Librarianship: Essays in Honor of Robert B. Downs*, 91–111. New York: Bowker, 1971.

Woodbridge, H. C. "Foreign Language Collection in the Small College Library." *Kentucky Library Association Bulletin* 18 (October 1954): 4 + .

Structuring Collection Development

Cogswell, J. A. "The Organization of Collection Management Functions in Academic Research Libraries." *Journal of Academic Librarianship* 13 (November 1987): 268–76.

Collection Development Organization and Staffing. Association of Research Libraries, Office of Management Studies, 1987.

Cubberley, C. W. "Organization for Collection Development in Medium-sized Academic Libraries." *Library Acquisitions* 11 (1987): 297–323.

Gamble, L. E. "Assessing Collection Development Organization in a Small Academic Library." In *Energies for Transition*, edited by Danuta A. Nitecki, 82–85. Chicago: Association of College and Research Libraries, 1986.

Quick, R. C. "Coordination of Collection Building by Academic Libraries." In *New Dimensions for Academic Library Service*, edited by E. J. Josey, 100–20. Metuchen, N.J.: Scarecrow Press, 1975.

Tools for Collection Development

Beckham, R. S. "Basic List of Books and Periodicals for College Libraries [in Anthropology]." In *Resources for the Teaching of Anthropology*, edited by David G. Mandelbaum et al., 77–277. Berkeley: University of California Press, 1963.

Books for College Libraries: A Core Collection of 50,000 Titles. 3d ed. Chicago: American Library Association, 1988.

Gardner, R. K. "*Choice*: Books for College Libraries; Its Origin, Development and Future Plans." *Southeastern Librarian* 15 (Summer 1965): 69–75.

Jordan, R. T. *750 Desirable 1959 Books for the Lower Division College Library.* Taft, Calif.: Taft College, 1960.

Kosa, G. A. "Profiling Techniques for Automated Retrieval Using LC Classification Numbers and LC Geographic Area Codes." *LASIE* 6 (September 1975): 9–12.

Mirviss, J. "Basic Book List on Physical Education for the College Library." *Journal of Health, Physical Education and Recreation* 34 (January 1963): 30–36.

New, D. E., and Ott, R. Z. "Interlibrary Loan Analysis as a Collection Development Tool." *Library Resources and Technical Services* 18 (Summer 1974): 275–83.

"Opening Day Collection." Rev. ed. *Choice* 6 (October 1969): 969–76; (November 1969): 1184–88; (December 1969): 1362–66; (January 1970): 1545–48; (February 1970): 1719–24; 7 (July–August 1970): 661–66; (September 1970): 807–10; 10 (December 1973): 1505–6+; (January 1974): 1675–92; (February 1974): 1831–36+; 11 (March 1974): 29–32+.

Parker, R. H. "Bibliometric Models for Management of an Information Store." *American Society of Information Journal* 33 (May 1982): 124–38.

Simmons, P. "Improving Collections Through Computer Analysis of Circulation Records in a University Library." In *Information Conscious Society*, edited by Jeanne B. North, 59–63. Philadelphia: ASIS, 1970.

Stubbs, W. R., and Broadus, R. N. "Value of the Kirkus Service for College Libraries." *Library Resources and Technical Services* 13 (Spring 1969): 203–5.

Contributors

Willis Bridegam received an undergraduate degree from the University of Rochester, an M.S. in Library Science from Syracuse University, and an honorary M.A. from Amherst College. He has been the Librarian of Amherst College since 1975. Before his arrival at Amherst he served as Director of Libraries at SUNY, Binghamton. Earlier in his career Bridegam held the positions of Continuations Cataloger, Head of Acquisitions, Medical Librarian, and Associate Director of Libraries at the University of Rochester. In addition to serving on the College Libraries Committee of the Commission on Preservation and Access and the Membership Committee of the Society for Scholarly Publishing, Bridegam has also been a consultant to a number of college and university libraries.

Charlotte B. Brown has been the College Archivist and Special Collections Librarian at Franklin and Marshall College since December 1983. Previously she held positions in the Archives and Manuscripts Department of the University of Maryland at College Park and in the Rare Books and Special Collections Department of the Countway Medical Library, Harvard University. Brown received her B.A. from Temple University, her M.L.S. from the University of Rhode Island, and an M.L.A. from Johns Hopkins University. She has published articles and conducted workshops on the preservation decision-making process and the establishment of preservation programs for college libraries.

Mary Casserly has been the Head of Collection Development at the University of Maine, Orono, since 1987. Before that she was Collection Development Librarian at the William Paterson College in Wayne, New Jersey. She received her M.S. in Library and Information Science from Drexel University and her Ph.D. in Library and Information Studies from Rutgers University. In addition to her work in the area of collection development, she has published articles on material availability, academic library self-study, and regional accreditation processes.

C. *Roger Davis* has been the Bibliographer at Smith College since 1975. Previously he was North American Bibliographer and Assistant Professor at the University of Virginia Library, 1972–75. His B.A. (1965) is from Yale University; his M.A. (1969) and Ph.D. are in Medieval and Renaissance English from Princeton University; and his M.S. (1972) in Library Service is from Columbia University. His dissertation was entitled "Petrarch's *Rime* 323 and Its Tradition through Spenser." Davis' publications include "The Complete Collection Developer," in *New Horizons for Academic Libraries* (1979). He has served as editor of several scholarly newsletters and has held offices in ACRL WESS and on the then-RTSD RS Collection Development Committee. Davis has also served on the jury for the Ralph R. Shaw Award for Library Literature and on the ACRL Planning Committee.

Peter V. Deekle, University Librarian and Director of the Honors Program, Susquehanna University (Selinsgrove, Pennsylvania), is also Director of the Blough-Weis Library. He was president of the Pennsylvania Library Association and program chair for the 1990 Pennsylvania Governor's Conference on Library and Information Services. He has also served as administrative officer of the Associated College Libraries of Central Pennsylvania. Deekle earned a bachelor's degree in English from the University of Pennsylvania, an M.S.L.S. from Drexel University (1973), and a doctorate in Adult Education from Temple University (1987). His publications include extensive research in the theory and practice of librarianship for liberal arts education. He has also written and consulted in the area of nonprint media collection development.

Wanda V. Dole is currently the Head Librarian of Pennsylvania State University's Ogontz Campus Library. Previously, she was Architecture Librarian at the University of Kentucky, Humanities Bibliographer at the University of Illinois–Chicago, and Assistant Director for Collection Development at the University of Miami. In addition to working in academic libraries, Dole has worked in publishing, bookselling, and teaching. She received a B.A. from Lawrence University and an M.A. in Classics and an M.S. in Library Science from the University of Illinois. Dole has published numerous articles and is working on a bibliography of British author Simon Raven.

Ronald H. Epp is currently Associate Professor of Philosophy at the University of Hartford. After receiving a doctorate in philosophy from the State University of New York at Buffalo, he taught at the U.S. Naval Academy and Memphis State University, where his research and publications centered on ancient philosophy and ethics. After completing his M.L.S., Epp moved to *Choice* where he was Managing Editor from 1985 to 1989. He has addressed the New England chapter of ACRL on faculty responses to changes in scholarly communication and presented a paper on the political and ethical issues of scholarly reviewing at the Fifth National ACRL Conference.

Evan Ira Farber graduated from the University of North Carolina and did graduate work there in political science and library science. His first professional position was Librarian of the State Teachers College, Livingston, Alabama. In 1955 he went to the Emory University Library where, under Guy Lyle's administration and mentoring, he was Chief of the Serials and Binding Division. In 1962 he became College Librarian at Earlham College in Richmond, Indiana, where he remains. Farber was Chair of the College Libraries Section in 1968–69, President of ACRL ten years later, and Co-Chair of ACRL's Fifth National Conference in 1989. In 1980 he received the ACRL Academic/Research Librarian of the Year Award and in 1987 the Miriam Dudley Bibliographic Instruction Librarian of the Year Award for his contributions to college librarianship.

Michael S. Freeman has been the Librarian at Haverford College since 1986. Before this appointment, he was Director of Library Services at the College of Wooster (Ohio) and held public service positions at the libraries of Dartmouth College and Illinois Wesleyan University. Freeman earned a B.A. from Brooklyn College (CUNY) and M.A.s in both Library Science and History at the University of Wisconsin–Madison. He was co-editor of the *Guide to Newspaper Indexes in New England* (1978) and has contributed to *Library Journal, College and Research Libraries, RQ,* and the *Journal of Academic Librarianship.* Freeman is currently on the Advisory Committee on College and University Libraries to OCLC.

William E. Hannaford, Jr., is the Director of the Gingrich Library and Professor of Philosophy at Albright College, Reading, Pennsylvania. A 1966 graduate of the University of New Hampshire, Hannaford has a master's degree (1970) and a Ph.D. (1972) in Philosophy from the University of Colorado and an M.S. (1975) in Library and Information Science from the University of Illinois. Hannaford has been Director of the Library at Castleton State College in Vermont, Head of Collection Development at Middlebury College, and Humanities Bibliographer and Assistant Dean for Collection Development at the University of New Mexico. Hannaford's published works include three books, several monographs and bibliographies, and numerous articles and papers.

Larry L. Hardesty is Director of Library Services at Eckerd College in St. Petersburg, Florida. He has a Ph.D. in Library and Information Science from Indiana University, an M.L.S. from the University of Wisconsin–Madison, and additional graduate degrees in History and Instructional Development. He directed two library-use instruction projects funded by the Council on Library Resources and served as a consultant for the Association of Research Libraries, Office of Management Studies. Hardesty has published many articles on such topics as bibliographic instruction, college library standards, library evaluation, collection development, and college library administration. He is on the Editorial Board and serves as Book Review editor for *Collection Management* and is Research Notes editor for *College and Research Libraries.*

Joanne Schneider Hill is Head of Collection Development at Egbert Starr Library, Middlebury College. A 1974 graduate of the University of Virginia, Hill has an M.S. (1976) in Library and Information Science from the University of Maryland. Previous positions include Special Projects Librarian at the American Bankers Association Library, Washington, D.C.; Reference Librarian at the Federal Deposit Insurance Corporation Library, Washington, D.C.; and Reference Librarian and Branch Head, the Jefferson-Madison Regional Library, Charlottesville, Virginia. During a year spent in India working with Tibetan refugees, she was a consultant to the Library of Tibetan Works and Archives in Dharmsala, Himachal Pradesh, and to the Drepung Loseling Library Society in Mundgod, Karnataka State. Hill has published articles on the topics of budget planning and the future of the book.

Thomas G. Kirk holds a bachelor's degree from Earlham College and an M.A. from Indiana University. Recently he completed an additional year of graduate study at Drexel University, where he studied informational systems in organizations and the behavior of organizations. After serving as Science Librarian at Earlham from 1965 to 1979 and Acting Director at the University of Wisconsin–Parkside during 1979–80, he moved to Berea College (Kentucky) where he has been library director since 1980. Professional contributions have been in the areas of bibliographic instruction and networking.

Thomas W. Leonhardt received his M.L.S. from the University of California at Berkeley in 1973, the year he began his career as head of the Gifts and Exchange Division of the Stanford University Libraries. Leonhardt also served as head of acquisitions at Boise State University and Duke University before becoming the Assistant University Librarian for Technical Services at the University of Oregon in 1982. He was appointed Dean of Libraries at the University of the Pacific in 1987. He is currently the editor of *Information Technology and Libraries* and is the author of numerous articles on technical services and collection development.

Katherine F. Martin began her professional career as a free-lance editor for the Manuscript Division of the Microfilming Collection of America. She later served as a cataloger in the North Carolina Collection at the University of North Carolina at Chapel Hill. Since 1982 she has been on the staff at the Donald O. Rod Library at the University of Northern Iowa, first as Bibliographic Control and Order Librarian and currently as Collection Management Coordinator. Martin holds an A.B. in history from Douglass College, Rutgers University, and both an M.A. in American History and an M.S. in Library Science from the University of North Carolina at Chapel Hill. Her publications include articles on archival security and a book review column for *Tar Heel Libraries*.

Ann Niles is Assistant College Librarian at Carleton College, where she is responsible for acquisitions and collection development. She received her bachelor's degree in Economics from Reed College and her master's degree in Library Science from the University of Minnesota. Her publications include *Index to Microform Collections*, volumes 1 and 2 (Meckler), "Conversion of Serials from Paper to Microform" in *Microform Review*, "Bibliographic Access for Microform Collections" in *College and Research Libraries*, and "Publishers' Toll-Free Numbers" in *Bowker Annual*.

Larry R. Oberg is Director of Libraries at Albion College, Albion, Michigan. Articles by Oberg have appeared in *College and Research Libraries* and *Library Journal*. His 1984 monograph, *Human Services in Postrevolutionary Cuba*, was a *Choice* Outstanding Reference Book of the Year. Oberg served as Assistant Editor of *College and Research Libraries* from 1983 through 1989. He holds an A.B. and an M.L.S. from the University of California, Berkeley, and is a member of Phi Beta Kappa. Before going to Albion in 1986, Oberg was Director of the Library at Lewis-Clark State College, Lewiston, Idaho, where he also taught in the School of Education.

Herbert D. Safford began his library career as a humanities cataloger at the Virginia Polytechnic Institute and State University. He was later promoted to Head of the Preservations Department. Following doctoral course work at Columbia University, Safford held associate director and director positions at Northern Montana College in Harve; Bowie State College in Bowie, Maryland; Muskingum College in New Concord, Ohio; and Kutztown University in Kutztown, Pennsylvania. Safford is currently Director of Library Services at the Donald O. Rod Library at the University of Northern Iowa in Cedar Falls, Iowa. He holds a B.A. from the University of Vermont, an M.A. from Yale University, and both an M.S.L.S. and a D.L.S. from Columbia University.

John R. Scudder, Jr., has been professor of philosophy at Lynchburg College, Lynchburg, Virginia, since 1967. From 1956 to 1967 he taught Philosophy and Religion, Education, and History at Atlantic Christian College, Wilson, North Carolina. He holds graduate degrees from Duke University, Lexington (Kentucky) Theological Seminary, and the University of Alabama, Tuscaloosa. His undergraduate degree is from Vanderbilt University, Nashville, Tennessee. He has published four books and numerous journal articles concerning the philosophy of education and health care.

Mary Clayton Scudder received her B.S. with a certificate in Library Science from the University of Alabama in 1952. In 1974, she received her M.L.S. from George Peabody College of Vanderbilt University. She holds the rank of professor at Lynchburg College, Lynchburg, Virginia, where she has directed the Knight-Capron Library since 1975. She has held previous positions in cataloging and public services. Recently she published an article on "Using *Choice* in an Allocation Formula in a Small Academic Library," and illustrated two rare book exhibit catalogs.

Kathleen Moretto Spencer has been Library Director at Franklin and

Marshall College since April 1982. Previously, she served as Assistant Head, Yale University Music Library, and has held positions in the Music Library, the State University of New York at Buffalo; the Philadelphia Musical Academy, now the Pennsylvania University of the Arts; and Notre Dame International School, Rome, Italy. Spencer holds both a B.A. and an M.A. in Musicology from the University of Pennsylvania, and an M.S.L.S. from Drexel University. She has cataloged the collection of the prominent American musicologist, Oliver Strunk, and has published articles on Virgil Thomson, the viola da gamba, and the collections of the Yale University Music Library.

Richard Hume Werking has been Director of Libraries and Associate Professor of History at Trinity University in San Antonio since 1983. He received his B.A. from the University of Evansville, his M.A. and Ph.D. in U.S. History from the University of Wisconsin, and his M.A. in Librarianship from the University of Chicago. From 1975 to 1977 he was a reference librarian at Lawrence University in Wisconsin, from 1977 to 1981 served as assistant director and acting director at the University of Mississippi Library, and from 1981 to 1983 was Associate Director for Collection Development at Trinity University. He has also taught history and has worked for the U.S. Civil Service Commission and the U.S. Department of State. Werking's interests in bibliographic instruction, collection development, library administration, and higher education are reflected in numerous journal articles.

Joan H. Worley is Director, Lamar Memorial Library, Maryville (Tennessee) College, a position she has held since 1984. From 1975 to 1984 she served as Reference Librarian at the John C. Hodges Undergraduate Library, University of Tennessee, Knoxville, after receiving her M.L.S. from the Graduate School of Library and Information Science, University of Tennessee, Knoxville. She also has a B.A. in History from Texas Technological University. Worley is active in several associations, including the Association of College and Research Libraries, and has published articles on college libraries, library instruction, reference, and collection development.